The In Crowd

Wilson Pickett

The In Crowd

The Story Of The Northern & Rare Soul Scene
VOLUME ONE

Mike Ritson & Stuart Russell

BEE COOL PUBLISHING (BCP) LIMITED

Published by Bee Cool Publishing (BCP) Limited
PO Box 16924, London SW18 4ZU

First published 1999

Copyright © Mike Ritson & Stuart Russell 1999

Printed and bound in Great Britain by Butler & Tanner Ltd., Frome, Somerset

A CIP catalogue record for this book is available from the British Library

ISBN 0 9536626 1 6

The moral right of the authors has been asserted

"To counterblast the Liverpool sound came along the Detroit sound known to the "in" crowd as Tamla-Motown... The punch of the big beat in a velvet glove"

Ron Boyle, Daily Express 1965

CONTENTS

ALVIN CASH

Dedicated to Donald Ritson and John Russell

Mike Ritson's interest in soul music goes back to his youth, listening to Atlantic, Stax and Motown at the local clubs in Carlisle. Moving to London, he met up with other like-minded soul fans who have remained friends to this day. Mike runs a successful printing company and is the co-owner of a publishing business. Still collecting records, he is married with four children and lives in Wimbledon with his family and over ten thousand 45s.

Stuart Russell was born in Worthing. He deejayed at soul promotions between '73 and '76, playing a mixture of current releases, US imports and Northern soul, before moving to London to work in advertising and graphics. After running a design company in Soho, he is now a consultant in both design and publishing. A lifelong soul and R&B fan, he lives with Teresa on the South coast.

Acknowledgments

THIS ALL STARTED over a drink in our friend Luigi's bar. With little more than a shortlist of people we thought were important to the story, we began something which would take over our lives. As we realised the scale of the project, the list grew longer and the idea of ever finishing seemed ridiculous. We did our best, but there are still people we didn't get to speak to – and we're sure there are some who we missed out completely. Please accept our apologies.

Everybody's input was invaluable, whether the simple confirmation of a date, or the verification of a record detail. And without the trust of those who lent us rare memorabilia and prized vinyl, "The In Crowd" would have been half the book it is. The encouragement of all the great characters on the scene, past and present, was priceless. It has been a fascinating, if exhausting, three years.

Thanks to: John Anderson at Soul Bowl for the tales of record hunting in the States, and for the best taxi ride we had; Chris Anderton; Les Ash; Tim Ashibende for his time and knowledge of the scene; Roger Banks for bad jokes, beetroot sandwiches, photographs, handbills, sheet music and the most amazing handwriting we have ever encountered – and thanks to Mr. Banks senior; Tony "Mr. Soul" Banks and his wife for their hospitality, and the eventual 12,000 word interview; Rose Batiste for the interview at Blackpool, and the opportunity of hearing "Hit And Run" live for the first time; Steve Bay; Rob Bellars; Mark Bicknell for the Jimmy Burns story; *Northern Essence's* Big Mick – sorry for not getting back to you; Alf Billingham for an entertaining and informative afternoon; John Bollen; Steve Bradley for tales about Major Bill Smith; Pat Brady for a great interview – if you don't like it, it's two against one!; Rowan Bray & Martin Low at Arena Digital; George and Ann Brown for memories of the Wigan Casino when it was the "Emp"; Goldmine's Tim Brown for the constructive criticism (it is appreciated); Kenny Burrell; Chris Burton for all his time and assistance – we hope you enjoyed Keith's drink; SBS's chairman in Hong Kong, Dave Burton for the laughs and the T-shirts which we'll sadly never be able to wear; Butch; Patrick Campbell for invaluable linguistic help, advice on grammar and for reading the book more times than was healthy; Sandra Carswell for all the transcribing; Nigel Caulfield for the X-Files record story; Steve Chadwick; original Velour John Cheatdom for the fascinating stories about the music business; Ian & Denise Clark for the 'phone numbers, articles, letters, and general help and advice – and the fun day in Norwich; John Clark for having such a fantastic memory!; Jimmy Claven for the stories; Neil Clowes; Trev Coates for the Liverpool connection; Dave Conway; Rick Cooper; Steve Cooper for Chateau Impney stories; Southgate's Randy Cozens for the drinks, the stories, the pictures, the Maxine Brown soundtrack – the list is never ending; reluctant DJ Ady Croasdell and Sylvia, for the amusing anecdotes – don't let him share your hotel room, he'll sit up all night watching the bloody cricket; Tony Cummings for giving us his side of the story; Colin Curtis for telling it like it is; Judy D'Abbertson; Keb Darge; Pete & Marie Davinson; Terry Davis for all the advice and, especially, the entertainment in Smithfield, and Maria, of course; Ian Dewhirst for hysterical Simon Soussan stories, and a wild West End evening; Kim & Phil Dick; Len Dopson; bad ideas man Bruce Doyle; Phil Eades; Steve Edgar; Tony Ellis for the use of the family album; Ian Emery; John Enright for proof-reading – now an expert on Northern soul; Stephen Evans; Dave Evison, John Farrell for the many conversations; Arthur Fenn; Ian Ferguson-Smith for *It Happened In Manchester*; Mick Flello; Steve Fletcher; the Flirtations – Earn'ee & Shirley Pearce, for their interviews, introductions, and support, and Vi Billups-Cadle aka Pearly Gates for the amazing voice overs (and we kept all the out takes!); Nigel Flood for introductions and Trentham transportation; Dave Flynn; Eddie Forshaw; Richard "Gilly" Gilbert; Rene Gelston; Steve Glover; Dave Goldswaine; Dave Greet for the background on Yate; Phil Grimshaw; Steve Guanori for *Blackbeat*; Pete Haigh for all the mentions in his *Blues & Soul* column; Tony Hall; Keith & Liz Hammond; Sean Hampsey; Andy Hanley for the Blackpool story; Sheila Hart; John Hassinger & Bob Kilbourn of *Blues & Soul* for archive pictures; Bob Harris for the longest fax, fashion advice, record titles and everything else; Neil Henderson; Keith Herschell for all your photographic skills and help – hoped you enjoyed reading all the old magazines and sleevenotes – thanks again; Paolo Hewitt; Alan Hindley for information on the Wigan music scene; Rob Holmes; Cleveland Horne of the Carstairs; George Hunt; Bobby Hutton; Jazz FM for their advertising help; Jim Hynes; Ion; Tony Jebb; Sylvia Johnson; Chris King for the interview; John

Knight for all his Modjestic memories; Gary Kingston for the loan of the records; Martin Koppell; Dave Krynski for the hours of work spent scanning record labels and memorabilia – thanks Dave; Chris Lalor; Glen Lambert; Angela Lawrence for the laughs when we were all shattered; Sheila Lazenby for never ending support and distribution of flyers all over the North; Michael Lee; Dave Leedham for introductions and photography – one of the best friends you can have on the scene; Ian Levine – sorry about the carpet!; Pat Lewis for the interview; Pete Lowrie for great tales of Detroit; John Manship; Dave McAleer for help in tracking down the elusive Tony Cummings; Keith Minshull – after four attempts, twelve pints, two meals and £100 in taxi fares, we got our interview – cheers Keith, it was worth it; Bob Morris; Judy Moss; Rob Moss; Kev Murphy and Bernie O'Brien at Lowton; Francisco O'Brien; Neil Oppegaard; Ian Palmer of *Manifesto*; the original "Night Owl" Dave Parris; Mike & Wendy Pattinson for the room, the "four curry special" – see you at the Perth book launch; Brian "45" Phillips; *Echoes'* Paul Phillips for all the Top 5s, the lunches on Mondays, Tuesdays, Wednesdays…the 50-1 outsiders, the tales of woe and misery, and keeping our names in lights – cheers Paul, get there early to make sure we get a table!; French soul brother Gilles Petard for the Ruth Brown picture; Graham Pither; Les Pyott; Barry and Sylvia Quinnell; John Ralph for always being available to give legal advice – even if it was always over lunch; Bill Randle for the introduction to Edwin Starr; Alan Reay for the photographic equipment that didn't work properly!; Clive Reed; John Reed at Sequel Records; Sally Reeves for the last minute transcriptions – volume two starts soon!; Clive Richardson for the interview at Stoke; *Soulful Kinda Music's* Dave Rimmer for the fastest Top 5 ever – see you in volume two; Beth Ritson; Tracy Ritson and Otis; Dave "The Legend" Rivers, who doesn't like sweets, doesn't tell lies, or steal records – Dave your help was invaluable in every way. Thanks for letting him out Mandy; Andy Rix for being a mine of information, thanks again; Kev Roberts for the information and promotional help, and the record deal; Brian Rae; Tony Rounce for great stories and other amazing feats of memory; Neil Rushton for stories about Brian Holland, Simon Soussan, US travels with Bill Baker, and introductions; Muriel Russell; Keith Rylett for Twisted Wheel stories; Shay and Jackie; the Catacombs' Allan Smith and Hazel for Blackpool, Stockport, Blackburn, and all the help and memories; Soul Sam;

Phil Saxe; merci beaucoup Phil Scott; Richard & Judith Searling for support and help in making it happen; Sanjay Shah; Dave Shaw for your encouragement and good luck with *Casino*; David Simpson for the publishing contacts and general business advice; Leigh Smart for contributions; John Smith for Mojo and Nite-Owl memorabilia; Mick Smith for brilliant stories – wish we could have printed them all; Pete Smith; Danny Spears; Phil Stables for Mojo information; Tony Stanhope; Graham Stapleton; Edwin Starr for the interview; Francis T; Tony Horn aka Tank of *Soulin* magazine; Barry Tasker and Dave White; Ginger Taylor; Ralph Tee; Terry Thomas; Kev Thomas; Rob Thomas for information; Dave Thorley for the loan of photographs; Richard Turner from Butler & Tanner; Jonas Unger for the great shots, and excellent company on our travels around the North; Alistair Urqhart; Luigi Venosi for all those free lunches we had to pay for; Russ Vickers; John Vincent; Lester Wardell; Graham Warr, for the brilliant Catacombs' stuff – and an extremely enjoyable drink after a great interview; Nick Washer, a life long mate whose help in this project was invaluable; Dick Watt, first there with advice three years ago, a mine of information and it was free – rare for a Scot!; Mick Webb; Pete Widdison; Jerry "Swamp Dogg" Williams for the chat and pictures; Russ & Doreen Winstanley for Pooles Pies, Simon's acetates, photos, stories and an introduction to London Weekend Television; Carl Woodroofe aka Carl Dene; and Keith & Maxine Woon.

We would like to give a special mention to Roger Stewart, whose help from day one has been invaluable. Accompanying us on many of our visits to the North, Roger provided us with more memorabilia than we could possibly have hoped for; when many others sent only photocopies, he gladly lent us rare and expensive originals. Thanks Roger.

And of course, Dave Godin, whose help throughout the whole project has been priceless.

Lastly, thanks to our family and friends, who have had to endure the trials and tribulations of long hours, weekends away, and yet still provided incredible support. Especially Su, Andrew, Matthew and William, and Teresa – without whose skills we would never have met our deadline.

Foreword by Dave Godin

BRITAIN IN THE post-war period, became a fearsomely insecure place, which manifested itself in a revival of all the various forms of snobbery to which the British have always been particularly prone, but which had been put on ice for the duration of the war. The latent anti-Americanism in the general climate of the times, was fuelled by resentment that a young, upstart country, ('which only came into the war once it was almost over'), was able to enjoy a much higher standard of living than ourselves, (which they lauded over us in their films), as well as the fact that the ultra-wealthy had had to sell off half of New York, which they'd formerly owned, in order to get precious dollars with which to win the war, (the debts of which you are still paying, by the way). All this ensured that the intellectual elite, or, as it is now termed, 'the opinion formers', would nearly always display a patronising and condescending tone when dealing with any aspect of American culture. (Stiff necked pride often being a virtuous replacement for action amongst the impoverished). Although jazz was conceded as acceptable in some circles, one wonders if this too wasn't a snobbish way of chiding the USA for its appalling treatment of its black citizens.

The fact that none of this cultural commentary was ever backed up with political comment, tends to show how basically cowardly it all was, and against this backdrop, a media elite began to develop in the 60s that decided it would stage-manage the less esoteric music of Blackamerica, and this too contained a nauseating element of colonial patronage as it was engineered into a 'personality niche' of the otherwise undistinguished.

Rhythm & Blues, according to their warped gospel, had to be 'authentic', and any move towards commercial success was seen as a betrayal of 'values' which were merely the feverish imaginings of white middle-class males who were prepared to help Blackamerican talent, but with the silently implied caveat that everyone should be quite clear as to the correct pecking order, and that those thus helped were suitably moist-eyed with gratitude. As

19

Trevor Churchill, Dave Godin
and Terry Chappell outside Soul City,
Deptford High Street, circa 1968

somebody once said several hundred years ago, 'We can all bear the sufferings of others with fortitude'. They knew all of Howlin' Wolf's flipsides, but nothing at all about Emmett Till.

What was truly phenomenal about 'Northern Soul' was not just its cultural implications, but also its political and sociological ones, and this most certainly informed most of my writing on the subject, even though circumstances often forced me to incorporate this factor on a subliminal level. There is a world of difference between those who 'live the life', and those who merely dream it, and the opprobrium and rank hostility many of the London-based, middle-class originated critics, commentators and card-carrying yuppies displayed towards it, was in itself revealing. There is no rage like that of a control freak losing control! All that hard work and brown-nosing gone to waste!

Like kids playing a game in which the big boys make up the rules as they go along, the London R&B Mafia first of all tried to scorn Northern Soul out of existence, and then, when this didn't work, sheepishly tried to court popularity within it. Like wolves in sheep's clothing, they checked out the scene, drank all the free booze, basked in the genuinely warm hospitality they were offered, and then returned to London to write their vitriolic put-downs.

Of course, careerists DJs, who cared more about their own egos than any record they ever played, were only too happy to play footsie with all this, (the precious 'name check' being valued above all else), but then their own track record in 'keeping the faith' was based on empty slogans picked up from me, which I in turn had picked up from the Blackamerican Civil Rights struggle, and their 'fame' was built on covered-up records, the occasional bootleg or

Emi-disc, which ensured such superfluous players as the artist, the composers and the record label who had actually originated it, (not to mention bank-rolled it), were kept anonymously waiting empty-handed as usual, at the back door. Where Blackamericans had generally been kept waiting ever since the days of 'emancipation'.

**Soul City Shop
Covent Garden**

But, despite all the manipulation, the venal deals, the bitchiness and the betrayal, Northern Soul thrived because it began as, and always continued to be, a movement that grew from the bottom up; firmly rooted in the British, white, working-class, (and, significantly, mainly male) collective experience, which instinctively and subconsciously saw the common causes and experiences that linked it to the Blackamerican collective experience. I was once asked by a Blackamerican if there was much colour discrimination in Britain, and I replied, 'No, not a lot. Over here they just discriminate against most everybody, regardless of race, creed or colour!'

The British obsession with class has, over the years, ensured that white working-class people have experienced a parallel kind of experience to

21

Blackamericans, but over here it is not the colour of your skin that counts against you, so much as the way you talk, or your educational disadvantages, or what Daddy does for a living, or whatever. The Dominant Ideology perpetuates itself by siphoning off the educational elite and kidding those so siphoned that they are now 'one of us', thus ensuring that anything wild, free or organic remains firmly under their control, because they're in a position to operate most of the levers. Should something build up such a compelling momentum that it simply has to be taken on board and can no longer be ignored, (like the Rock & Roll music revolution), then it is conceded temporarily, but only because this is the best means by which to ensure that it is subsequently successfully sequestered. Just as the Soviet Revolution was years before.

But, one of the greatest aspects of Northern Soul is that this never happened, (although a few did try, and oh, deary me, they tried so hard!), and, as it resolutely determined to stay wild, free-wheeling and calling its own shots, so the elite packed their bags, and, with sneers on their faces, they moved onto more 'meaningful' fields in which their lust for power and glory could perhaps find some hope of achievement. Some found it in religious superstition, some in ersatz copy-catting; whatever it was, it was always shallow and empty. Some High Priests even spoke *ex cathedra* and proclaimed that Northern Soul was dead. And the Northern Soul scene would never entirely be forgiven by them, because it in turn had stung them by putting them on notice, and saying, 'not off our backs, mate!'

Prominence as a DJ, (much like justice), was always on the side of those with the longest purse-strings, since money paid for the US trips, and bought

the cheapo records that then added 'glory' to the DJs name. But, despite all strenuous and concerted efforts to make it seem otherwise, people are not mugs, and, as these people exploited the scene for the sake of their own frail egos, so too a double-whammy on their part ensured that by never logging the records they played, the very artists and composers they were supposed to be paying homage to, never saw a red cent by way of royalties either.

But another, more positive aspect of the Northern Soul scene that also hardly ever gets mentioned, is the vast reservoir of genuine love and mutual affection it generates amongst it grass-roots adherents. Although this is seldom noticed in the abrasive, no-nonsense world of 'media and cultural studies' in which a word like 'sentiment' is just about the worst  swear word you can use, those on the ground know exactly what I am talking about. And I particularly know it because I have been privileged and humbled to have been the recipient of a goodly proportion of it for more than a quarter of a century.

If my writing has, over the years, shown any degree of strength and conviction, it is simply because I was given strength by the brothers and sisters at grass roots level. You can't buy something like this, and neither should you pander to it, try to solicit it, or claim it as a right just because you've given a few 'head figures' or prime locations a name check. No, this is a reflection of so many of the lyrics that have swept into our collective consciousness via the music. People who are all 'intellect' with little heart or imagination, might think a line like 'turn on your lovelight' is cute, but the real Northern Soul fan; the true Soul brother and Soul sister; knows it is beyond mere significance; it's an essential part of walking the walk.

Another aspect of the Northern Soul scene which is seldom, if ever, commented upon is that it is, (as indeed Blackamerican music itself once used to be), what I term 'non-lookist', which is my way of saying that its value judgements were hardly ever made on appearances. Instead of style triumphing over substance, substance was always the one element that was most sought after, so how one actually looked, had little bearing on what was important. Just as Blackamericans once used to judge a recording solely on the criteria of how a person cut the mustard within the record's grooves, and not on how the Company's publicity machine implied their potential for cutting the mustard in bed, so on the Northern Soul scene, people were accepted as fellow Soul brothers and sisters because the inner characteristics were

valued more than the external. Soulfulness cannot be defined, it is recognised.

I didn't invent 'Northern Soul', but merely coined the term to define the kind of music that young people from the north of Britain were preferring to those in the southern parts, who were falling under the spell of the changing direction that the US R&B and Soul charts were taking in the late 60s. What this did do however, was give the music a national, as opposed to regional, identity, and unified various disparate locations into one collective endeavour.

No two locations were identical; in fact, it was their uniquely mixed play-lists that attracted the crowds, but had I not coined the term, and publicised the various locations in my column in 'Blues & Soul', the scene might well have split into tribal factions, much as football still does, and, as a result, never moved into mainstream consciousness. Of course DJs had a vested interest in tribalism. Being self-appointed chieftains, their massive egos often made them themselves at least, think their 'creativity' was more important and meaningful than that of the poor souls who had originally made the records they were spinning. Like the dealers who, having a record for £2.50 on their list, would, after I'd rave-reviewed it, make sure it was a £25 item on their next list. But, as Barbara Lynn so cogently reminded us, money can't buy you love!

But, despite all this freakishness and neurotic misplaced energy, it was the music itself that actually gave the Northern Soul scene its momentum, inspiration, idealism and life-force, and it is the music that will endure into the future, long after the DJs, the wheelers and dealers, the bootleggers and other assorted scallywags and carpet baggers, and journalists like myself even, are long since forgotten! Northern Soul has always consisted of two distinct worlds, attracting, as Bernard Shaw once said in reference to anarchism, people who are apparently too good for this world, or people who are hardly fit for any civilised world!

This book is unique in that it is a tribute both to the grass roots music and the grass-roots fans who made the scene so special and unique in Britain's cultural history, and, as such, it is to be treasured. Mike and Stuart have done their research from the bottom up, and, like so many treasures, its true significance and magic will probably always remain at best partially underground. But, it will be of inestimable value to those who lived the music and the life, as opposed to those who, (to quote Little Anthony & The Imperials), were always 'on the outside, looking in'. The vast majority kept the faith, a few betrayed it, but, it happens.

And Northern Soul sure did happen!

DAVE GODIN, July 1999

Alvin Cash & The Crawlers' played
The Twisted Wheel in early 1967.
Their on-stage dance routines, including
backdrops, were copied by avid soul fans

Alvin Cash

Twine Time The Barracuda The Philly Freeze
Alvin's Boo-Ga-Loo Keep On Dancing

One Degree North

THE NORTHERN SOUL scene wasn't classified as a new culture until Dave Godin had written the defining article for *Blues & Soul* in June 1970. But by the time most people had read "The Up-North Soul Groove", an underground rare soul scene had taken root across the Midlands and North of England. While the rest of the country was busy throwing itself beneath the juggernaut of progressive rock, teenagers in the towns and cities of industrial Britain side-stepped the beast and stuck with what they loved best.

The Golden Era of Soul became the blueprint for a lifestyle which was exciting, amphetamine-fast and resolutely underground. The Northern scene had been spread almost exclusively by word-of-mouth and had managed to avoid the attention of a national music press, preoccupied as ever, with events in the capital. There was no barometer of youth culture or equivalent style magazine such as *The Face* to blow its cover, and the secret would remain undisclosed until events at Wigan Casino some years later turned Northern Soul into a media circus.

Teenagers would travel hundreds of miles on scooters, crammed into the backs of Minis and vans, or take the "Night Train" to raves held in dingy basements where you didn't dare lean against the wall as the condensation would ruin your mohair suit. In your first pair of Levi's, a trilby or beret, and Tuff "T" boots you were so cool you were straight out of the 'fridge. Even though the clubs were as black as the ace of spades you wore sunglasses – which of course made it that much easier for the drug squad to mark your card.

When the Metro at Wakefield was raided and one hundred and fifty all-nighter fans were arrested, it made the national press and television news, but aside from the drugs, the outside world had no idea what it was all about.

Soul disciples flocked in their hundreds to the new temples of Cool.

Nightspots like the Birdtrap near Brierfield, and the Golden Disc at Keighley where Darrell Banks' "Open The Door To Your Heart", Joe Simon's "No Sad Songs" and the Velvelettes' "These Things Will Keep Me Loving You" raised the temperature on the dance floor. Rows and rows of scooters were parked outside the Spinning Disc in Leeds, while "I'm Gonna Miss You" shimmered on the turntable; and Roy Tempest's "Original" and "Fantastic" live acts drew the soul crowd to the Nite-Owl in Leicester. Future recruits to the soul army knew they already had their finger on the pulse, at the Earlseaton Youth Club.

It was wall-to-wall mohair strutting to Chubby Checker's "(At The) Discotheque" at the Blue Gardenia in Leeds; risking life and limb leaning out of the rickety wooden windows at the Bin Lid in Dewsbury, to shout to your mates as Inez & Charlie Foxx walked that "Tightrope"; and thousands of mods crammed like sardines into the Burnley Mecca. Doing the "Twine Time" to Peter Stringfellow's "USA Import & Classic Soul Show", at the Tin Chicken in Castleford; soul heaven in Sheffield was the Esquire and King Mojo; and Manchester's legendary Twisted Wheel was *the* essential pilgrimage for any discerning mod. The midnight-to-six nighthawks flew in from all points of the compass to slip 'n' slide to "Spinning Top", "Get On Your Knees", "Breakout" and "Cool Jerk".

Suedeheads stomping in the dust to Little Richard's "I Don't Wanna Discuss It" in a disused chicken shed in Bletsoe, powered by portable generators; Ben Shermans and the smell of Brut as everybody clapped on the beat to Frankie Valli's "You're Ready Now"; "Swoop Down On You" and "Skiing In The Snow" echoing off the brick walls at Wolverhampton's Catacombs; and the blow of the Sunday come-down was always softened by "Farmer Carl" Dene at the Chateau Impney in Droitwich. It was going up the escalator to the Blackpool Mecca's Highland Room and the hairs standing-up on the back of your neck as you heard Earl Wright's "Thumb A Ride" for the first time; DJs who never introduced the records or even spoke into the microphone unless they were trying to get a car moved; and getting trampled-on while paying to get into the Golden Torch when Rose Batiste's "Hit And

Run" came on. You'd have thought somebody had thrown twenty pound notes on the dance floor, so desperate were people to get dancing.

Steamy all-nighters at Up The Junction in Crewe; soul clapping to "Tainted Love" at Va-Va's in Bolton; the Central in Leeds with Tony "Mr. Soul" Banks; Karman Ghia cords, Spencers' bags, bowling shirts and Solatio shoes as you joined the scrum fighting its way through the Casino's double doors; and laughing your head off on the coach from Southampton as it passed the "REDUCE SPEED NOW" sign turning off the M6 to Wigan. And, of course, it was all about that great feeling of knowing "We're In This Thing Together".

As soon as new releases became popular they were dropped. There was no way a chart record would be played at any of the "In" crowd's haunts. When Arthur Conley's "Sweet Soul Music" was released it was played sixteen times in one night at the Wheel, yet when it charted it was never heard again. The Showstoppers tore Plebs in Halifax apart when "Ain't Nothing But A House Party" was first released, but as it climbed the charts they were already history, despite an unbelievable live act.

The R&B soundtrack was Detroit's Motown, Ric-Tic, Golden World and Revilot; the suave Chicago school of the Impressions, Tony Clarke, the Artistics, the Radiants; the Big City sheen of Lou Johnson, Garnet Mimms and Little Anthony & The Imperials; "That Driving Beat" of Memphis' Willie Mitchell and the dance craze anthems of Alvin Cash & The Crawlers and Jerry O; the City of Brotherly Love's Candy & The Kisses, Volcanoes, and Bunny "Follow Your Heart" Sigler; the Hollywood pile drive of Mirwood's Fred Smith productions; the swagger of Jimmy Robbins, Little Hank, the Flamingos, Alexander Patton, Bobby Freeman, Sam & Kitty, Morris Chestnut and the OKeh adrenaline of Sandi Sheldon, the Triumphs, the Autographs and Major Lance's "You Don't Want Me No More". Everybody knew that Aretha was the Queen of Soul, but only the North knew the Ladies-In-Waiting – Cindy Scott, Dena Barnes, the Vel-vets, Christine Cooper and Lorraine Chandler. All 100 Proof Aged In Soul, and ninety nine and a half just wouldn't do.

As the heartbeat came close to cardiac arrest, rarer and rarer 45s surfaced – the Inspirations, Al de Lory, Jay D. Martin, Gwen Owens, Herbert Hunter,

Don Gardner, Danny Monday, Lenny Curtis, Sam Williams, Bernie Williams, Frank Beverly…and just trying to find your own copy of those seven inches of black magic became seriously bad for your health.

Waiting for Brian "45" Phillips' list, praying that nobody else would get their hands on that mint copy of "I Dig Your Act"; sending seventeen shillings and sixpence to F. L. Moore's in Bedfordshire for Dean Parrish's "Determination"; finally getting "Out On The Floor" – even if it was on Jeff King's Soul Sounds label; cursing on the 'phone as Groove City's line was permanently engaged; checking out the latest batch of pressings from Selectadisc and paying over the odds for white label acetates with hand-written titles. And in the days before cheap flights to the States, there were the seriously dedicated who crossed the Atlantic to scour through piles of forgotten vinyl in warehouses and cut-out stores.

Ian Levine and Colin Curtis pioneered the change to modern soul and for a while it was record boxes at twenty paces as the Mecca-Wigan feud kicked up a storm. Casino DJ Russ Winstanley banned records like "Shake 'n' Bump" and "The Ladies Choice", the scene split asunder and everything looked shaky for a while. Once the dust had settled the Carstairs, Black Nasty, Kim Tolliver, James Fountain and other Seventies recordings were played alongside the old-style stompers.

On the East coast, Mary Chapman took up the challenge, and with the Lincolnshire Soul Club's all-nighters at the pier, Cleethorpes did the unthinkable by putting pressure on Wigan – the Casino's Mike Walker was forced to run all-nighters on somebody else's turf. The torch was passed on to Richard Searling, and with the help of John Anderson he broke "I Don't Like To Lose", John & The Wierdest, Mr. Soul, Al Williams and dozens of unheard of grooves. "Do I Love You" escaped from Motown's vaults and the Southern Soul Club turned things upside down with the Northern fans' exodus from the heartland of the scene down to Yate near Chipping Sodbury.

The production bug had bitten Levine, and by 1977 the Mecca had converted to one hundred per cent disco. Commanding less attention in the pages of *Blues & Soul* and *Black Music*, the Northern scene went back underground. The Casino finally closed for the last time, and another memorial tattoo was added to the arms of the devotees. It wasn't just the end of an era, it seemed like the end of the Northern soul world. In fact, the story just opened on a new chapter.

The 100 Club moved the boundaries and put a twist on everything, pointing the way for the future – Top Of The World at Stafford, Central Pier at Morecambe, Neil Clowes' all-nighters at Keele University, a new circle of DJs and a single-minded breed of super collector prepared to pay thousands for elusive vinyl.

The needle is still in "The Up-North Soul Groove", and the commitment to Keep The Faith has never been stronger.

Come And Get These Memories!

John and Marisa Anderson, Edwin Starr and Soul Sam

31

Ruth Brown

CHAPTER 1

Two Steps From The Blues

RHYTHM AND BLUES was non-existent in Britain during the early Fifties. With a firm grip on its broadcasting monopoly, the BBC's Light Programme ensured that listeners were fed an endless diet of Frankie Laine, Mantovani, and Rosemary Clooney. *Melody Maker* and *New Musical Express* – the only pop papers – gave scant reference to any black American music other than jazz, and it was a miracle that 78s by the Orioles, Muddy Waters and Big Joe Turner had sold any copies at all in Britain. Ironically, any interest within the UK for black music was usually for material that would have been deemed unfashionable and out-of-date in the States. When guitarist Big Bill Broonzy played for the London Jazz Club in September 1951, the audience wanted to hear him recreate the dazzling virtuosity he had shown on his recordings from the Twenties, even though Broonzy had always followed trends in black taste and moved a considerable way from his original folk blues roots.

British traditional jazz, essentially a diluted recreation of Dixieland and other pre-war styles, was in full swing by the mid-Fifties. Leading exponent Chris Barber toured the States in 1956 on the back of Lonnie Donegan's hit "Rock Island Line", and arranged for blues singers Broonzy, Josh White and Brownie McGhee to perform recitals in small British clubs. Blues was viewed as an adjunct to the jazz world, and it was two German blues fans who promoted jazz concerts – Horst Lippman and Fritz Rau – who brought the first American Folk Blues Festival to Europe in 1962. The line-up included John Lee Hooker, T-Bone Walker, Memphis Slim, Willie Dixon, Sonny Terry and Brownie McGhee. The impact of the tour that followed triggered tremendous interest in black American music amongst young white teenagers – for once outside the elitist jazz circle.

Adolescents in the USA had discovered R&B by tuning in to black radio stations, but in the stultifying climate of post-war Britain, it was pretty unlikely that a young teenager in Kent would get to hear the vibrant sounds of urban black America. However, in 1953, Dave Godin wandered into the Silver Lounge ice cream parlour in Bexleyheath to hear Ruth Brown's "Mama He Treats Your Daughter Mean" booming out from the jukebox. Together with LaVern Baker, Brown was Atlantic Records' biggest female star in the USA, and although her recordings were issued by Decca on their London-American label, all had failed to make an impact in this country. Godin asked the lad who had put the record on what it was. He duly pointed it out and asked Dave if he liked it. When Dave replied that the record was "amazing", he was informed that this was "rhythm and blues".

Dave Godin's unexpected introduction to this new world changed his life forever. In 1983, *Blues & Soul*, (in which Dave wrote some of the most heartfelt, radical and upfront articles ever published about black American music), recognised his efforts with a special award for "a life of tireless endeavours in the furtherance and development of soul music in the UK". He was instrumental in the launch of the Tamla-Motown label in this country, ran the ground breaking Soul City shop and record label, was the first journalist to put the quotation marks on the underground rare soul scene in the North of England, and compiled the critically acclaimed "Deep Soul Treasures" collections – another genre he identified. It is hard to imagine the face of soul music in this country without his immense contribution.

Howlin' Wolf

Born in Lambeth, Dave Godin won a scholarship to Dartford Grammar School, where fellow pupil Mick Jagger was one of his earliest converts to R&B. Dave was walking home from his local record shop, having just collected the "Bo Diddley Is A Gun Slinger" album, when he met Jagger, who was interested in hearing the album. It was Godin who introduced him to the delights of Muddy Waters, Little Walter, Howlin' Wolf and Arthur Alexander. An early driving force behind the Rolling Stones was a guy called Bobby Beckworth, and the young R&B enthusiasts would meet and hold impromptu jam sessions at Beckworth's house – Godin playing harmonica. But, there was no love lost between Godin and Jagger. Dave became more and more unhappy with the Stones' later appropriation of black American music and made his

feelings known at a recording of *Ready, Steady, Go!* The group were on the same show as Marvin Gaye, whom Dave had befriended the previous year in Detroit, and Jagger's request to be introduced to the Motown star was flatly refused.

A fervent opponent to National Service, Godin registered as a conscientious objector and spent his two-year stint as a hospital porter. On his return to Civvy Street, he and a friend toured the States in a $40 van witnessing breathtaking R&B revues. "I first saw Fats Domino in 1957 at the wildest Rock & Roll concert I've ever been to in my life in the USA. Held in an enormous auditorium, it was a memorable line-up with acts like LaVern Baker, Johnnie & Joe, Chuck Berry, The Bobbettes, The Spaniels and just about anyone who happened to have an R&B hit at the time. The audience (mainly white college kids) were about the noisiest you could imagine, but the more they yelled the more the amplification was turned up and the more the artists responded. It was a shattering experience and left me vibrating for a week."

In 1959, when Bo Diddley's "Go Bo Diddley" was issued in the UK, Godin's first letter to *Record Mirror* appeared complaining that the album had been overlooked by their reviewers. As a consequence, fellow R&B fans, noting a kindred spirit, wrote to him and friendships were quickly formed with other pioneers such as Norman Jopling, Mick Ashby, Graham Ackers, Jess Pender and Gloria Marcantonio. It was then that Dave acquired his missionary zeal.

"In those days, cassettes were still in the future, so to 'share' sounds, one had to visit one another's homes. Again, the 'beleaguered minority' syndrome was probably at work, (when for instance I first became vegetarian in 1953 as well, it was two years before I even met another vegetarian, and when I did, I had this impulse to hug and embrace her simply because our shared belief made us automatic comrades), but this in some ways was the start (I suppose) of the 'disco'. They were house parties, where we were often as different as chalk from cheese in many respects, but that shared worship of black American music bound us together. There is no doubt at all in my mind about this, and although it still sort of exists to a degree, like all 'new' things when they are new, it was so intense. We'd seen the Promised Land, and, like all good missionaries, set out to make as many converts as we could!

Bo Diddley

"The only place you could hear black American music in the Fifties was low-life juke joints, and strange as it may now seem, funfairs. Getting records from the USA in those days was almost impossible thanks to the Copyright Protection Agencies who were assiduous in seeing to it that no unpublished music was imported. This chimed with an overall anti-American climate, where the BBC dominated broadcasting exclusively, and could always be relied upon to select the home-grown version over the original. The Musicians' Union too was a deeply reactionary force since they prevented nearly all American artists from appearing over here, and only allowed them to perform if there were reciprocal bookings for UK artists in the USA. This is the main reason why Elvis Presley never visited the UK; it was just too much hassle to negotiate. It is interesting to note how 'socialist altruism and principles' went slap bang out of the window as soon as UK acts later started the British invasion of the States, but tell me the old, old story."

Contemporary R&B remained the exclusive province of a coterie of die-hard fans until the early Sixties. Blues fans such as Mike Leadbitter, Simon Napier and John Broven had founded the Blues Appreciation Society whilst still at school in Bexhill. The society's journal, *Blues Unlimited*, concentrated on post-war blues and the coverage of modern R&B was slight. The perceived wisdom amongst many blues fans was stubbornly against recent developments in black American music. As a minority they had developed their own rigorous standards of judgement and taste, an attitude that at times Dave found disturbing. "Records which strayed too much from formulaic blues or R&B patterns were deemed 'commercial' and hence not worthy of critical consideration, and this annoyed me considerably. For instance, when the Chantels' "Maybe" was issued on London, I was the only person I knew who bought it and adored it, and was actually mocked and chided because of it!"

Record Mirror's James Craig reviewed R&B sporadically. Bo Diddley, Ray Charles, Chris Kenner and Bobby Lewis all received favourable comments in October 1961. But this wasn't enough for fans Robert Heywood and Phil Warner from Blackpool, who asked for an appreciation society to be formed to help promote black American music. Reader David Holt from Bramhall, Cheshire added his views on the subject: "I gather that rhythm and blues is gaining popularity fast Stateside. If you were to look at their top selling singles, there are three notable R&B records selling extremely well. I have been sent these: Gary "US" Bonds "School Is In", Lee Dorsey's "Ya Ya" and the Marvelettes' "Please Mr Postman". I feel I should let your readers know how great these are, and would strongly advise spinning them when they hit the European market. I only wish that rhythm and blues would catch on here also – it would make a pleasant change from some of the platters waxed recently in Britain."

Whilst the early pioneers in the UK struggled just to hear the records, events were taking place in the States which would lead to Dave making another memorable trip.

On Friday 26th October 1962 in Washington, D.C., compere Bill Murray walked on stage at the Howard Theatre to introduce a young all-girl singing act, that was yet to have a hit record the Supremes. They were the first act of the Motor Town Revue – featuring the mouth-watering line-up of Mary Wells, the Miracles, Marv Johnson, Marvin Gaye, the Vandellas, the Contours, the

Marvelettes, the Temptations, Singin' Sammy Ward and the twelve-piece Choker Campbell Show of Stars Band. The entourage had travelled from Detroit in a convoy of cars and a bus with "MOTOR CITY TOUR" emblazoned on the side. This was the first night of a one-week engagement at the Howard Theatre, which would be followed by a gruelling tour taking in over thirty cities across the USA, and culminating in a ten-day stint at the Apollo Theatre in New York.

Just two days before the Revue's first night, James Brown and The Famous Flames had recorded a typically dynamic performance on the legendary Harlem stage. Released in 1963 as "The James Brown Show Live At The Apollo", the album would eventually spend an incredible sixty six weeks on the *Billboard* Pop chart and stake its claim as one of the greatest live albums ever recorded. The Motown entourage were following a week's show by Brown and were determined to win over the testing audience. Like James Brown, their penultimate performance was taped and the live album "Recorded Live at The Apollo, Volume One", issued in April of the following year, captured the raw promise of Detroit's young R&B artists who were set to alter the course of musical history.

Berry Gordy's stars in the making had begun to make an indelible mark on the charts – Mary Wells' "You Beat Me To The Punch" and Marvin Gaye's "Stubborn Kind Of Fellow" were both riding high on the *Billboard* Hot 100, the Contours' rocking "Do You Love Me" was getting massive radio airplay and would shortly top the R&B chart and the Miracles' "You Really Got A Hold On Me" released that November, would repeat the Contours' success. The whirlwind tour helped drive home the sound of Hitsville USA into the hearts and souls of young America. But as 1962 came to a close, it was a different story in Britain.

Whilst beat groups were doing their best to recreate the grit of Chicago's Southside, some British bands had recognised Motown and other early uptown R&B as a great source of new material; the Beatles' albums featured many covers of black American records which, although released in the UK, had largely gone unnoticed by the British public – The Miracles' "You Really Got A Hold On Me", The Cookies' "Chains", Arthur Alexander's "Anna (Go To Him)" and The Marvelettes' "Please Mr. Postman", the latter making a telling impression on Dave Godin.

"It seemed to me that these brilliant records were simply going to be lost and forgotten if nobody took them up. When the Marvelettes' "Please Mr. Postman" was issued on Fontana, I just thought it was one of the greatest records I'd ever heard, (I still do!), and that started me thinking about setting up some sort of network of fans to help spread the word. One of the few ways in which radical records could get some air-play, (which everyone has now forgotten about), was record request programmes on the BBC, and the Sunday show *"Two Way Family Favourites"* had a listenership in millions playing records between the UK and members of the armed forces serving in West Germany. Also *"Housewives' Choice"* each weekday morning. Under various pseudonyms, I'm proud to recollect that I was responsible for getting what were probably the only UK air spins on records such as "Hide And Go Seek" by Bunker Hill, "I'm Missing You" by Loretta Williams, and "When the Lovelight Starts Shining Through His Eyes" by the Supremes, which I recall presenter Jean Metcalfe said, (with some predictive foresight from today's viewpoint), after it had played, 'it sounds like a chorus from a beat opera'."

Although an acquired taste, Godin was not alone in his love of the early Motown releases and they were appreciated by a few pioneer collectors, music fans and danced to by precocious mods in the all-night clubs of London. A few Motown releases by Marv Johnson, Paul Gayten, Barrett Strong and the Miracles had been issued on Decca's London-American label, and in November 1961 the rights were acquired by Fontana, a subsidiary of Philips. Only four singles were released before John Schroeder lured Motown to the fledgling Oriole label.

Oriole's only previous success had been with Maureen Evans, a singer who had started her career recording covers of current

39

popular hits for Woolworth's budget label Embassy. The connection with Motown seemed a rather surprising decision on their part, however, they were determined to promote the discs with vigour and publicised their new releases with a weekly fifteen minute show on Radio Luxembourg. The nineteen releases failed miserably in the British charts, although Marvin Gaye's "Stubborn Kind Of Fellow" and the Contours' "Do You Love Me" sold reasonably well. The latter could well have become Motown's first UK chart entry, if it had not been covered by Brian Poole & the Tremeloes, who took it on to be a number one hit. It was then that Godin started the Tamla-Motown Appreciation Society (TMAS).

Run from Bexleyheath in Kent, the association was originally to be called The Mary Wells Fan Club & Tamla-Motown Appreciation Society, but Godin quickly changed this as he realised that it could work better as an umbrella organisation for all of the Motown artists.

Clive Richardson was a keen and active member of the group. He later ran the Don Covay Fan Club, and edited *Shout*, the acclaimed R&B fanzine which ran for well over one hundred issues, before becoming a regular contributor to the newly launched *Black Echoes*. "I'd bought the Contours' "Do You Love Me" single and album from my local record shop in Bromley – funnily enough, the Oriole representative was in the shop at the time. Like many R&B enthusiasts, I read *Record Mirror* as it was the only place that gave any coverage to it and I remember winning the Olympics' "Dance By The Light Of The Moon" album in a competition set by Trevor Churchill. Amongst the fan club addresses, I saw an advertisement for the TMAS. As Dave Godin lived only a few miles away, I went over to meet him, and plied with cups of coffee, I was converted to the cause."

The co-operation TMAS received from Oriole was practically zero. The only encouragement was in the form of a few leaflets to insert in the society's *Hitsville USA* newsletter – one of the first R&B fanzines. Undeterred, Godin approached Motown in Detroit, and much to his surprise, in the summer of 1964 received a three page telegram from Motown's owner Berry Gordy asking him to visit the company's headquarters.

SCHEDULE

THURS.   FRI.   SAT.

Bobby Bland

CHAPTER 2

Hitsville USA

RANDY COZENS' FIRST all-nighter was at a basement in London's Charing Cross Road called the 79 Club. He was fifteen, already buying records like Major Lance's "The Monkey Time" and the Miracles' "I Like It Like That", and he was distinctly unmoved by the live act featured that night, the Downliners Sect. "It was a long-haired thing. R&B music, yes, but it was British R&B."

His elder brother, Gil, had been one of the early mods. Growing up in West London, Randy remembers the ebb and flow of the fashions; pointed shoes with chisel toes, one-button box jackets, 14" trousers, matelots' bell-bottoms, scooters and *Titbits* doing a special feature on the mods at the Wimbledon Palais. It all made a big impression on Randy who once waited for a shop to open in Drury Lane just to buy a pair of cuban heels.

The original mods, or modernists as they styled themselves, were an aloof tribe who aspired to an idealist hybrid of European chic and US Ivy League, all wrapped up in what was described in the language of the time as "the imagined cool of the Negro". They gathered in coffee bars drinking *espresso* and topics discussed might range from the films of Truffaut and Goddard to the latest Blue Note album. Louis Brown's club La Poubelle (The Dustbin) in London's Great Marlborough Street became a favoured haunt as it was frequented by French expats, students and au pairs. The mods' fashion sense was highly tuned, and the music that accompanied the clothes and lifestyle had

to be just right – New Wave soul from the Impressions, the Miracles, the Shirelles, the organ grooves of Jimmy Smith and Brother Jack McDuff, ska from Prince Buster, Derrick & Patsy and the R&B of Jimmy McCracklin and Hank Ballard.

Randy Cozens had heard the first Beatles' album and wanted to hear the originals. "I was on to it. We'd moved to Winchmore Hill in North London and I used to get my hair cut at Clubmans in Grand Parade, Haringey. They were the only hairdressers that could do the French cuts. A few doors away was a lighting shop that sold records. The guy who ran the place, Dave, was a soul collector and he had cardboard labels in the window with the titles of the latest records. I remember he had Johnny Nash's "Love A'int Nothing" and things like James Brown's "Prisoner Of Love". I'd read all the reviews in *Record Mirror* and order everything. Norman Jopling would review something like Eddie Holman's "This Can't Be True". You didn't know that it was a soul record but the name sounded right. I'd buy blind nine times out of ten unless I knew the artist. And then the thing that pissed me off, was when they started running an R&B chart, and I didn't want to share it with anybody. I didn't want it to go massive and get ruined.

"I was one of the few who bought Bessie Banks' "Go Now" when it came out. There was a little shop in Palmers Green where I picked up a few things like Earl-Jean's "I'm Into Somethin' Good". And if there wasn't much out I'd order back catalogue stuff. I went to Transat later in Lisle Street but the imports were more expensive. I first heard "In The Midnight Hour" in 1965 but it was like ten shillings for the single and I was only paying thirty bob for an album. Because I worked at Chancery Lane I used to go into Harlequin in Holborn. They never had import singles but they had LPs from people like Chuck

Jackson. If I'm right, Dave Nathan, who used to be at Soul City and *Blues & Soul*, worked there. And then I heard about the Tamla-Motown Appreciation Society and got the newsletters off Dave."

On his return from Detroit, Dave Godin was interviewed by Norman Jopling for *Record Mirror* in an article entitled "A Great Visit To Hitsville USA". The trip had been organised by Margaret Phelps, who ran the Motown Artistes' Fan Club and who subsequently introduced Dave to many of Motown's stars and less-well known acts, including Marvin Gaye, Martha Reeves, Choker Campbell, Kim Weston, Stevie Wonder, and Jackie Hicks of the Andantes. A photograph shows him being presented by Berry Gordy Jr with an Edwardian mug and pair of cuff links.

Dave recounted his visit to Jopling: "When I was in Hitsville USA, Berry took me to where there were four new sides cut by Martha & The Vandellas. He asked me to pick their next single. I said I thought two were about as good, but he made me actually pick out one track ("Dancing In The Street") and he said it would be Martha's next single!" Given Dave's memories of hearing R&B during the Fifties at funfairs he was taken to a fairground, visited a Playboy club and witnessed the Motor Town Revue live. The Supremes' new 45 "Where Did Our Love Go" was played to Godin while he was being driven in Berry Gordy's car.

Pirate radio stations, moored beyond British waters, and so outside government jurisdiction, were important to the early promotion of Motown and R&B. Ronan O'Rahilly, who owned London's Scene Club and was the manager of Georgie Fame, owned Radio Caroline. In March 1964 the station began broadcasting off the coast of Harwich and listeners first heard Jimmy McGriff's instrumental "Round Midnight". This later became the Radio Caroline anthem played at closedown each evening. Within three weeks a Gallup poll survey discovered that the radio station had almost seven million regular listeners, and this did not include those under the age of seventeen. It was estimated that Radio Caroline had a prospective listening audience of nineteen million people.

Godin spotted the potential and on his return to Britain, armed with advance copies of the Supremes' "Where Did Our Love Go", set about getting them played by the pirates. Because the BBC would not give airtime to Black American records, it was a golden opportunity as the listening figures for the

off shore stations were considerably higher than the BBC or national media would admit. As well as the Supremes' disc, records by Dionne Warwick and Etta James were successfully aired and entered the Top 50. Radio programmes such as Caroline's *All Systems Go* featured two hours of both the British and American Top 50 charts together with the best R&B; *The American Top Fifty Down Beat* comprised of R&B and standards by artists such as Ray Charles, Wes Montgomery and Della Reese; and *It's All Happening*, and *The R'n'B Show* were great outlets for Black American music. Mike Raven's popular programme on KING had the highest rated listening figures at the time.

Pirate radio unlocked the door to black American music for a growing legion of young listeners, of which Torch and Mecca DJ Colin Curtis was one. "My parents had bought a pub in Kidsgrove, and there was a record shop literally three doors away. Well, I say a record shop, they'd sell Hoovers, anything electrical. Even as a kid at grammar school, the big thing for me was coming home, because of the records upstairs in this shop. They had them in these mouldy old toaster racks, in the original sleeves. My parents weren't wealthy, but money used to come to me. Beg, steal or borrow, I mean whatever it took. I was a wheeler dealer all the time, and I'd target funds to get the records I wanted.

"It happened to me very early in life, I suppose I was about nine or ten and one of my best friends' sister was playing these records. You go back to pathetic stories, but there was an electric torch that used to have a flashlight on the front, and like a red or a white light on the top. We used to play around with this. And we were heavily into listening to pirate radio, even at that age. You know, things like Mike Raven. And so we would try and emulate this in my friend's front room. We'd have all the latest pop records that we could get our hands on, and we used to take this torch thing to pieces to use as the microphone. This is the button to press when the jingle's coming on, or whatever. Probably treading on the Subbuteo pitch at the time. But his sister used to lend us these records on Tamla-Motown. And they'd fit in, you know,

Major Lance

we'd have the old Dansette, and you'd put six records on, and five would drop at once. Or play the wrong one.

"But all of a sudden, I was listening to lyrics like Stevie Wonder, the Temptations' "The Way You Do The Things You Do". I don't know when the actual turning point was, but I started to develop a need to hear this type of music, and that got me more and more into pirate radio. My grandfather used to own a huge Bush radio. I used to spin this thing around and it used to light up, it was colossal. And I'd flick around, and you'd have Radio England, Radio Wessex, Caroline. This great music was coming out, with this R&B feel. It'd be "Barefooting" by Robert Parker, then they'd play the B side. Then they'd play the same record again, and this was amazing to me. I couldn't believe it. Then we moved to Kidsgrove, and that was when we made connection with the local shop.

"In those days, shops used to have these leaflets printed with the new releases. I used to list everything that was potentially worth listening to. You know, anything on Bell or on Stateside. And one day, the guy in this blue overall with Ever Ready on it, said 'I don't believe this'. And he went out the back and he came out with another list. And he put my sheet down, and then he put down another sheet, and he said 'Look, you want about eighty per cent of the same records as Keith.' And I'm like, 'Who's Keith?, What's going on here?' He said, 'Yea, the guy with the limp'. I'd seen him around in Kidsgrove, but I didn't put two and two together. He turned out to be Keith Minshull."

IN 1964, Dave Godin was working for the Continental Telephone Exchange, but was put on Motown's payroll as a full-time promotional agent. Between them, Gordy and Godin plotted to engineer a 'label' identity for the UK, as opposed to the promotion of individual acts, because although several acts had had hits in the USA, it was difficult to be sure who would be the first to make the breakthrough over here. By marketing it as a 'sound' and 'label concept' it did not matter which individual act made it first, because all the others would be dragged into the spotlight alongside them.

By October 1963, EMI had acquired the rights to release Motown products and started to issue releases on its Stateside label, the first being Martha and the Vandellas' "Heatwave". The label had been set-up specifically for the release of American recordings and had replaced Top Rank. Various names had been proposed for the label including Javelin and Discus, although EMI eventually stuck with the more evocative title Stateside – featuring the dollar sign, in contrast to its sister label Parlophone's pound sign logo.

Given the society's original name, it was ironic that the first Motown artist to make their mark on the British charts was Mary Wells. As it was Dave Godin had no regrets. "In the event, it was "My Guy", but my decision proved even more useful and apt when it was announced shortly afterwards that she would be leaving the company. I'd never anticipated this of course, but under the circumstances it was a brilliant stroke of luck that we had followed this path rather than just putting all our efforts into promoting Mary Wells. Again, it must be stressed that, like all ideas which in retrospect seem reasonable and sound because they turned out to be successful, my concept of selling a 'label', as opposed to an artist, was met with fierce opposition from EMI. In those days however, Berry Gordy had implicit trust in me and my awareness of the UK market, which was, in so many ways, different from that in the US, and so whatever advice I gave, he knew it was genuinely given and honest, so it was a situation like 'If Dave say's it's right, that's good enough for us'."

TMAS member Clive Richardson remembers magical evenings at EMI's Manchester Square headquarters. "The Motown artistes would circulate among us. There were never more than 100-150 present, so there was every opportunity to speak to the stars. If I remember correctly, the first time it was the Supremes, and at the second evening, Marvin Gaye turned up with Harvey Fuqua and Berry Gordy Jr. I've still got my signed copies of the four "R&B Chartmakers" EPs. Another evening the Marvelettes came. Dave ran the TMAS in a very open-handed and friendly manner. He had the necessary get-up-and-go to pull the whole thing off. We were all regularly informed of the latest Motown news – *Hitsville USA* was a well-produced publication, there was nothing else like it."

Motown showed their gratitude to the Tamla-Motown Appreciation Society by pressing a limited edition single featuring snippets of songs and votes of thanks. Margaret Phelps of the Hitsville USA fan club introduced Berry Gordy Jr., who expressed his gratitude and hopes for the future success of the company with "Greetings to all you swingers and friends…". Smokey Robinson, Stevie Wonder, Marvin Gaye, Gladys Horton of the Marvelettes and Melvin Franklin of the Temptations closed the first side of the single.

"Quicksand" opened the other, with Martha Reeves thanking the society for their birthday card, even though it was early. The Contours, Eddie Holland, Kim Weston and finally the Supremes thanked Dave for being a "swinging fellow", before fading out to "Where Did Our Love Go". Some of these discs were given out during the Motown Revue's visit. Northern Soul DJ Leigh Smart recalled that his cousin was given a copy by Earl Van Dyke at Birmingham Odeon, an evening that Dave Godin believed had happened too early.

Godin's advice to Gordy to delay the Motown Revue's trip to Europe went unheeded. "I truly felt that Britain was not yet ready for it and consequently reported back that we should wait until the time was more ripe. This was the first time Berry Gordy rejected my advice, and in my heart I knew it was the beginning of the end...so the Motown Revue came, and flopped even more disastrously than press clippings from that era would indicate."

Although Stevie Wonder, Martha & the Vandellas, Marvin Gaye and The Supremes had been to England before, this was the first time that the whole package, touring together since 1962, had appeared outside the States. The Miracles, Martha & the Vandellas, The Temptations, Little Stevie Wonder, Earl Van Dyke and his Soul Brothers and token British artist Georgie Fame (now managed by promoter Arthur Rowe) opened at the Finsbury Park Astoria on Saturday 20th March 1965. Every soul fan in London came and packed the place out.

Clive Richardson saw the Revue at the Finsbury Park Astoria. "It was a great evening, which now all seems a bit of a blur. These were our idols on stage, and what must have struck the Motown artistes was the almost sepulchral atmosphere. It pre-dated screaming fans and was certainly no Harlem Revue. There was no call-and-response from the audience, it was almost like a recital."
Outside the major cities there was considerably less

50

Maxine Brown

**Garnet Mimms
and John Abbey**

interest, and *Melody Maker* reported that Bristol promoter Charles Lockier
had to give away 1,000 free tickets to the concert to "coloured immigrants and
their friends". Despite the poor attendances, *Billboard* in the USA reported
that the tour was playing to 'standing-room only' audiences in the UK, when
in reality, at Kingston-upon-Thames for example, the theatre was two-thirds
empty. Nonetheless, those who witnessed the shows were won over by the
performances.

Martin Barnfather, who would later become better known as Northern
Soul DJ Soul Sam, remembers seeing the revue. "Well the venue was half full,
but I can tell you that it was the best live act I've ever seen. They actually
sounded better than on their records. Georgie Fame, who was good by UK
standards was on the same bill and he sounded like an amateur by
comparison." At some venues, Fame was booed off stage by soul fans who had
come to witness the real thing. Fans like early R&B collector Dave McAleer
and his friends, who thought that they were the only people in the country
who knew about R&B. Although he was later to express doubts about whether
Motown was soul music or simply pop music sung by black people, Dave was
impressed by Stevie Wonder's performance.

McAleer ran one of the earliest soul music fanzines during the Sixties and was instrumental in establishing the first Northern Soul label for Pye Records in 1974. He had started collecting rock 'n' roll in 1956, but gradually progressed towards R&B when it had started to sound tame, to his ears. At thirteen McAleer had bought Ray Charles' "What'd I Say", at fourteen the Isley Brothers' "Shout", and before long had progressed to the early funk of James Brown's "Think" and Hank Ballard & The Midnighters' dance craze smash "Finger Poppin' Time".

Many classic R&B hits were covered by more acceptable faces in the Fifties; Pat Boone drained all the guts out of "Ain't That A Shame", "Tutti Frutti" and "Long Tall Sally" and the McGuire Sisters whitewashed the Moonglows' "Sincerely". Dave became something of a purist, determined to unearth the American originals of the UK covers. "I was hooked on American R&B. Your collection didn't date, which was a real plus, and I knew that it would still sound tough when compared to Adam Faith or Bobby Vee and, of course, as a teenager it was pretty elitist." Before pirate radio came to the rescue of soul fans and helped to spread the word, collectors had to be more enterprising in their efforts to get their hands on the precious vinyl. *Billboard*, the American music industry's magazine, contained information not readily available in Britain, so Dave started to subscribe. This way, he would at least know of any records issued in the States way before they came out in Britain. He also ordered items by mail-order from Randy's Records in Gallatin, Tennessee run by Randy Wood, the owner of Dot Records. And then there was American Forces Network which was a great source of inspiration as was the Dutch radio station Hilversum, which broadcast a mixture of R&B and American pop, light years ahead of the staid BBC.

Exclusive Recording
Artist
BIG HILL RECORDS

LOU JOHNSON

Personal Manageme
Richard Simpson
1630 Broadway

CHAPTER 3

Rhythm & Soul

TELEVISION EVENTUALLY OFFERED salvation to R&B fans in the form of Rediffusion's *Ready, Steady, Go!*, which was launched on 9th August 1963. As well as the current pop acts of the day, it regularly showcased many of the visiting greats of R&B and soul. American artistes included the Miracles, James Brown, Inez & Charlie Foxx, Dionne Warwick, Stevie Wonder, Chuck Jackson, Ike & Tina Turner, Otis Redding, Marvin Gaye and many more. Although the earlier performances were mimed to records, from Friday 2nd April 1965 the acts were recorded live. Randy Cozens remembers how the show kick started the weekend.

"*Ready, Steady, Go!?* Ready Steady fucking excellent! I used to work on Friday evenings helping at these dinners with people like Quentin Hogg, the Queen Mother and all the rest of it. I can remember seeing James Brown on the television at work, we had to have it on in the kitchen. But Friday nights for me, if I missed *Ready, Steady, Go!* and someone like Lou Johnson was on, it was the fuck-ups man. The dancing wasn't that good. Dancing down the club you'd go on one leg and slide along the floor. No real acrobatics that I can remember, but it was pretty cool. On the TV they used to have people come up and do things like the Block, which was shit. And *Top Of The Pops* was fatal. There was nothing cool about that because they tried too hard, but *Ready, Steady, Go!* was the bollocks. Not so much when it started with people like Manfred Mann, but when Vicki Wickham got the soul and R&B thing going it was great."

The programmes dancers, Sandy Sergeant, Teresa Godfrey and Patrick Kerr, were regular visitors to a well-known Mod club, a few hundred yards from Piccadilly Circus. The Scene Club in Ham Yard, was where DJ Guy Stevens worked the turntables. His esoteric playlist could include Louisiana Red, Boogie Jake, Lazy Lester or Little Al, and the club became a haunt for the early R&B enthusiasts. Stevens used to import records and sell them in the club's cloakroom – it was one of the few places that had American 45s. The club closed around three in the morning, but in 1965, Brian Peters took over the deejaying and Saturdays became all-nighters.

Dave McAleer was a regular at The Scene. He was deejaying at the Ready Steady Go in Dean Street, where he spun R&B releases and the occasional rock 'n' roll record – Gene Vincent was a regular visitor. Guy Stevens had his finger on the pulse and Island Record's owner Chris Blackwell gave him the task of running a planned new R&B label.

Chris Blackwell was born in London. His father was Irish and his mother, Blanch Lindo, was the daughter of an old Jamaican trading family. The family moved to the West Indies and after an education in the UK, Blackwell joined them. After being aide-de-camp to the Governor General Sir Hugh Foot, and a succession of other jobs, Chris became involved with the jazz circuit in New York where he befriended Miles Davis. He became involved in the Jamaican music scene and released the first album "Lance Hayward At The Half Moon" on his own label, named after the film *Island In The Sun*. In 1963, whilst on a visit to Jamaica, Blackwell heard Inez & Charlie Foxx's "Mockingbird" on the local radio station. He recognized the potential of the disc, and saw this track as the perfect vehicle to enter the R&B market which was then enjoying a revival through the mod scene in London. The brother and sister act had recorded the track for Henry "Juggy" Murray's Symbol label, a subsidiary of the main company, Sue, which Murray had named after his daughter. Based in New York, the label's first success had been in 1958 with ex-Drifter Bobby Hendricks' "Itchy Twitchy Feeling". Later US hits from Ike & Tina Turner, Jimmy McGriff and Barbara George helped establish Sue as one of the first labels to make the crossover from the rawer R&B to more commercial soul.

Within 24 hours, Blackwell had flown to New York and negotiated the rights to "Mockingbird" from Murray. The deal included the extensive back catalogue of Sue Records, together with its subsidiary label Symbol and Harold Battiste's New Orleans-based AFO which the company distributed. Credited solely to Inez Foxx, "Mockingbird" became the first UK release on the distinctive red and yellow Sue label.

As label manager, Guy Stevens' knowledge of black American music was put to the test as he became responsible for all the releases on the new label. Although many of the first issues were taken from Murray's US labels, material from other companies was soon issued, and from December 1963 until its eventual closure in June 1968, Sue made a diverse collection of classic R&B, soul and blues available to British fans.

The first chart success for the company came via Inez & Charlie Foxx's "Hurt By Love", which reached number forty in the summer of 1964. This was followed by a reissue of the Phil Upchurch Combo's "You Can't Sit Down" in May 1966 which reached number thirty eight. This had been a particularly in-demand club track which had first been released without success on HMV five years earlier.

Not enamoured with the music he had heard at the 79 Club, Randy Cozens wanted the real thing and the "Disc" promised more. La Discotheque was a few numbers down from the Flamingo and All-nighter Club in Wardour Street. "You'd pay your money and went up some stairs. Apart from the Limbo, which was up near the 100 Club, most of the all-nighters were downstairs. The thing that I can remember the most about the "Disc" was the music – it was pounding. On the sides of the dance floor were mattresses like you would get in a gym. You could crash out, or lay there with a girl. Heaven. In the evening before, we would go to places like Coco's, which was a coffee bar in Wardour Street and another place called Samantha Jo's. You'd do your little deals or whatever. That little stretch from Shaftesbury Avenue to Leicester Square was buzzing. You could hear music in all the coffee bars. People walking up and down, lots going on, meeting mates. It was cool. Seeing all the clothes. But then the *Mirror* ruined it all with that article."

In May 1964, *Sunday Mirror* investigators Ronald Maxwell and Lynn Lewis exposed the "Drug Menace" which was sweeping through "all-night clubs and dives". La Discotheque's owner "Swiss Albert" was named in the House

57

of Commons by Ben Parkin, Labour MP for Paddington North as being behind this insiduous evil.

The clashes with Rockers at Clacton, Brighton, Margate and other seaside resorts, represented the spiritual death of mod. The resulting media attention killed it for the originals and the whole scene in turn was exploited by commercially run nightclubs like Tiles in Oxford Street, pop groups appropriating the fashions for their own end and short-lived magazines which cashed-in on the scene such as *The Mod's Monthly*.

This level of media attention ruined it for Randy. "After the *Mirror* article it was invaded by hoards of Parka boys on scooters. And that had all gone. That was something out of 1963 really. I know we're only talking about 1964 but it was all over by then. When people talk about mods that's all they talk about, but that killed it. The "Disc" was over. But then I found the Last Chance, and that was heaven."

The Last Chance Saloon, at 19-21 Oxford Street, held all-nighters on Fridays and Saturdays and, unlike many of the other London clubs, the musical policy was one hundred per cent soul. Based upon a Western saloon theme, the interior of the club was decorated with swinging doors and rope nooses. "You went down a couple of flights of stairs to a main room with a few

rooms leading off. Can you imagine hearing Fred Hughes' "Oo Wee Baby" for the first time, or "Getting Mighty Crowded" by Betty Everett? That was a massive sound then. I mean they're easy stuff to get now, but they were such great records."

Finally, thanks to Godin's enthusiastic efforts and promotional skills, EMI launched the Tamla-Motown label in March 1965. Its first release was the Supremes' "Stop! In The Name Of Love", which was then the number one record in the USA.

Motown artists were continuing their assault on the American charts; Junior Walker & the All Stars were at number six with "Shotgun" and The Temptations were at number nine with "My Girl".

"Stop! In The Name Of Love" entered the British charts at number forty seven and singer Dusty Springfield welcomed

Motown Stars
In London 1965;
The Temptations,
The Miracles,
Martha & The Vandellas
and The Supremes

the Tamla-Motown acts to a party, at fellow singer Dana Valery's flat. Dusty had met and befriended Martha Reeves whilst touring in the States, and on her return persuaded Vicki Wickham, the producer of *Ready, Steady, Go!*, to put together a show dedicated to the Motown acts. On April 21st 1965, Rediffusion showcased *The Sound of Motown*, presented by Dusty Springfield. Recorded at Wembley Studios, it featured the Supremes, Martha & the Vandellas and Earl Van Dyke.

Dave Godin's love for R&B encompassed more than just Motown. "It was after the Motor Town Revue flopped that I began to think about expanding this base to include all Black American performers, and so eventually the Tamla-Motown Appreciation Society transmogrified itself into the Friends of American Rhythm & Blues Society (of which Dusty Springfield became a member), and I published *Rhythm & Soul USA* magazine. This was very popular, but, although Motown had given me a degree of financial support for TMAS, I was on my own in this venture, and, not being rich, it only ran to four issues."

The first issue was published in April 1966 and featured articles on Irma Thomas, Tammi Terrell, Wilson Pickett and Billy Stewart. Dave continued his crusade against those he viewed as determined to keep soul music to themselves. In the second issue, he clarified the editorial board's policy of not including matrix numbers in the magazine's discographies. "Although listings of recordings and the rest are all very interesting, it is not our intention to cater to the minority who want to keep R&B their exclusive esoteric territory. We are out to popularise R&B and

Soul music – to rescue it from the realm of rarified pseudo intellectualism that prevents it from gaining a popular following here. Our motto is that 'it's what's in the grooves that counts' – not whether the disc has a hand-scratched matrix number or not!"

Tiles, in Oxford Street, was the exact opposite of the cellar bars that the mods had frequented. Inside, it had fashion shops, coffee bars, and a huge sound system suspended from the ceiling. Throughout 1966, Tiles resounded to the soul sounds of visiting American artists: Billy Stewart, Rufus Thomas, the Orlons, Alvin Cash, Solomon Burke, Otis Redding, Robert Parker, Edwin Starr, Ben E. King and Bobby Hebb. Soul music was taking the country by storm.

In March 1967, the Stax/Volt Revue visited Europe for the first time playing in the UK, Paris, Oslo, Stockholm, Copenhagen and the Hague. The crop of chart riding R&B artistes included Otis Redding, who had made his first trip in the autumn of the previous year, Eddie Floyd, whose "Knock On Wood" was easily the most played soul record in the UK at the time, Carla Thomas, Sam & Dave, Arthur Conley, Booker T. & The MGs and the Memphis Horns. Everybody in the entourage was overwhelmed by the reception given to them by the European audiences; in Scotland, Otis Redding had to be rescued by security guards and stewards from being dragged into the audience by an ecstatic crowd. Guitarist Steve Cropper's bemoaned the quality of British cigarettes and lack of soul food. Interviewed for *Record Mirror* he said "The food's maybe all right, but in America we get more sauces and spices. Food is kinda naked here."

Otis Redding's manager Phil Walden, who had arranged the tour with British promoter Arthur Howes, craftily altered some of the advertisements for the "Hit The Road Stax" tour to read as "The Otis Redding Show", which inevitably caused some resentment. Even the *Record Mirror* review of the first night at the Finsbury Park Astoria, expressed surprise at how this had mysteriously happened.

Sam & Dave clearly made the greatest impact on reviewer Norman Jopling with a performance which he described as "exciting and entertaining" and which included a "spine-tingling rendition" of "Hold On I'm Coming". He seemed disappointed by Redding's act which he felt might have gone some way to "exploding the soul myth" surrounding him. Jopling's review angered Atlantic Records' manager Frank Fenter and divided many of *Record Mirror's* readers. Jopling had been a keen supporter of R&B and soul music writing a "Great Unknowns" series in the paper about lesser known American artistes. After his criticism a whole page was devoted to "The Stax Controversy".

Fanzines aimed at collectors desperate for more information began to appear. One of the earliest was Mike Vernon's *R&B Monthly*, for which Dave Godin wrote one of his first articles on Mary Wells. Pete Wingfield, of "Eighteen With A Bullet" fame, produced *SoulBeat* in 1964, and a sixteen-year-old from Plymouth called Tony Cummings, with a friend Derek Brandon, commenced publication of *Soul* magazine. Tony, who now works as a producer and presenter on Cross Rhythms, Britain's first contemporary Christian music station, recalled those early days.

"I first became interested in R&B at the age of thirteen when I bought my first records. I was simultaneously also fascinated by blues music. There was a record shop doing mail order in Plymouth, where I lived, called Pete Russell's Hot Record Store which had all the US imports of people like Howlin' Wolf, Bo Diddley, BB King etc right back to Robert Johnson and Blind Lemon Jefferson. But as an avid listener to Radio Luxembourg, I also listened to R&B as it became "soul music" and it was the latter – the Isley Brothers, Mary Wells, the Dells and thousands more – that eventually became my passion. I contributed to discographies and wrote letters for blues fanzines like *Blues*

63

Stax HQ, Memphis

Unlimited and *R&B Monthly*, but couldn't find much coverage of soul music save for Pete Wingfield's *SoulBeat*. So I started my own fanzine called *Soul*. I had voluminous correspondence with the other soul music nuts but didn't meet up with most of them until I relocated to London."

Although the first two issues were originally produced on duplicators using typed stencils – a laborious process which thankfully vanished with the advent of photocopiers and desk top publishing – the third issue in April 1966 was professionally printed. Contributors to the magazine included Mike Vernon, John Abbey, who would later run *Home Of The Blues* – the forerunner to *Blues & Soul,* Trevor Churchill, who went on to become label manager at EMI's Bell label and now at Ace Records, journalist Roger St. Pierre who started the Beacon label a few year later, and Kurt Mohr, a Swiss national based in Paris who compiled the most in-depth discographies on air-mail paper.

Price 2/6 **SOUL** No. 3
April
1966
THE MAGAZINE FOR THE R. & B. COLLECTOR.

Sam & Dave

Editor: Tony Cummings, 102, Beaumont Road, St. Judes,
Plymouth, Devon.
Assistant Editor: Derek Brandon.

The magazine changed its name to *Soul Music Monthly,* and by the time Tony had moved to the capital, he had joined forces with other like-minded soul freaks: Dave McAleer, who had produced four issues of a fanzine dedicated to the music of Memphis and Muscle Shoals titled *Fame-Goldwax Survey*; John Philibert, who ran *The Organisation* geared towards jazz organists and Mick Brown, who had taken over the reins of *SoulBeat* from Pete Wingfield. Helpers included Bill Millar, Charlie Gillett, a teacher who had just returned from studying in the States, and Clive Richardson, who would eventually take over the editorship of the publication when it had become *Shout.*

Clive recalls that one of the gang had spotted a headline in a music paper where Cliff Richard had spoken of "His Kind Of Soul". They were desperate not to be associated in any way with Richard, so they compiled a list of alternative names which would create an image, as far as possible away from that of the pop star. Tony Cummings' favourite 45 – the Isley Brothers' "Shout" – saved the day. Richardson thought the London R&B scene was very close knit. "It was like a brotherhood, a gathering of like-minded souls." A fact Tony Cummings remembers well.

"Soul music buffs back then really felt they were on some sort of religious crusade. The music of African Americans was being plundered and copied by a white music industry and the British cover versions of US R&B songs were loathed by us. We had the recorded evidence that "Money" by Barrett Strong or "Go Now" by Bessie Banks were vastly superior to the Beatles and the Moody Blues and hundreds more and our mission was to spread the word about the originators. Our intense belief that black music was always better than white music made us an odd little purist clique, and it was embarrassing when we occasionally discovered that one of our heroes like a Righteous Brothers or a Dean Parrish were, in fact, white."

John Abbey's *Home Of The Blues*, launched in 1966, irritated the hell out of the R&B clique, with its inclusion of articles and reviews of country and western artists and white rockers like Jerry Lewis. In fact, Abbey wrote a regular feature for *Record Mirror* on country music. Surprisingly, given the soul crowd's low opinion of Abbey, it was his publication *Home Of The Blues*, later *Blues & Soul*, which survived the longest. More commercially minded, Abbey put less emphasis on the facts and information, and had no qualms about putting the Four Tops or Otis Redding on the front cover.

Originally duplicated, after financial input from a mysterious character called Delazlo, the magazine was professionally printed and distributed. In October '67, the title changed to *Blues & Soul*, and Abbey added another string to his bow, by selling imports through their retail business, Contempo. The office in Burlington Street became a regular haunt for soul fans, who used to clamber up four flights of stairs to rummage through boxes of records. It was a logical move, when the publication relocated to Hanway Street in January 1970, to sell records on Saturday mornings, and as the demand grew they were soon open every day.

"Suddenly, amidst the Beatles and the Dave Clark 5, came a song that was to change my whole life forever. The handclaps, that 'OOOH', and I was in another world listening to "Where Did Our Love Go". From that moment on, soul music would become a way of life for me..."

$tateside

STATESIDE IS THE TRADEMARK OF THE GRAMOPHONE CO. LTD.

MADE IN GT. BRITAIN

$tateside

45 R.P.M.

SS 327

Belinda
(London) Ltd.
BIEM
45KR-4355
A Tamla-Motown
Prod.

Recording first
published 1964

SOLD IN U.K. SUBJECT TO
RESALE PRICE CONDITIONS
SEE PRICE LISTS

WHERE DID OUR LOVE GO
(Holland—Dozier—Holland)
THE SUPREMES

E.M.I. RECORDS LIMITED

$tateside

STATESIDE IS THE TRADEMARK OF
THE GRAMOPHONE CO LTD
ONE OF THE E M I GROUP OF COMPANIES

EMI

THE GREATEST RECORDING
ORGANISATION IN THE WORLD

"The only way of finding out what was good in music was by scanning the newly-formed pirate radio stations, especially Caroline, who broadcast a Sunday afternoon Top 100 USA Chart Show, which was even more trendy than *Beyond Our Ken*, which was broadcast on parallel on the Beeb. Also, the new release section of *Record Mirror* listed all the items that I knew I would want to order from my little record shop. The guy who ran the shop was in his sixties, and usually a little grumpy, but he did seem to know what I wanted. There can't have been many kids in Bromley, Kent who walked in there with their pocket money to find a copy of the Velvelettes' 'Lonely Lonely Girl Am I' waiting for them. I've still got it with 6/8 chalked on the top of the sleeve.

So with the help of the aforementioned, it soon became clear which labels were going to be of interest, and before long a nice collection of Tamla, Stateside, Capitol, Polydor, HMV and President was made.

In 1968, I discovered Soul City. So my collection sprouted – Revilots, Golden Worlds, Drews, Solid Hits, Brunswicks and many other treasures. Suddenly all the shops were getting US singles, just as I was earning good money. By the early seventies, stocks of '60s records were to be had at ridiculous prices. I remember seeing over twenty copies of Mike & the Modifiers on Oriole in Woolworth. Record Corner in Balham, had taken over as one of the top importers of soul and a regular visit ensured one's collection stayed topped up with a very high percentage of all US releases on major and minor labels. At this stage in life, I don't think that I had heard the term 'Northern Soul', but this was about to change.

Firstly, one Saturday in the West End, I entered a Harlequin record shop and there I met Dave Burton, and to the strains of Rose Batiste's "Sweetheart Darling", first realised that I was not the only person in the world who raved over Motown-esque music. Thanks to Dave, I was introduced to the term 'Northern Soul', and a whole lot of new sounds that I had never heard of before.

I gave Dave a copy of the recently found Otis Smith disc, 'Let Her Go', his face was a picture – a deflated pumpkin with eyes! Dave took the record to Blackpool, and I believe that was my first step into the scene. However, far more gems were to appear from another source in the not too distant future.

I had written to *Record Mirror*, pointing out that the UK issue on Track of the Debonaires' 'I'm In Love Again' had the wrong writer credits, and anyone interested in this kind of music to write to me. The response was unbelievable – a guy from Sunderland who collected the Track label; a couple from Northampton who appeared more interested in bondage; and lastly, a chap from New Jersey who had a spare of the original Solid Hit issue – would I like it? His name was Kurt Schwartz, and we had exactly the same taste in music. He obviously hadn't heard of the Northern scene, but found duplicates, with ease, of records that nobody in this country knew of. Exchanging six or seven discs every fortnight, some of the gems included Patti & the Emblems 'I'm Gonna Love You A Long Long Time', Pat Lewis 'No One To Love', Doni Burdick 'Bari Track', Cissy Houston 'Bring Him Back' and Edwin Starr 'You're My Mellow'.

I remember taking into Dave's shop one record in particular – Dean Courtney's 'We Got A Good Thing', and Dave playing it to Ian Levine over the 'phone. The whole shop could hear Ian, at the other end of the 'phone, shouting 'I must have it, I must have it, I MUST HAVE IT!'

A week later, another copy arrived, and he did indeed have it."

NICK WASHER

CHAPTER 4

I'm Gonna Be A Wheel Someday

A MYTH THAT has been perpetuated for years is that the Beatles, and others behind the Mersey Beat, obtained early R&B and rock 'n' roll records from merchant seamen coming into the Liverpool docks. This early exposure to American vinyl has been said to have been the spark that ignited Liverpool's musical prominence in the Sixties.

Aside from the fact that many of the examples often cited were issued by British companies, Liverpool's days as a centre for transatlantic shipping had long gone by the Fifties. By this time transatlantic cargo was likely to have been unloaded down the Ship Canal, through Cheshire and into Manchester. The area around Trafford Road is known as "The Barbary Coast" – a reference to the variety of goods dropped off there. Alan Lawson, in *It Happened In Manchester*, has said that although records were not part of the official cargoes, there are a lot of locals who still own American singles which came from the Ship Canal. If there is a basis to the merchant navy connection, it would seem rather than Liverpool that Manchester would have been the beneficiary. While Liverpool may continue to be seen as the most musically influential city in the North West, Manchester certainly had the wilder night life, having over two hundred clubs during the early Sixties.

A thriving coffee bar scene had been developing in Manchester since the late Fifties and exotically named establishments such as The Mogambo, Zanzibar, The Cona, La Cave, Jungfrau, Pacific and the Hi-Fi became popular haunts for teenagers. At night, many re-opened as clubs.

One such place was the Left Wing coffee bar, at 26 Brazennose Street, a

71

favourite haunt of beatniks. When this shut down, the premises were acquired by the Abadi brothers, and in March 1963 it re-opened as the Twisted Wheel. At the opening night a local group, Dean West and the Hellions, debuted at the club. After a few months, on Saturday 23rd September, the Twisted Wheel held its first all-nighter, featuring the Graham Bond Quartet and the Spencer Davis Group. The club instantly became the flagbearer for the change to the harder-edged music which was becoming popular – Rhythm and Blues. News spread about the Wheel, and by 1964 the club's membership was fourteen thousand strong.

British R&B copyists, such as Jimmy Powell & The Dimensions, Long John Baldry, Alexis Korner, Zoot Money and John Mayall's Bluesbreakers became regular acts at the club. American artists started to visit the country, and early visitors to Brazennose Street included Champion Jack Dupree, John Lee Hooker, T-Bone Walker, Screamin' Jay Hawkins, Little Walter, Solomon Burke and Charlie & Inez Foxx. Many of the performances were reviewed in the fanzine *R&B Scene*, edited by the club's DJ Roger Eagle.

Described as "Britain's Leading Rhythm & Blues Magazine", it was professionally printed and sold for one shilling and sixpence. Eagle was aided by Neil Carter and *Blues Unlimited*'s Mike Leadbitter. While the London fanzines were concentrating on the world of soul music, Manchester's *R&B Scene* was defiantly blinkered to the contemporary black music arena. Homesick James, Sonny Boy Williamson and Screamin' Jay Hawkins were given far more prominence, and the Sue label was singled out for praise because of the many blues sides issued. Dan Joffey, who ran the Screamin' Jay Hawkins' Fan Club, made the mistake of calling *R&B Scene* a Mod magazine. This earned a swift

Pye International launched the R&B Series in March 1963

72

rebuke from Roger Eagle: "Where you got that idea from, we don't know, but nothing could be further from the truth." There was a fear within the editorial team of *R&B Scene* that the "mod" influence would somehow ruin appreciation of R&B – but it was too late. The mod scene had quickly spread from the capital and the New Wave of soul music was becoming increasingly popular. The Blue Gardenia in White Horse Street, Leeds was advertising Thursday "Soul Sessions", and the Twisted Wheel was becoming *the* club to be seen at.

The arrival of Eagle rapidly elevated the Wheel's status, from being just another beat and jive coffee bar to a club capable of competing with the R&B strongholds of the capital, such as the Marquee and the Flamingo.

Local lad, Phil Scott discovered the Wheel after going there to see John Lee Hooker. "The club, with its cavernous rooms and distinctive 'wheel' decor generated an electic atmosphere. By 1964, it had become home for the first generation of Northern Mods. Every Saturday night, rows and rows of scooters would be parked outside, whilst inside mohair-suited Mods and die-hard R&B fans listened and danced to records that couldn't be heard anywhere else. Although under Eagle the Wheel had established a firm R&B policy at Brazennose street, the demand from Mods for more soul music was not ignored and a wonderful blend, as only Roger could do, of R&B and the emergent sounds of young black America was played. The Wheel became the benchmark that scores of clubs would follow. The dancers were second to none. The records played could not be heard anywhere else, and the crowd were unique. The club belonged to the 'In Crowd', quite simply because it was the birthplace of the Manchester soul scene."

John Mayall's Bluesbreakers played at the last night in Brazennose Street and the club moved to Whitfield Street, a few hundred yards from Manchester's Piccadilly railway station. The majority of the late night venues in Manchester were originally coffee

"The Esquire Club in Sheffield is great – on a visit there a few weeks ago we heard a very good selection of records indeed, here's one club where the 'mod' influence has not ruined the appreciation of R&B..."
Roger Eagle,
R&B Scene, April 1965

bars which charged a membership fee, and so qualified as private clubs. As many of them became havens for young runaways, and drug use became rife, there was a fear that the city's clubland was running out of control. This caused consternation in the Manchester Vice Squad, and an Act of Parliament was passed in 1965. Many clubs in Manchester were closed down, but the Twisted Wheel avoided this fate. With the police station directly opposite the new premises, it was perhaps felt that the club would be easier to control.

An all-nighter, with the Spencer Davis Group, re-launched the Wheel in 1966, with many of the members doubtful that the Victorian building would be able to capture the atmosphere of the original site. Roger Eagle found the demand for uptempo soul prevented him from presenting a broader range of black American music, so he eventually left to open the Stax Club in Fountain Street. Eagle's fears about the mod influence were realised, and the Twisted Wheel was left to develop its reputation as one of the foremost soul clubs in the country.

During the mid Sixties, the club entrance opened to a passage leading to a coffee bar, with the dance area in the basement. The stone floor downstairs was divided by painted brick walls into a series of alcoves, each with speakers wired up to the club's sound system, which was powered by a thirty watt amplifier. The DJ was stationed in a cage, made of bicycle wheels, and the theme was carried on to the walls where cartwheels were hung. Today, the listed building is a gay club. The exterior is similar to how it appeared in its heyday, but the inside has changed considerably over the years.

John Knight, a teenager from Halifax, first went to the Wheel soon after it had opened in Whitfield Street – what John recalls as the mod's Jerusalem. He recalled his impressions for Howard Earnshaw's *Soul Up North* fanzine.

"Living in West Yorkshire, Whitworth Street was highly accessible and virtually from its opening in 1966, the year when I first went there, packed out at every all-nighter. If you didn't get in the queue early, when a star attraction like Junior Walker & the All-Stars were appearing, there was little hope of getting in through the doors if you were at the tail end. Don't believe the tales of sneaking in through the fire doors, that never happened.

"If you arrived by scooter, they were usually parked up an alleyway behind the club. Chromed panels weren't usually brought along. Scooter thieving

"The Twisted Wheel was, without doubt, the 'in' place in the mid to late 60's. Anyone who hadn't made the pilgrimage to this chapel of soul, was just a plain unfortunate, or worse, playing at being a mod. Unpardonable, either way in those elitist days. Being a mod was all about style. What you wore, how you wore it, how you danced and what records you danced to at the all-nighters. Only Soul would do. Soul was stylish, and being a mod was all about being stylish and having a good time, every time!"

John Knight

happened regularly, whole scooters, occasionally a few at a time, went missing – not just tasty accessories! Generally, most goers turned up by train as it was convenient for the club and also for meeting up at Piccadilly. It was also not the done thing to turn up looking wet and bedraggled from a rainy ride across the Pennines. Guaranteed piss taking would usually follow from those arriving looking sleek in their dry crombies, instead of a soaking wet parka. As

appearance was all important, it was important to carry around spares. Usually shirts and socks in air travel bags or holdalls. The really flash brought hand towels, soap and other clean up bits. No girl ever turned up without the ubiquitous vanity case filled with god only knows what.

"The interior decoration of the Wheel wasn't particularly interesting and would not survive close scrutiny from the more fastidious in respect of cleanliness. When it rained, it leaked and in summer, in the middle of the night, the place could overheat badly. Even with the best personal hygiene around, and perfume, as well as after shave and talc there was a distinctive body odour aroma! The row of spoked wheels separating the DJ from the dancers, is probably what most Wheel goers remember. This was at the opposite end from the stage. Requests were constantly being made. Some people would turn up with interesting new records to play. Surprisingly, rare soul anoraks didn't seem to exist quite like they do these days, and this might have had something to do with the mod culture and cool attitude. But I tell a little white lie, there were always at least two mohair-suited individuals outlined with anorak halo's standing in a corner never dancing and disdaining everything they heard with the type of comments regularly heard from present day anoraks, 'What a lot of shite. What's this rubbish he's playing.' They were a seriously endangered minority."

However, Wheel regulars did begin collecting the sounds being spun at the club. The Detroit Spinners' "I'll Always Love You" was an elusive 45, and in late 1967, an entrepreneurial regular managed to get hold of a dozen import copies. These were quickly snapped up for thirty shillings each. Tina Britt's "The Real Thing", the Miracles' "That's What Love Is Made Of", the Drifters'

"Baby What I Mean", the Vibrations' "Talkin' 'Bout Love" and the Olympics' "We Go Together" were just some of the recently deleted singles that began to pick up plays, and high prices. Like other clubs at the time, blue beat made it on to the turntables and tracks like Prince Buster's "Al Capone", "The Ten Commandments", the Folks Brothers' "Carolina" and Roland Alphonso's "Phoenix City" were mixed in with the R&B records.

As John Knight remembers, it was not only the music that had the strongest pull. "Legend may also have it, that everyone went to the Wheel just to dance and listen to the new rare sounds making an appearance on the turntable. Whilst this is not untrue, others were there to see who they could pull and a lot of that happened at the all-nighters. These were generally the folk who weren't pill heads. How pairing seemed to take place, almost without any warning or indication, could be a mystery to those who had not sorted out the eye-contact routines. Heavy snogging sessions were normal with pairs so close together a ten shilling note wouldn't have slipped between them. It was one way to break up the all-nighter with a groping session, while you rested your legs from the dancing. If you were into voyeurism you might have got to see more!"

Dozens of live acts played at the Wheel, from Ike & Tina Turner and the Ikettes, together with their ten piece band, to a Roy Tempest girl group, misleadingly billed as the Shiffons. Even Jimi Hendrix dropped by one night, to see the Spellbinders live on stage – the New Jersey group's "Help Me" was a massive Wheel record.

"Two records that particularly remind me of the place" John Knight recalls "and seemed to typify it, were "Soul Sauce" by Cal Tjader and "Soul Serenade" by Beau Dollar, two classy and haunting instrumentals. At the time, they seemed to reflect the smart, classy, cool mod attitude that prevailed."

However, it wasn't always possible or even necessary to get to Whitworth Street to be the style kings or queens. "There were lots of excellent small clubs in the North that held regular all-nighters with top acts on the bill."

77

remembers John. "One such venue was the Plebeians Jazz Club, more commonly called 'The Plebs', in Upper George Yard in Halifax. You knew you were onto a good thing as soon as you arrived, in nearby George's Square, by the sixty or so scooters parked there on a typical Saturday night. The Pierre Cardin suited crews, with twelve inch vents in the back of their jackets, making their way into the Plebs for an all-nighter *were* Dobie Gray's 'In Crowd'. You could almost hear them silently singing, Robert Parker's "Let's Go Baby (Where The Action Is)". The Plebs attracted Mods from all the local towns and cities, even from as far away as Sheffield and Burnley. And what a place! It was an early 19th century warehouse cellar virtually in the centre of the town. You went down stone stairs, paid and got the obligatory pass-out stamp in the bright red light of the entrance, before entering the club which was almost pitch black, apart from the brightly lit stage. Today's fire regulations would never have allowed a place so tightly packed to get a licence – the place heaved! And a cloud of sweat literally turned to steam before hitting the ceiling and turning into running condensation.

"The all-nighter's were legendary – like the Twisted Wheel but on a far smaller scale. Inez and Charlie Foxx, the Drifters, Herbie Goins, the Alan Bown Set, Mike Cotton, Jimmy Cliff, the Ferris Wheel, they all played there. The playlist was something else too. Whatever was being played at the Twisted Wheel, was played at the Plebs, but with the added attraction of its own unique selection of all time goodies, some rare and some not rare at all. As long as the floor stayed packed, the DJ knew his job was getting done. Any record out of flow, or tempo, was guaranteed to clear the floor, as the dancers hit the freezing cold night air to cool down.

"In 1965, the Plebs playlist was heavily dominated by Motown, Stax and Atlantic. The music was fresh and vital – tailor made for dancing. However, it didn't take the DJs long to go out hunting for something different. By early 1967, records from rarer labels were featuring very heavily on the club's playlist. Chubby Checker's "(At the) Discotheque" was *the* big Soul rarity. The DJ who owned a copy, like the Plebs' "King" Arthur, was guaranteed to regally command the dance floor. Bunny Sigler's "Let The Good Times Roll" was another one – much sought after – that had feet going. The really hard-to-find "Incense" by the Anglos, with Stevie Winwood, was another superb slice of white soul which was guaranteed to raise the temperature. The Impressions' "I Can't Satisfy", "Meeting Over Yonder" and "You've Been Cheatin" were all floor fillers. James and Bobby Purify's emotionally charged soul anthem "Let Love Come Between Us" kept the dancers moving, as did their other classic "Do Unto Me". Homer Banks telling us all about "A Lot Of Love" helped the sweat turn into steam and hit the ceiling in the same way that Bobby Wells described it on "Let's Copp A Groove". The Showstoppers' "Ain't Nothing But A House Party" with the Bandwagon's version of "Breaking Down The Walls Of Heartache" (not to mention the flip side "Dancin, Master") all ensured high energy raving into the early hours.

"And who didn't enjoy Bob Kuban & The In-men telling you all about "The Cheater"? Big beat stompers that blasted out of the speaker's included

Rex Garvin's "Sock It To 'Em, JB" with it's companion "You Can't Sit Down" by Phil Upchurch. Almost anything by Willie Mitchell, on the London label, got a wholly credible response as did the guru of the organ, Billy Preston. Lee Dorsey's "Ride Your Pony" and Donnie Elbert's "A Little Piece Of Leather" were instant classics and rarely off the turntables. But it was the unusual and off-beat discs like Cozy Cole's "Big Noise From Winnetka", that made the Plebs outstanding in its selections of soul. On a packed dance floor it was no wonder that "Getting Mighty Crowded" by Betty Everett struck the right notes. And some tracks played at the "Plebs" never lost their allure. The Fascinations "Girls Are Out To Get You" and Darrell Banks' "Open The Door To Your Heart" remain definitive soul tracks."

Jimmy Claven, a familiar face on the soul scene during the Sixties, lived in Todmorden during this time, and his first visit to the Plebeian was a memorable event. "I was thirteen and the first niter I went to was at "Plebs". As soon as I'd begun, there was no stopping me! Week after week, during what I consider to be the truly golden years, there was the Cavern at Burnley, the Birdtrap at Brierfield, the Wheel, of course, and the sadly underrated Blue

Note and Top 20. I had the dubious honour of being Todmorden's first chemist raider and got six months in a detention centre for my first offence. And due to appalling abuse, I missed the last night at the Wheel."

In the summer of 1965, the rock 'n' roll veteran Larry Williams toured the UK with the relatively unknown Johnny "Guitar" Watson. To the disappointment of his British fans, Williams' act was light years away from his Fifties hits "Short Fat Fannie" and "Bonie Moronie", and the despondent singer was forced to relive the past for his British fans, who were unwilling to accept the new direction his career was taking. Williams would became a producer for Columbia's OKeh label a couple of years later and enjoy limited success duetting with Watson. Their vocal version of jazz saxophonist "Cannonball" Adderley's "Mercy, Mercy, Mercy" would be a minor R&B hit in 1967, and the storming flip-side "A Quitter Never Wins" would later gain approval in the North.

Their performances were seen by Roger Eagle and reviewed in *R&B Scene*: "Two great artistes with a tremendous amount of talent, and yet this recent tour was not the wild success it could have been by any means. I saw Larry four times in the North, and on each occasion there was something missing, although the early performance at the Wheel in Manchester did give some idea of what the man could do." Eagle had heard that their London appearance had been great and "well-attended by the faithful."

Williams and Watson's appearance at the Ricky-Tick in Guildford was witnessed by Allan Smith, an R&B enthusiast from Wolverhampton. "Distance was no object, as I worked for British Rail and could buy train tickets at a quarter of the normal fare. After the Ricky-Tick, I caught the train to London and went to the Flamingo in London's Wardour Street. This was my first all-nighter and appearing live were Georgie Fame and Herbie Goins & The Nightimers. It was incredible!"

The Flamingo in Wardour Street was owned by Rik and John Gunnell. It attracted a predominately West Indian crowd, which was bolstered by black American GIs. Also in attendance were a variety of Soho nightlife – local gangsters, pimps and prostitutes. Visiting jazz musicians from members of Duke Ellington's orchestra and Count Basie's group would drop by when in the UK. In June 1963, when Cassius Clay came to fight Henry Cooper, he asked where "the brothers hang out". Georgie Fame, who was a regular performer at the club, played the night of Clay's visit. There were regular blue-beat nights, live sessions from acts like Zoot Money's Big Roll Band, and American acts such as Solomon Burke. Then there was a stabbing at the Flamingo, which prompted the American air force authorities to ban servicemen from the club. It quickly became packed with Mods.

Allan had first been interested in rock 'n' roll and had graduated through blues to R&B and soul music. After his experience of the Flamingo, he started going to the all-nighters at the Whisky-A-Go-Go in Birmingham, seeing Ike & Tina Turner with the Ikettes on his first visit. He became a regular, catching many of the best live acts of the day – Steam Packet, Brian Auger Trinity with Julie Driscoll and a number of R&B stars. As Allan recalls, one performance almost did not take place. "Robert Parker appeared once, although he had trouble getting in because they thought that he was trying to get in for nothing. They kept him at the door for ages."

It wasn't long before Alan made it to the Twisted Wheel. The trek to the club would begin at a coffee bar in Wolverhampton called the Milano. "It was frequented mostly by Mods and we used to meet there before going to Manchester. We used to hitch hike or go on the train if we could afford the fare." On his first trip to the Wheel he had expected to see Charlie & Inez Foxx but they cancelled and were replaced by The Alan Bown Set, a very popular act throughout the Sixties – their cover of Little Anthony & The Imperials' "Gonna Fix You Good" was a crowd pleaser. British bands appeared at the Wheel regularly during the summer, when there tended not to be many visiting American acts.

"I then went about seventeen or eighteen weeks on the trot. There were so many great live bands – The Action were really good. The biggest sounds I can remember from the Wheel were Sam & Dave's "You Don't Know Like I Know", The Astors' "Candy", Willie Tee's "Walking Up A One Way Street", Alvin Cash & The Crawlers' "Twine Time" and the Sharpees' "Tired Of Being Lonely". The tempo was slower then, they weren't like the 100 mile-an-hour racers that would come in later. After it closed in the morning, we used to walk to a coffee bar behind Victoria Station, where there used to be a soup kitchen that gave out free coffee from the back of a wagon."

Johnny Sayles

CHAPTER 5

Got My Mojo Workin'

THE PSYCHEDELIC EXPERIMENTS from the West Coast of America began in the mid-Sixties with tracks like the Byrds' "Eight Miles High" and the Beach Boys' "Good Vibrations". It was an excuse for some Mods to grow their hair and pull on kaftans and flowery shirts. The music policy at a few nightclubs began to reflect the promised New Dawn; Soft Machine's jazz doodlings at the Happening 44 Club and Pink Floyd's all-night raves at the UFO got the underground movement idiot-dancing in the blobby coloured light shows. Not surprisingly, Tiles jumped on the bandwagon and organised a rock festival, which turned out to be a financial disaster.

Even Guy Stevens lost faith in soul and R&B. He left the Sue label to work with Hapshash and Coloured Coat, and would occasionally return to Island to help out with their growing roster of progressive bands. After a brief emergence in 1979, as producer of punk band the Clash, he died two years later of a suspected drink and drugs overdose.

Soul acts from the States continued to tour the UK, but were beginning to notice less interest in London. Garnet Mimms made his first appearance in the country and was the support act to The Jimi Hendrix Experience. The accompanying review in *Home Of The Blues* of his show at the Saville Theatre ended with: "The closing act, Jimi Hendrix Experience, brought us back to the world of reality. Thump, crash and a trio of long-haired gentlemen. No comment." This strange mixture of styles had been preceded by other unlikely pairings – Ben E. King with Bo Diddley, and the astonishing combination of Lee Dorsey and Pink Floyd.

In April 1967, Charlie & Inez Foxx appeared at a modernised Flamingo, with Barbara Gaskins, one half of the Barbara & Brenda duo. In a brief interview with Peter Trickey of *Home Of The Blues*, Inez Foxx expressed disappointment at the poor attendance. Their shows in the provinces had caused hysteria amongst three thousand or more at a time. At the Flamingo there were only two hundred.

After Stevens had gone, John Abbey maintained standards at the Sue label with first-rate soul releases by the Lamp Sisters, O.V.Wright and Bobby Bland. When Island sold their West Indian music labels to entrepreneur Lee Gopthal, Sue became a victim of Island's revamp and changed its identity to Action. Abbey continued his work under Gopthal's B&C umbrella.

The summer of love was beginning to take its toll on the capital's soul clubs, and its influence was being felt in the North. The popular all-nighter the King Mojo, blossomed into The Beautiful Mojo. Phil Stables, from Doncaster, recalls the strange times when joss sticks burnt in the club.

"The summer of '67 marked a watershed for the youth of Britain and also for the King Mojo. Slowly, but with gathering speed as the summer wore on, the papers were full of reports of love, flowers, San Fransisco and LSD which was reflected by Stringfellow at The Mojo. The club was repainted with flower

The Fantastic
JOHNNY C

designs and some members started to appear wearing kaftans, beads and even cow-bells. Generally this was regarded as a bit of fun, but some took this new philosophy very seriously. The whole scene did not change completely, but to the dismay of the serious soulmen, some pop records with the "Peace & Love" theme began to infiltrate the play list. The club became a curious mixture of modernist soul fans and those who had 'freaked out'. The dance floor could be full of foot slides, spins and back drops, "Boogaloo" and "Funky Broadway", then almost in an instant, "All You Need Is Love" or "Let's Go To San Francisco" would come on, and the hippie element would lift up their arms and sway around in what seemed an early version of the Mexican wave. Despite these differences, the mood of the crowd was still amicable. That summer of '67, was all at once, interesting, tragic, amusing and silly. Things seemed to settle down by the autumn but it was becoming too late for The Mojo." Owner Peter Stringfellow took to wearing a kaftan, and would often stop records half-way through to philosophise on whatever subjects took his fancy. The crowd at the club took it all in good spirit.

The playboy proprietor of Stringfellow's nightclub in London's West End was an amiable host, and was revered by teenagers in the Sheffield and Doncaster area. As Stables recalls: "The atmosphere in the club was always warm and friendly, due in the main to the casual and unassuming approach of

ARTISTICS

Personal Management
Carl Davis
1449 S. Michigan Ave.
427-0828
Chicago, Illinois

Peter. His influence was obviously strong – he was rated, having an easy manner on the decks, and would dance and chat between records." However, it was a different kind of record that became the turning point in Stringfellow's life.

After a three-month prison sentence for selling stolen carpets, Peter Stringfellow began to organise dances in Sheffield, first running the Black Cat Club and then The Blue Moon from local church halls. He would black out the windows with chipboard, hang red light bulbs from the ceiling and plug his mother's radiogram to the choir's speaker system to play records in between the local beat groups. Having successfully promoted the Beatles at the Azena Ballroom in Gleadless, Stringfellow was approached by a local businessman, Ruben Wallis, and asked if he wanted to buy a derelict Victorian house that had once been Day's Dance Hall. The asking price of five thousand pounds was too much for Stringfellow, so he agreed to rent the building for thirty pounds a week. Stringfellow named the club after Muddy Waters' "Got My Mojo Working", a favourite song of his that Long John Baldry would perform at the Blue Moon. Stringfellow assumed that his regular crowd would follow

IN EARLY 1967, little known American acts came to the UK masquerading as more famous stars. Promoted by Roy Tempest, the groups performed in many of the UK's soul clubs. At Klooks Kleek Klub in Hampstead, the Invitations hoodwinked R&B fans into believing they were the Original Drifters. An article in *Home Of The Blues*, revealed that the Invitations third single for Dynovoice, "Ski-ing In The Snow" featured the lead vocal of Roy Jolly. Their first two songs for the label had been Top 100 R&B hits, but the hat trick was not completed.

The Steinways, whose "My Heart's Not In It Anymore" was a Torch favourite, and subsequently bootlegged on Out Of The Past, performed as the

THE VELOURS

Platters. The Velours' of "I'm Gonna Change" fame played clubs as the Fabulous Temptations, although they did announce to the audience before each show that they were not the Motown act. John Cheatdom of the Velours remembers that Motown sent over a spy to check the group out. "Motown sued us, but they dropped it once they found out we weren't doing that much damage. When we had become the Fantastics we were working at Louis Brown's Valbonne, when Eddie Kendricks and Melvin Franklin came in, sat down and watched the whole show. We were in the dressing room and word gets to us that they'd like us to come over to their table. We said 'We aren't coming out of that dressing room for anything. But after an hour, I said OK, I'll break the ice – I'm the smallest one! I went over to their table and Eddie Kendricks said "Hey man you ain't bad. Sit here and have a drink.

"Phew! I went back, got the rest of the group to come front – it wasn't bad, we became friends".

And Sam, Erv & Tom who also recorded as the Diplomats, spent the evening at a club in the Midlands, trying to meet with their idols the Isley Brothers, before being told that they were the advertised act.

him to the Mojo, but the club attracted a new clientele of Mods desperate to hear blues and R&B. Phil Stables evoked the spirit of The King Mojo, in *Come And Get These Memories* – a fanzine edited by soul fan Keith Rylett.

"The first impression once inside the club was of the coffee bar area, selling Coke, soft drinks and coffee, which was furnished with barrel tables and a few chairs dotted about. This was the only area in the Mojo that was well illuminated. Moving on to the right brought the main dancing area and the heart of the club into view. Typical of many clubs of the period this was not large by modern standards. The club had a capacity of only a couple of hundred or so, but many more would squeeze in, especially for the live acts.

"Walking onto the dance floor immediately to the front was a large stage on which Peter Stringfellow had his decks to the left hand side near the wall. To the left of the stage was a smaller stage area, which was mainly used as a raised dance area or an elevated position to view the live acts when they appeared."

The Mojo went through many transformations during its short life; African warriors were painted on the walls with small mirrors in their eyes; the stage was covered with dolls which Stringfellow had encouraged club members to bring in; everything, including the grand piano, was once painted in PopArt black and white stripes; and a Thirties theme with murals of American cars and gangsters, probably inspired by the popular television series *The Untouchables,* led to a few regulars turning up at the club in three-piece pinstripe suits and trilby hats.

Image was all, as Phil Stables recalls: "The members of The Mojo were modernists, stylists and soulmen, the term "mod" was becoming less used apart from the younger kids at school. There was also a core of the older "swingers" whose dress probably reflected the styles of Swingin' London, rather than the street cred of the modernist in long vented mohair suits. Bud Harper did sing "my suits are all mohair" and he *was* Mr. Soul! Levi's jeans and suede and leather jackets, Italian style casual shoes and the English brogue, all set off with neat cropped hair."

Garnet Mimms

Bob Harris, from Sheffield, who met Stables whilst travelling to the Blue Orchid all-nighter in Derby, remembers that the different fashion trends were very important. "At the early clubs, everybody wore Levis and Wrangler denims and cords which were complimented by accessories such as pork pie hats, trilbys, berets and gloves. The style of shoes varied, but dark brown or green Tuff 'T' boots were popular. And definitely sun glasses. These were essential, especially at the Esquire, where unless you wore shades, you could be accused of knowing where you were. They also neatly advised the local drug squad that you were a potential suspect. Clever weren't we?"

Invariably, when no live act was appearing, girls would get up on stage to do their dance routines to "Let The Good Times Roll" or "Philly Freeze". The essence of the atmosphere at The Mojo was one of a big house party. On occasions, Stringfellow would hand over the DJ spot to "Dinky Dawson", who despite the nickname, was anything but dinky. From Worksop, Stuart "Dinky" Dawson was a local personality who ran promotions, similar in style, to Stringfellow's earlier efforts. The Pendulum, in Rotherham, was held in a rented church hall, and members of another club, Lemon B. Jefferson's, could see "Art, Dinky & Dave" dancing as a team on stage to their own individual favoured styles of music – a curious blend of progressive rock, rock 'n' roll and soul music. Dawson became a DJ at the Broken Wheel in Retford, and later sound engineer for Fleetwood Mac, the Byrds and Steely Dan. He now lives in the USA.

89

The King Mojo played host to a string of American and British acts. The Alan Bown Set, Amboy Dukes, Zoot Money, Amen Corner, Root and Jenny Jackson all played the club. However, the most popular acts were the American visitors; Oscar Toney Jnr, Edwin Starr, Junior Walker, J. J. Jackson, Stevie Wonder and Garnet Mimms.

Edwin Starr made his UK debut at the Mojo. "I first came over in 1966 with "Agent Double-O-Soul", and immediately found my footing. I felt comfortable because everybody was so receptive, knowledgeable – they'd all done their homework. They knew all my records, they knew about the record company and the other artists on the label, it was astonishing." Starr later recorded for Stringfellow's Hippodrome label in 1985.

As with most clubs during this period, the majority of the records played were new or recent releases, and Phil Stables reckons that out of the two hundred and eighty singles released during the last nine month period of the club, almost all were played. In his article for *Come And Get These Memories*, he compiled a Mojo Top Ten, which is a good indication of the most popular tracks played. The playlists on the Northern soul circuit were similar, but each club had tracks peculiar to that club alone. At the Mojo, it was Billy Stewart's cover of "Exodus", from his "Teaches Old Standards New Tricks" album. In addition to the new releases, Stringfellow would often play the older R&B tracks such as Little Willie John's 1956 hit "Fever".

The club was situated at the end of a row of impressive Victorian houses that overlooked Abbey Field Park, and local residents began to complain about the noise, alleged drug use, and the sexual antics of the teenagers. Inevitably rumours began to circulate that the club was going to close.

The last all-dayer at the Mojo was on 8th October 1967, and featured a live appearance by Stevie Wonder. At the time, the track "Love A Go-Go", taken from the "Uptight" album, was a big favourite, so it was inevitably packed.

ARTHUR FREEMAN
Fame Records

DIRECTION
Phil Walden
Artists and Promotio

REDWAL MUSIC BUILDING 535 COTTON AVE

THE KING MOJO

MARKEYS "Last Night"

HOMER BANKS "60 Minutes Of Your Love"

DRIFTERS "Baby What I Mean"

BRENDA HOLLOWAY "Just Look What You've Done"

WILLIE MITCHELL "That Drivin' Beat"

CONTOURS "It's So Hard Being A Loser"

WILSON PICKETT "Funky Broadway"

HOWARD TATE "Look At Granny Run Run"

STEVIE WONDER "Love A Go-Go"

BILLY STEWART "Exodus"

KING
MOJO
CLUB
(SHEFFIELD)

Telephone 2 3 5 1 6

An application for a music and dancing license was rejected and despite Stringfellow's appeal, the club eventually closed. One local resident, Dougie Birge gave evidence, saying that he had counted fifteen used condoms in the club's car park one morning, and even worse, as an avid budgie breeder, stated that his birds had not hatched a single egg in four years because the volume of the music had cracked them all.

Phil Stables, along with others, had taken time off from school and gone to the proceedings. Even though the court case was boring, and the evidence was continually interrupted by legal niceties, they felt compelled to go. Everybody was devastated at the news that the Mojo would close. Stables recalls that he intended to daub Sheffield Cathedral with red paint, but was talked out of it by his friends. "In our eyes, the cathedral was where the city's old people went to worship, and I thought that my protest would demonstrate how fed-up we were at our temple being taken away."

Jr Walker

CHAPTER 6

Soul As Deep As You Like...
And Then Some!

JUNIOR WALKER & The All Stars had been advertised to appear at The Mojo on 25th October 1967, and their appearance was re-scheduled for the Sheffield City Hall. Stringfellow opened a new club, Down Broadway, in the city centre, but this was seen by the soul members as a disappointing alternative with little atmosphere. The club with a reputation which had been growing in stature was The Twisted Wheel in Manchester, and seemed the perfect substitute for the King Mojo. Whereas the Mojo was a friendly place where there was rarely any trouble, the Wheel had more of an edge. There were certain characters at the club who were infamous for "rolling" unsuspecting punters. But as Phil Stables recalls: "The Wheel's members were one hundred per cent dedicated, seriously fashion conscious, almost professional in their approach. Brogues were worn with tailored jackets over Levis. It was a stylish place."

John Smith, who now lives in Oxford, remembers his first visit to the Twisted Wheel. "The previous Sunday I had witnessed the final session at our adopted home The King Mojo in Sheffield. The last all-nighter had been a week earlier. We got to Manchester, courtesy of British Rail, catching the train from Sheffield Victoria Station, which, following a leisurely journey over the Pennines, deposited us on the platform at Piccadilly station. A quick exit from the station was the order of the day as there was always a large number of those friendly boys in blue only too keen to make the acquaintance of the mohair-suited foreigners. Down the ramp from the station we went, across the road and round the corner into Whitfield Street, and there on the right was the entrance to the Wheel. Membership cards were shown – we had written off for these in advance – monies were paid, and in we went.

"The cloakroom was to the right and in front were tables and chairs with a bar serving soft drinks to the left. Beyond this descending to the right was a staircase leading to the lower level and through an opening on the left was a cold dark and almost empty room with the toilets in the far corner. The music was piped up from below to these areas and out of the loudspeakers could be heard the familiar strains of Charlie Rich's "Love Is After Me", Bobby Bland's "Call On Me", Googie Rene Combo's "Smokey Joe's La-La" and other similar goodies. On down the stairs, turning back on yourself, and you were confronted by another rabbit's warren of rooms. To the right was the main room with the stage on the far side, and there were areas of raised flooring on the left to enable more people to see the stage more easily. Turning to the left, after descending the stairs, led you down a corridor formed from wooden and iron wheel shapes with small dance areas on the other side and at the end it opened out in front of the record decks. Here nameless DJs – I never knew their names anyway – played all the best sounds: Roscoe Robinson's "That's Enough", Chubby Checker's "(At The) Discotheque", the O'Jays' "I Dig Your Act". If any unfamiliar sounds were played, the DJs were only too pleased to tell you all the details.

"The club soon filled to bursting point due to the crowd pulling power of the live act, Junior Walker & The All Stars, plus the fact that at midnight the doors were shut and no further admittance was allowed. A rule strictly applied due to the proximity of the police station directly opposite the club. Old friends were greeted. 'Hey, the Notts crowd's upstairs', 'Fred from Scunthorpe's here with the Lincoln lads', together with many displaced from the Mojo. It became a regular home from home. The crush wasn't too bad, the atmosphere was definitely good and the great sounds kept coming; Dean Parrish's "Determination",

Fascinations' "Girls Are Out To Get You", Travis Wammack's "Scratchy" and many more.

"But then, as the clock sped past 2am, everyone began drifting towards the rear room and as the time approached for the All Stars to appear, things got very cramped as the contents of the whole club forced its way into the room to witness the live performance. They bounced on stage and immediately struck up with "Roadrunner", followed by "Shake And Fingerpop", "Cleo's Back", "Shotgun" and many more. It was well over an hour before they were suddenly gone leaving the audience gasping for air and a little more elbow room. The rest of the club was gradually re-populated and records again took over the task of keeping the customers satisfied. Bobby Moore's "Searching For My Baby", the Dynatones' "Fife Piper", Marvin Smith's "Have More Time" and Bobby McClure's "Peak Of Love" replaced the live Motown sounds. The remainder of the night was spent talking, dancing and looking through the few records for sale. By now the limbs were getting tired and empty seats were impossible to find, so every resting place was eagerly sought after as the pace in the club slowed slightly.

"Then it was all over. 7.30am and the double doors alongside the stage was opened and slowly and reluctantly everyone spilled out of the back of the club, up an embankment and onto the car park. Small groups built up around various cars, record boxes appeared and Discotrons did their best to recapture the sounds of the last eight hours, Art Freeman's "Slippin' Around" on red Atlantic changed hands for thirty shillings, Fontella Bass & Bobby McClure's "Don't Mess Up A Good Thing" for £1. Gradually people drifted away, cars departed on their journeys home and the car park emptied. We made our way back to Piccadilly and the 9.45am train to Sheffield.

"This had been our first Twisted Wheel visit, but it wasn't to be the last. To begin with, we only went occasionally, alternating between the Wheel and the Nite Owl in Leicester. But the last session at the Owl happened just seven weeks later on the 2nd December, and from then on there was only the Wheel left. So by default I became a regular for the next two years and an occasional visitor for a third year before the inevitable fate also befell the Wheel. In this

Junior Walker at
The Ram Jam Club,
Brixton

period though I had made many new friends. Ike & Tina Turner, Edwin Starr, Ben E. King, Billy Stewart and Oscar Toney Jnr. being the very best of the visiting artists. But for ten months out of the year, you could almost guarantee the best American live acts each week. We became convinced that the management wrote into the artists' contracts that they had to perform "Knock On Wood", as week after week every act trotted out this well worn soul standard. But if the clock could be turned back to those old days, I'd be happy even if it meant hearing "Knock On Wood" live every week again."

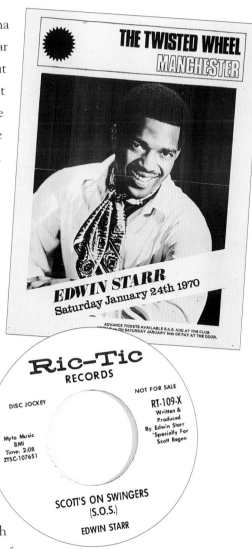

Phil Stables remembers that half the buzz was simply going to Manchester – a big event for teenagers. On Saturday night, they would congregate at the Coffee House in Doncaster. With a juke box full of decent soul sounds, it was the perfect meeting place before the trek to the Wheel. A new all-nighter ran for a few months on Fridays, in the spring of 1970, at a country club in Draycott, just outside Derby.

"The Blue Orchid was in the middle of nowhere. On arrival at Derby's railway station, we would catch the last bus to Nottingham. This would be packed with young people, all shouting and laughing, throwing gear from one end of the bus to the other. Then they'd all pile off at the end of a country lane, in pitch black and walk about a mile and a half to this modern building. Inside it had a fish tank in the wall, was carpeted throughout, had a rostrum DJ and a dance floor. It was £1 to get in and you were given two tickets, one blue and one yellow, with which you could claim a meal in the restaurant area. As the Orchid's all-nighter was on Friday, it was complimentary to the Wheel on Saturday. It was unusual to take a girl to all-nighters, but the exception was the Orchid, it was a great place to impress a girl about the scene. A lot of the Wheel crowd would be there, and you knew that the next night in Manchester it'd be the same thing all over again."

"...we trust you will all become true SOUL CITIZENS..."

Dave Nathan, Soul From The City – sleeve note 1969

Transat, in London's Lisle Street, had been one of the few places it was possible to get American R&B imports. When it closed, salvation arrived with the opening of Dave Godin's legendary Soul City. The first shop, situated at 21 Deptford High Street, was opened by author Brigid Brophy, who gave a memorable speech linking the music to aspirations of freedom.

Dave was in partnership with Dave Nathan and Rob Blackmore. Godin still remembers the visit to the store by his heroine Big Maybelle, who almost stopped the traffic when she sang along with her record "Do Not Pass Me By". Following a burglary in which the shop was cleaned right out, the decision was made to move to the West End, and 17 Monmouth Street, Covent Garden became the next home for Soul City.

Godin decided to set up the Soul City label, and, after what was blamed in ads as "an unexpected hitch in the printing stage", the first disc appeared in April 1968 – a reissue of Don Gardner & Dee Dee Ford's "Don't You Worry", first issued by Stateside six years earlier. The distinctive mauve and blue label was designed by a friend of Dave's, Henry Giles. It was one of the few multi-coloured labels, though the heat of the pressing process did have a strange effect on the printed colour. Over the label's eighteen month life, nineteen singles were officially released. The second release was Gene Chandler's "Nothing Can Stop Me". Dave wrote in Rod Dearlove's *Voices From The Shadows*: "Previously out on Stateside, I'd decided to put it out because it was constantly being asked for in our shop and, as a result of getting so many in-the-past spins on the Northern circuit, it made, to everybody's surprise (not least of all my own!), the UK Top 50!" The record had sold well through specialist shops, and reached number forty one in June 1968.

The label issued singles taken from a variety of American outlets, classic soul and R&B acts such as: Bessie Banks, the Valentinos, Billy Preston, Mighty Sam, Erma Franklin and the Staple Singers. Chris Bartley and Van McCoy persuaded Detroit singer-songwriter Chris Jackson to send Godin a tape. The song "I'll Never Forget You" became the twelfth Soul City release. Also released were two OKeh 45s, previously unissued in the UK – Billy Butler's "The Right Track" and Major Lance's "The Beat" – which were popular Northern dancers, and another from the Chicago label was destined for release. Van McCoy, who had produced the Chris Jackson disc, sent Dave a copy of Sandi Sheldon's "You're Gonna Make Me Love You", but the track was never released.

101

Chris Bartley

As a small label, Soul City did not have the financial muscle or resources of the larger companies; as a goodwill gesture, Dave would personally take artists like Chris Jackson to visit the pressing plants. The second Soul City disc by Jackson, "Since There's No Doubt", was never issued, and Godin thinks that three acetate copies existed. In a letter to *Record Collector*, Dave revealed more: "Chris Jackson, of course, subsequently wrote "You Little Trustmaker", but – make of it what you will – I thought that it was significant that he didn't write the Tymes' follow-up single! Our own relationship was, to put it kindly, somewhat turbulent!" Dave also set up the Deep Soul label, and had plans to press the discs on blue vinyl, though this had to be called off due to a

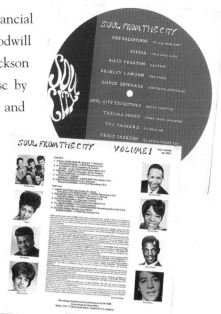

lack of coloured material at the time. The label and shop closed in August 1970, but Dave was soon approached by a Dutch financier about setting up a new venture.

The proposed label was to be named Four-Forty-Four, after the company's address in London's Strand. Dave negotiated a list of material for release on the label, and everything was set. Lou Stallman, who had written the Supremes' hit "Everybody's Got The Right To Love", sent Dave a copy of Sam Nesbit's "Black Mother Goose". This was due to be released in the States on the Amos label, and Dave distributed twenty five copies of the disc to DJs, in readiness for the track's UK release.

However, certain views of a racial nature held by the label's backer proved to be a stumbling block. It was an issue that Dave felt could not be resolved and the label was shelved. A demonstration copy of "Black Mother Goose" was found by Ady Croasdell in London, sold to a soul fan in Market Harborough, promptly sold to a collector in Leicester, and never seen again.

The 444 Label

"...the soul scene is booming still in the North, where the kids are less concerned with creating an effect than with having a good time."

Dave Godin, Blues & Soul 1970

CHAPTER 7

The Up-North Soul Groove

IN EARLY 1970, Brian "45" Phillips, a regular DJ at the Twisted Wheel, was running a record sales list from his home in Middleton, a few miles north of Manchester. A typical mail-out, in March of that year, contained some of the more expensive English label items that had become in-demand on the growing rare soul scene. These included the O'Jays "I Dig Your Act", a high price item at thirty two shillings and sixpence, the Artistics "Girl I Need You" and the Platters "Sweet Sweet Lovin", both for sale at twenty two shillings and sixpence each. An import label copy of Bobby Bland's "Call On Me" was on offer for sixty five shillings – then more than nine times the cost of a new release. Bland's soft Latin shuffle, an American R&B and pop hit in 1963, had long been a favourite at the Wheel, having been played off the Vocalion album of the same name. Import copies of the rarer items that had been released in the UK were now becoming more common, and were starting to be viewed as cheaper alternatives to the British issues. The addition of a wheel symbol on Phillips' list signalled to the Manchester club's regulars, discs that would be of particular interest.

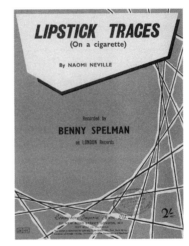

There was an insatiable demand for oldies. Bunny Sigler's "Let The Good Times Roll – Feel So Good", a frantic medley of two R&B hits originally recorded by Shirley & Lee in the Fifties, had been issued on Cameo Parkway in 1967, but was then reported to be changing hands for £2 a copy. An enterprising dealer found cut-outs in the States, which were quickly imported, and the price rapidly dropped. Other in-demand tracks included Leon Haywood's "Mellow Moonlight", the Velvelettes' "Needle In A Haystack" and the eternally popular "Nothing Can Stop Me" by Gene Chandler. Little

105

Hank's "Mr. Bang Bang Man", which had appeared in 1966 on London and been swiftly deleted on the grounds that the lyrics were offensive, was reissued by Monument due to club demand and briefly entered the Top Fifty. When this had first been issued in December 1966, John Abbey reviewed it in *Home Of The Blues*: "Shotgun sounds on a nonsensical item about a character who strolls around town with a pistol in his hand. Well-made and a very strong beat."

The beat was the deciding factor. The dancefloors of the North wanted the uptempo, four-beats-to-the-bar, that the legendary R&B rhythm sections had committed to wax. Motown's Funk Brothers had led the way; James Jamerson's fat bass lines and Benny Benjamin's driving snare drum were the heartbeat of countless hits from Hitsville USA. Fellow Motown percussionist, Jack Ashford, interviewed in *Bass Player*, marvelled at the duo's relentless groove. "You really had to stay on top of the beat to keep up with them. If you laid back, they'd leave you in the dust. They were so bad, you could make a chicken squawk on *two* and *four* and if those two guys were playing behind it, it'd be a hit." A fact that became obvious to the many small record labels that mushroomed in the shadow of the mighty Motown Corporation. The forgotten gems from Detroit's Ric-Tic, Golden World and Revilot were some of the first imports to get played in the Northern clubs. The less-is-more simplicity of the Stax groove machine, Duck Dunn and Al Jackson Jr., was never better than on Wilson Pickett's "In The Midnight Hour". Jerry Wexler demonstrated the

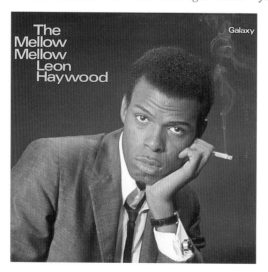

popular New York dance "The Jerk" to bass player Dunn, and throwing his arms around said "That's where the beat should be – where the arms get thrown!"

Chubby Checker's "(At The) Discotheque", another track that had been issued by Cameo Parkway, was then possibly the most in-demand item fetching £10 a copy.

Two records by American pop groups had also caught the scene's attention, "The Fife Piper", a flute instrumental by the Dynatones, a white group from Clarksburgh, West Virginia and the Blendells' cover of Stevie Wonder's 1962 single, "La La La La La".

In June 1970, Dave Godin dedicated the whole of his column to the first part of a special feature on the oldies and rare soul scene. Inspired by three of his readers, Dave was prompted into writing about "The Up-North Soul Groove" – and thus inadvertently created the term "Northern Soul". Ironically, amongst many of those on the scene, the favoured phrase was "Rhythm & Soul", the title Godin had given to his own early fanzine.

Criticising the insularity of the capital's citizens – their tendency to ignore anything happening outside of London – Godin poured scorn on its apathetic inhabitants – "Jaded by a surfeit of novelty and sensation, the sad fact is that whatever 'scene' could once be said to exist in London is now bored out of existence". Again he criticised the media's lack of interest in soul music generally, as the capital continued to be enthralled by the rapid growth of progressive music. To give readers some idea of the records being played in the clubs, Dave ran through a few of these "regional breakouts" from Marvin Smith, the Fascinations, Earl Van Dyke, Bobby Sheen, Dean Parrish, Chubby Checker, the Blendells, Rosco Robinson, Barbara Randolph and the Velvelettes.

Barbara Randolph's "I Got A Feeling" and The Velvelettes' "These Things Will Keep Me Loving You" were two deleted Tamla-Motown 45s. Dave took the opportunity to urge EMI to reissue some of the in-demand Tamla favourites: "Wake Up EMI – think of the time when the Tamla-Motown contract is due for renewal! Exploit it NOW!".

Godin received many letters and telephone calls, enquiring about the records that he had mentioned, and to further whet collectors' appetites, listed more of the same in the second part of "The Up-North Soul Groove". All the discs listed were records that had been issued

107

previously in the UK; the Poets' "She Blew A Good Thing", the Elgins' "Heaven Must Have Sent You", the Incredibles' "There Is Nothing Left To Say", Bettye Swann's "Make Me Yours", Benny Spellman's "The Word Game", Mary Wells' "What's Easy For Two Is So Hard For One"/"You Lost The Sweetest Boy", the Radiants' "Hold On", Inez & Charlie Foxx's "Tightrope" and the Ad-Libs' "The Boy From New York City". He rounded off the piece with a reminder of the tracks that used to be in-demand, but which had since been reissued or made available at more affordable prices. The Flamingos' "Boogaloo Party", Billy Butler's "The Right Track", Leon Haywood's "Mellow Moonlight", Jackie Wilson's "Higher And Higher" and Little Hank's "Mr. Bang Bang Man" – which was where he came in.

These deleted UK releases had been popular in the soul clubs for the previous few years, but as US imports began to filter on to the scene, the more

THE AD LIBS
Night Clubs– TV–Records

Exclusive on

PHILIPS

DOSHAWNS MGT. INC.
BILL DOWNS, PRES.
212-Un5-9795

dedicated DJs like the Midlands' "Farmer Carl" Dene, became relentless in the search for the rare and unusual. Carl Woodroofe owed his agricultural nickname, to a farmer's hat he wore when he deejayed. Having first bought R&B in 1964 from shops like The Discery in Birmingham, Carl deejayed Sunday afternoons at the Chateau Impney in Droitwich Spa. The Chateau's discotheque was in the darkened basement, and every Sunday afternoon from four until seven o'clock, it became a favourite rendezvous for teenagers. By placing advertisements in *Record Mirror*, Carl managed to unearth copies of records which were gaining in popularity on the club scene. When Tony Clark's "The Entertainer" was a sought after item, he discovered the whereabouts of a copy by telephone, and immediately drove to the seller's house to buy the record. This same commitment was applied to discovering imports. Carl had heard, from a friend in the States, about Leon Haywood's "Baby Reconsider". Liking the Haywood singles that had been issued in Britain by Vocalion, Carl went to importer F. L. Moore and found a copy. "Baby Reconsider" was first played at the Chateau in 1968, and was the first of the big money records on the soul scene. Others, such as Jackie Lee's "Darkest Days", Edwin Starr's "Backstreet", the Sharpees' "Do The 45", Dobie Gray's "Out On The Floor" and the San Remo Strings' "Festival Time" became the original Northern Soul rarities. As they were heard, collectors like Graham "Docker" White and Richard Selwood would track copies down and introduce them to the DJs at the Twisted Wheel. Brian Rae deejayed at the club in 1967, and in an interview with Dave Evison on Radio Signal, he noted how on his return to the club in 1969, the music policy had changed.

Sandi Sheldon's "You're Gonna Make Me Love You" was another major discovery at this time – though, who first played it on the Northern scene, is open to debate. Graham Stapleton, who with John Thorpe ran a soul mail-order business from Fulham, and later had the Cheapo Cheapo market stall in London's Berwick Street, remembers buying a pile of records in a bin bag from Radio One DJ John Peel. In amongst them, was the Sandi Sheldon 45, which Graham sold to Wolverhampton DJ "Froggy". The

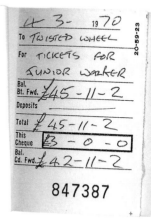

producer, Van McCoy, sent a copy of the record to Dave Godin for possible release on the Soul City label. Although the record was not issued, Dave introduced it to the Northern scene.

Among record dealer Brian "45" Phillips' customers was a young lad called Ian Levine, who would knock on his door at the crack of dawn to make sure he got the records that he had ordered by post.

Like many teenagers in the mid Sixties, Levine discovered an affinity for Motown records whilst listening to the pirate stations; in Ian's case, his introduction came through Radio Caroline's DJ Kenny Everett. Levine's favourite disc had been the Supremes' "Reflections", but it was hearing Rita Wright's "I Can't Give Back The Love I Feel For You" in 1968, that inspired him to begin collecting the entire Tamla-Motown catalogue. A girl assistant at a small record shop in Levine's hometown of Blackpool, helped him to get those releases which were still available like the Miracles' "Going To A Go-Go", the Isley Brothers' "This Old Heart Of Mine" and the Velvelettes' "Needle In A Haystack". Gary Wilde, who deejayed at a casino in Blackpool, ran a cigarette kiosk in Victoria Street, where he also sold secondhand copies of records such as the Flamingos' "Boogaloo Party", Jamo Thomas' "I Spy (For The FBI)", and the deleted Tamla-Motown singles that Ian needed for his collection. These were already already fetching up to fifteen shillings a copy.

At school, Levine met an older boy, Stuart Bremner, who introduced him to the undiscovered world of soul music beyond Motown. "I became his protege, which was unusual in a grammar school with its rigid caste system. It was very odd to fraternise with an older pupil, however, we met socially and he introduced me to Curtis Mayfield and the Impressions, and tracks like "I Need You", "You've Been Cheatin'", "Can't Satisfy" and "Since I Lost The One I Love". And newer soul releases like The Stairsteps' "Stay Close To Me"."

Levine's father ran a casino, and Ian was lucky enough to go on regular holidays to the States. "In New Orleans, it was over one hundred degrees and humid, but I began to scour second-hand stores for the gaps in my Motown collection, and from fan club newsletters, I had discovered that Motown had bought the local Detroit labels – Ric-Tic and Golden World.

111

My first Ric-Tic discoveries in the States were Edwin Starr's "Stop Her On Sight" and J. J. Barnes' "Please Let Me In". I guessed that the latter would be similar to J. J. Jackson's gritty "But It's Alright", but I was so surprised when I heard it. The Marvin Gaye-style voice, with crooning backing vocals, epitomised my own taste in soul music and I remember playing it over and over again."

Through the son of a business colleague of his father's, Levine made a memorable first visit to a club in Manchester, and recalled hearing a disc that had gained a cult following in the area's clubs and discotheques. "Lester Hare and I went into this club, I don't know which one, but they were playing "You're Ready Now" by Frankie Valli. The smell of Brut hit me as I went in. This would have been in September 1970, before I had been to the Twisted Wheel. And as I walked into this club, I noticed that they all had Ben Sherman shirts with button-down collars, short clean-cut haircuts, and they were all clapping together on the chorus "You're ready now...(CLAP), you're ready now...(CLAP)". It was an atmosphere that I had never seen before...and I got kind of hooked." Frankie Valli's disc was one of the first to be reissued as a result of Northern club demand, having appeared with little interest back in 1966 on Phillips. It subsequently went on to become a top twenty hit towards the end of 1970.

Levine finally made it to the Wheel, during the club's final months. He befriended Rob Bellars and Phil Saxe, who had both deejayed at the club. "Rob Bellars' knowledge is staggering. He remembers everything. He was the first person to cover records up. There was a British release on Pama by Bobby Patterson called "What A Wonderful Night For Love", and he covered it up. The mentality was that, if a record was on Pama, it did not have the prestige of other labels – so he covered it up as Benny Harper, who had a record on the American label Phil La of Soul. I started taking my records in, things like Sonny Stitt's "Agent Double-O Soul", Rose Batiste's "Hit And Run", Bob Wilson's "All Turned On", then fairly obscure American imports.

"I was going to university in Manchester, and my father would drop me off at the station, and as soon as he was out of sight, I would hitch to Manchester, skip the lectures, and spend my fare on records found in junkshops."

Blues & Soul was still the only regular source of information about the Northern soul world. Billy Butler, who had been DJ at the Cavern in Liverpool, outlined his week's schedule and mentioned that his favourite group was the Sandpebbles. DJs John & Michael Harris listed their most requested 45s as Tammi Terrell's "This Old Heart Of Mine", Jackie Wilson's "I Get The Sweetest Feeling", Chubby Checker's "(At The) Discotheque" and the Formations' "At The Top Of The Stairs". Top sounds at the Wheel then were Leon Haywood's "Baby Reconsider", Timmy Willis' "Mr Soul Satisfaction" and Sandi Sheldon's 'You're Gonna Make Me Love You".

In October 1970, owner Ivor Abadi distributed a flyer to all the members of The Twisted Wheel Club announcing that the hours of opening and closing at the club had been restricted by Manchester Corporation. In effect, this meant that the all-night sessions would have to stop, and Abadi stated he would be appealing against the imposition and that it would be business as normal pending the findings of the appeal. A petition was drafted which members, and their parents were invited to sign to pledge support for the club. Resident DJ Les Cokell contacted Dave Godin at *Blues & Soul* and next to the announcement of Ben E. King's forthcoming UK tour, which included a future appearance at The Twisted Wheel on 14th November, readers were urged to counteract the threatened legislation.

The North was not alone in this developing scene and "Oscar Michael", one of the Midland's better known soul DJs, was spinning oldies and rare sounds at many venues including The King's Head at Bearwood near Birmingham, the Gladstone Club in Dudley, The Kingfisher Country Club at Wall Hearth and The Plaza Ballroom at Old Hill. His most requested 45s included: the Impressions' "Nothing Can Stop Me"; the ubiquitous "Baby Reconsider" by Leon Haywood which was then selling for £25 a copy; Jackie Wilson's "I Get The Sweetest Feeling" and Darrell Bank's "Open The Door To Your Heart".

An interesting reply to a *Blues & Soul* reader's request about the proportion of records sold from Contempo, stated: "There can be no disputing the facts that soul begins north of Birmingham, which is unfortunate for the southern soul lovers because they have a very bleak time being surrounded by progressive music lovers".

113

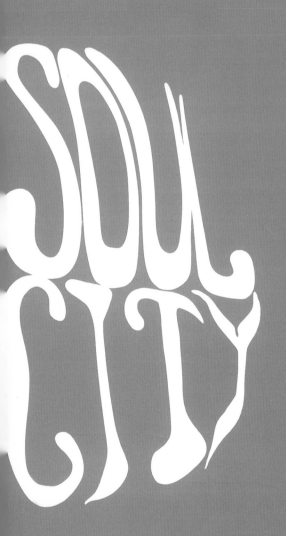
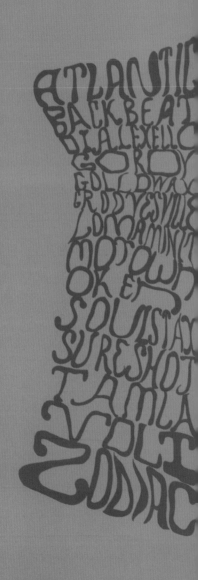

CHAPTER 8

Land Of A Thousand Dances

DAVE GODIN WAS not the only one at *Blues & Soul* aware of the growing rare soul scene. Editor John Abbey had recognised the interest in Sixties recordings from all points North, and selected a picture of Motown's session star Earl Van Dyke for the cover of the first issue of 1971. To the majority of the magazine's readers, Van Dyke was definitely a name from the past; his last US single release, a version of the Temptations' number one soul hit "Runaway Child, Running Wild", had been issued two years previously, and his most recent album – "The Earl Of Funk" – was a live recording which Berry Gordy had issued to appease the disgruntled musician. Nonetheless, to the clubgoers across the Midlands and North of England, Van Dyke's Hammond organ grooves over Motown rhythm tracks were in-demand

cuts. EMI had just reissued two of the most popular on Tamla-Motown – "Six By Six" and "All For You" – the latter being the tune which had opened the Motown Revue's first British tour in 1965.

The unique taste of the Northern soul fans was clearly evident in Dave Godin's columns whenever he featured readers' favourite tracks. Many dance floor fillers were appearing with an almost monotonous regularity: the Incredibles "There's Nothing Else To Say Baby", Dean Parrish "Determination", Bobby Sheen "Doctor Love", Mickey Lee Lane "Hey Sah Loney", Al Kent "You've Gotta Pay The Price", and Tami Lynn "I'm Gonna Run Away From You". Lynn's old black Atlantic label release was fetching five pounds a copy, and would shortly be reissued on John Abbey's imminent new soul label – Mojo.

Blues & Soul's mail order oldies service was doing brisk business offering, at fifteen shillings each, Northern club treasures such as Timmy Willis "Mr Soul

Twisted Wheel, Manchester

Satisfaction" and the Tams "Hey Girl Don't Bother Me" which would be a surprise number one hit when reissued by EMI on Probe that summer. Of the many clubs that were mentioned in the magazine, either in Godin's column or in the frequent DJ updates, it was Manchester's Twisted Wheel that was the firm favourite. Under the banner headline "Land Of A Thousand Dances", Godin reported on his first pilgrimage to the club about which he had written excitedly a few weeks before.

Dave had been invited to Manchester by John Bollen, a student at Middlesex Polytechnic exiled in London. As a soul fan marooned in the capital, John had found refuge at the Soul City shop, which he had first discovered in 1969 when the Soul Children's hypnotic ballad "The Sweeter He Is" had catapulted them into the R&B Top 10. Dave had been alerted to the goings-on North of the capital by frequent visitors. Saturday was always a busy day at the small shop and Dave, together with co-owners Dave and Rob Nathan, would regularly audition the new releases for customers. It became apparent that visiting soul fans from the Midlands and North of England, quite often football fans attending away games, had different tastes to those in the South. Current new releases were overlooked unless they sounded like the oldies favoured in the Northern clubs, and those that did bear the distinctive hallmarks would be categorised in the shop as "Northern". What was initially little more than an internal catalogue system within the Soul City shop,

would soon be used to identify the growing rare soul scene. The shop's own record label had issued tracks by Major Lance, Billy Butler and Gene Chandler which had become scarce, and it was inevitable that Godin would eventually write about the subject in his fortnightly column for *Blues & Soul*.

After regular visits to the store, John befriended Dave and suggested he attend an all-nighter at the Twisted Wheel, which Bollen had first visited at Christmas, 1967. John had been introduced to the soul scene whilst still at school by Denis Blackburn, who was a few years older and worked as an apprentice at the Rolls-Royce factory. A first trip to the Burnley Mecca, packed to the rafters with mods, was as John remembers "pulsating". The scene in the North was then well established and records like the Flamingo's deleted "Boogaloo Party" were big sounds. It was not long before he became a regular at the Birdtrap at Brierfield, and the Golden Disc on the Skipton Road, Keighley. John recalls seeing the Velvelettes popular 45 "These Things Will Keep Me Loving You" for the first time on the American Soul Label. Few people in London were aware of the growing cult, and a friend visiting the capital asked John's advice about where best to shop for soul records. Bollen replied that there was little chance of getting any of the current in-demand tracks. Much to John's amazement, his friend asked over the counter at Contempo for

117

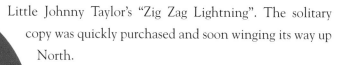

Little Johnny Taylor's "Zig Zag Lightning". The solitary copy was quickly purchased and soon winging its way up North.

On arrival in Manchester, Godin met a group of Wheel regulars, which included Les Cokell, one of the DJs at the club, at John Bollen's flat in Whalley Range. Dave had also been corresponding for some time with another Wheel regular Francisco O'Brien who he met for the first time. The evening was purported to be the final all-nighter. Rumours flew round that the police had planned to herd any undesirable members, seized in the expected raid, into specially constructed wire pens at the back of the club. The club had endured countless raids by the police and fire brigade acting under the powers granted by Parliament, and by the time of Godin's visit, the Twisted Wheel was one of only two all-night clubs in Manchester. The party gathered in the White Hart, on the corner of Whitfield Street until closing time, before joining the seemingly endless queue. Godin provided a vivid description of the club, the fashions and the dancing which he considered to be the finest he had ever seen outside of the USA.

With many dressed in mohair suits, to occasional cries of "Right On Now!", clenched fists in single black racing gloves would punch the air. Dave was probably deliberately overlooking the dilatory effect of drugs when, commenting on the subdued light of the club, he wrote: "Naturally such scarcity of illumination tends to have a widen effect on the pupils of the eyes". Given the threat of closure that was hanging over the club, it was portentous that the record that stuck in Dave's mind was Jackie Lee's brooding "Darkest Days". At the time of Godin's visit, the appeal to the Crown Court had yet to be heard and the club was continuing to hold its all-nighters until a final ruling was made.

Gloom and despondency overshadowed the country, as 1970 drew to a close. The work-to-rule and overtime ban by electricity supply workers continued and a special Cabinet committee was considering emergency measures to restrict and ration the use of power. Radio One was off the air in London for seventy minutes and St. Helen's police manned the station by candlelight. The *Manchester Evening News* asked "What's gone wrong with glamour club Manchester United?", who were in the uncomfortable position of fifth from the bottom in Division One – manager Wilf McGuinness was facing the sack. And following on swiftly from the power workers' dispute, the Union of Post Office Workers went on strike in January.

On Thursday 28th January, a classified insertion in the "Dancing Modern & Old Time" section of the *Manchester Evening News* announced that the Twisted Wheel's appeal date had been set for 2nd February. The advertisement warned the club's members that, if it lost, the 31st January session would be the last. The star attraction was Edwin Starr and advanced tickets were available at the club from 9pm on Saturday night. Owner Ivor Abadi needed a drinks license to be able to compete with other clubs in the city and the police were reluctant to issue one to an all-nighter.

Edwin Starr, who played at the Twisted Wheel seven times remembers the final night well. "Funny, but it didn't feel like the last night. It was as exciting and as much fun as the first time I played there. Ivor Abadi and his brother were adamant that the show would start at the same time as usual. There were a lot of internal problems with the police, and circumstances beyond their control with the authorities. They did everything that they could not to antagonise the situation. They had to admit defeat, but in a way, it was a defeat with triumph. We conducted ourselves well that night, and went out in style. I went on around two o'clock and made no concession to the special circumstances of the event, it was business as usual, let's just get on with the show. It was only at the end, when there was a kind of quiet echoing – and everybody realised it was the end of an era." Les Cokell was deejaying that night, and some members cried as he played the last record.

Godin returned again to his readers' favourites in February, and due to the national postal strike and production delays at *Blues & Soul*, his articles continued to feature the Wheel despite the fact that the club had already closed. Ste Butt from Royton chose the Invitations' "What's Wrong With Me Baby" a favourite at the Richmond Club in Heywood, Lloyd Findlater selected Major Lance's "The Monkey Time", big at the Motown Club in Shaw, and

Chuck Wood

Peter Tarnawskys opted for Little Anthony & The Imperials' "Gonna Fix You Good" which "really gives The Wheel a fantastic atmosphere". "Flash" Atkinson from Keighley picked Mary Love's "You Turned My Bitter Into Sweet", and Steve Kelly wrote from Carlisle recommending the Twisted Wheel's Brian Phillips as one of the best DJs around. Other tracks included Major Lance's "The Beat", Earl Van Dyke's "I Can't Help Myself", and a record which was a big favourite at the Catacombs in Wolverhampton, Lorenzo Manley's "(I'm Gonna) Swoop Down On You".

Contempo International, the organisation behind *Blues & Soul* announced the launch of the Mojo label, and although technically a subsidiary of Polydor, the repertoire and promotion were to be handled by Contempo. Many of the soul acts on Polydor were transferred to the new imprint and the first releases were scheduled to tie in with the forthcoming James Brown concerts in March. The first Mojo 45, announced for release on March 19th 1971, was a double header by James Brown featuring "Get Up, Get Into It, Get Involved" and "I Need You". In the event, this record came out on Polydor, and the J.B.'s "These Are The J.B.'s" became the label's debut.

John Abbey's label catered for soul fans in both the North and South of England. Although the majority of the label's releases leant towards contemporary funk and US Southern soul artists from the likes of James Brown, Bobby Byrd, the JBs, Vicki Anderson, ZZ Hill and Freddie North, Abbey did not fail to acknowledge the demand from the North of England to reissue in-demand records that Mojo had access to within the vast array of US companies that Polydor distributed. The labels now at Abbey's disposal included MGM, Atlantic, King, Money, Moira, Tico, Roulette, Bank, De-Lite, Whit, Jewel, Ronn, Paula, Spring, Calla, Canyon and Brownstone.

Throughout 1971, Mojo reissued many sides which were popular amongst Northern fans: the Fascinations' anthem "Girls Are Out To Get You", which Abbey had reissued previously when working with Guy Stevens on the Sue label, came out in June; two earlier MGM releases, the Formations' "At The Top Of The Stairs" and the Fantastics' "Baby Make Your Own Sweet Music" re-surfaced in the summer; Doris Troy's "I'll Do Anything" reappeared in September; Chuck Wood's "Seven Days Too Long" and Jamo Thomas' "I Spy (For The FBI)" both followed in October; and before the year was out J.J.Jackson's British recording "But It's Alright" and Willie Tee's brassy amble

Moses Dillard

"Walkin' Up A One Way Street" were back in the shops again. Mojo's biggest success was one of the label's first reissues, Tami Lynn's "I'm Gonna Run Away From You", which sold over 250,000 copies reaching number four in 1971.

Lynn's infectious hit had originally been released in the UK in 1966 by Atlantic, and covered at the time by Kiki Dee. Since its deletion, demand had grown through repeated plays in the clubs, and Leicester-based record dealer Jeff King bootlegged the disc on his own Soul Sounds label selling hundreds of copies before Polydor, which owned the UK rights got wind and successfully prosecuted him. Abbey promptly reissued the disc and brought about a brief revival in Tami Lynn's career, giving her the chance to tour the UK on the strength of the hit. With veteran producer Wardell Quezerque, John Abbey produced her follow-up "That's Understanding" but this failed to repeat the success of "I'm Gonna Run Away From You" and Lynn returned home to the States. Abbey managed to get extra mileage out of the song when his Contempo label put the disc out at the height of Northern Soul's commercialisation in 1975, and again it entered the Top 40.

Al Kent's Ric-Tic instrumental "You Got To Pay The Price" was scheduled for release in December 1971, but was never issued.

After the Twisted Wheel closed, the search began for another venue to take its place, and the first candidate was a weekly all-nighter held at a club called Lord Jim's in Huddersfield. The DJs were the Twisted Wheel's Les Cokell and Julian Bentley. It did not last long, as Dave Price from Llandudno remembers. "I would say that about a quarter of the Wheel regulars had made it there. It was a brilliant night, or should I say half-a-night, because at around four o'clock in the morning it was raided by the police. They had obviously decided that we were undesirables and we were all escorted out of town on foot." The management of the club altered the musical policy at the club and Cokell and Bentley were fired. The Northern crowd were on the look out for somewhere else, and on the grapevine Dave Price heard about another all-nighter, this time at Wakefield in a basement club called the Metro Bistro.

"A few of us from Wales went along and again most of the Wheel crowd were there. It lasted for a few Saturdays until that was raided. This time we really made the news! By the standards of the day, this was a serious raid. It made the national press, TV and radio. They sent everything but the SAS in that night – dogs, riot police, even sealed off the town centre. We were all escorted to the local nick in coaches. But the ironic thing was that everybody reckoned it was one of the best all-nighters we ever had. We were all off our heads, it was green and clears and bombers in those days, we didn't give a fuck where we were. After the initial police action, and by the time everybody was locked up back at the police station, the local plod soon realised that they had been rather misled by their superiors and that these people were quite friendly – they hadn't raided some terrorist base. The relations improved and quite a few of the cops were introduced to Northern soul. There was even some dancing going on. A bit bizarre really." Dave Godin mentioned the Metro incident in his column and reported that one hundred and fifty "brothers and sisters" had been detained during the raid whilst Chuck Jackson's "Chains Of Love" was playing. The seventeen-year-old Ian Levine was amongst those charged, a fact which did not go down too well with his parents.

Following the raid on the Metro, Dave Godin tackled the drug issue in a report entitled "AMPHETASOUL". The use of amphetamine-based drugs such as Benzedrine, Dexedrine, Methedrine, Preludin and Drinamyl, which were available only on prescription, was widespread. Not wishing the article to sound like a sermon, Dave ended the article offering to provide information about organisations which might be of help to any of his readers. He was to return to the subject of drugs over the years, once replying in 1977 to a letter in *Blues & Soul* about a lad spied carrying a holdall emblazoned in white letters with the legend "Filon reaches the parts of the body other gear cannot reach": "Psychologists have proven that drugs are, in effect, a flight from sexual anxieties about oneself...drug users are more in need of compassion than scorn because it is an inner pain that they seek to quell...".

Record shops and dealers across the country began advertising Northern soul in the classified section of *Record Mirror*. F .L. Moore in Dunstable was selling soul packs of one hundred R&B imports for £12.50, and Selecta Disc in Nottingham had copies of the Prophets' "I Got The Fever" for 75p, Donald Height's "Talk Of The Grapevine" for 50p, and Billy Harner's "What About The Music" on Kama Sutra for 75p, all on a "first come first served basis". Soul Control in Chiswick tempted customers with the opening line "Darkest

Days"…we haven't got it (wish we had). We just wanted to catch your eye to tell you we have got Joy Lovejoy, Al Kent…". In September, Selecta Disc finally obtained copies of the Jackie Lee track – "the greatest discotheque record of all time" – which they advertised for sale at £1. Graham Stapleton used the cryptic "Backdrops from Soul Uprising" to promote his soul business in London.

Dave McAleer, who had published *Fame-Goldwax Survey* fanzine in 1966, had left the music publishers Chappells to work in the copyright department of Pye Records. After a spell at RCA, where he issued two compilation albums "Just A Little Bit Of Soul" and "Funky Bottom Congregation", he moved back to Pye to work in their A&R department. Through his soul connections and feedback received from *Blues & Soul*, Dave arranged for two popular Platters' tracks "Washed Ashore" and "Sweet Sweet Lovin'" and Charlie & Inez Foxx's "Tightrope" to be reissued in July 1971. The discs failed to crossover into chart success but still sold reasonably well, each achieving sales of about 10,000 copies.

In the summer of 1971, Martha "The Queen" Jean, a DJ on the Detroit radio station WJLB, broadcast a message requesting information as to the whereabouts of four local women who had sung together as the Fascinations. They had recorded the uplifting "Girls Are Out To Get You" for Curtis Mayfield's eponymous label. The record, which featured Donny Hathaway on piano, became a Top 20 R&B hit, briefly entering the *Billboard* Hot 100. Despite three more attempts to repeat the success of "Girls Are Out To Get You", the group finally disbanded in 1969 and the women returned to work. Joanne Leavell was working in real estate, Shirley Walker was a secretary at the Chamber of Commerce, Bernadine Boswell was a doctor's receptionist and Fern Bledsoe, who had formerly been a secretary at Motown, was now at the Ford Motor Corporation. Martha Jean was advising the girls to get in touch "cos they got a hit in Britain y'all!"

On the strength of the reissued "Girls Are Out To Get You", the hastily reformed Fascinations made their British debut on August 8th at The North Park Country Club in Kettering. Their tour dates included clubs and venues across the country and the inevitable spot at a US Air Force Base at Upper Heyford. The record reached number thirty two in July 1971.

Dave Godin finally made it to the Blackpool Mecca on August 21st 1971. Amongst those accompanying him on the trip up North were Alf Billingham, and London DJ Terry Davis. Terry had experienced the scene at first hand when stationed in Preston with the Civil Service six months earlier. He had read about it in *Blues & Soul*, and had persuaded a colleague to come out to try and find a Northern soul club. The Ad-Libs' "The Boy From New York City" booming out from a cellar bar called the Stax Club was his first introduction to Northern Soul. Davis, along with Paul Tibble, had run a well-respected soul night at the Fountain in London's East End, which Godin occasionally visited. Dave came one evening and told a group of the pub's regulars that he had been invited to the Mecca and wondered if anyone was interested in joining him. Terry, his brother Pete, and two other Fountain regulars joined Dave and Alf Billingham on the train to Blackpool. Dave was keen to record the event but as the flash on his camera was not working, he lost his temper and threw the camera out of the window. The party was met at Blackpool by Ian Levine, Steve Appleby, Harold Grounds and Les Cokell, who Dave had met on his previous trip to the Twisted Wheel.

Terry recalled the great welcome bestowed upon the party by manager Bill Pye. "It was quite a reception, we were given free admission and made to feel

126

like special guests, real VIP treatment. As I went into the Highland Room the first record I heard was Barbara Lewis' "Someday We're Gonna Love Again". And out of the next twenty I probably only knew about four, but Pete and I were definitely up for it. The other two guys who had come were more into funk and new soul releases, and thought it was very strange – the fashions, the dancing, and the accents. They weren't overwhelmed by it, more bemused."

The DJs on the night of Godin's visit were Tony Jebb and Stuart Freeman, and Godin wrote in *Blues & Soul* that on entering the Highland Room, Denise LaSalle's "A Love Reputation" was being played – a record that Dave had listed as one of his favourite releases of 1967. John Bollen had first introduced LaSalle's disc to the North after hearing Godin's copy. Boogaloo was trying to persuade Godin to start a fund to buy The Twisted Wheel as a Soul Co-operative and swore that it was for sale for £5,000. Other notable characters included Tubby from Accrington, who had the Detroit record label "Ric Tic Records" tattooed on his upper arm, and old friend Francisco O'Brien. Godin observed: "Maybe there are some who read this in the Southern part of England who find it hard to understand just why I rave about the Northern Soul scene, and perhaps this is because they have never been there and seen it first hand for themselves, because believe me, there is just no equivalent in the South, and until you've been there I don't think any mere written word can fully convey to you that special and unique vibration that generates amongst the brothers and sisters. Until August 21st 1971 I had always thought of Blackpool as The Tower, but from then on in, I shall always and forever remember it as The Mecca – Soul Heaven here on earth, and a pious pilgrimage that I would urge all the faithful to undertake as often as they possibly can."

"The pop Press have suddenly wakened up to a situation that the specialist soul Press has been carrying on about for a long time now, that in the North clubs pack 'em in playing soul."

Tony Cummings Record Mirror, 20th November 1971

CHAPTER 9

Soul Civil War

Record Mirror's Tony Cummings had known Dave Godin for years. Since the early Sixties they had run into each other at various soul events in the capital and often crossed swords. Alf Billingham, who has known Dave since the Soul City days remembers a typical disagreement the two had when a society had been formed called The R&B Association of Great Britain.

"We would meet upstairs in a pub in Covent Garden called the Lamb and Flag. People like Tony Cummings and Clive Richardson were there. And at the time Dave had an artist on his Soul City label called Chris Jackson. A great artist but a total pain in the arse. Now, you'll probably be aware of the Country and Western Association of Great Britain – they have this once-a-year do at Wembley, Country has never had the caché or oomph that black American music has in this country. It's not that viable commercially, but then we had this fantastic opportunity when CBS, and all the major labels, said that they would get involved in a similar type of project. They would bring artists over. 'Not expecting you to pay. We'll put one central gig on somewhere. It would be a great opportunity to just push the music.' And don't forget, you had this serious evangelical thing going on with all these people. They were all determined to push the music forward – it was all very Baden-Powell, for the good of the cause. Here we had a fantastic opportunity to promote soul music and all the major labels wanted to support it. And because of all the in-fighting that went on, it failed. I'll give you an example, this was the level of banality that made the thing implode.

"They had a Hall of Fame at the R&B Association, and every year they'd elect someone. Now, I think it was Dave, who came up with the idea of Sam Cooke. And I think it was Cummings, who came up to him and said you can't have Sam Cooke. And Dave said 'Why not? He made great records and a few duff ones, but don't they all? And Tony Cummings' refusal had been based on the fact that Cooke had strings on his records! I don't remember the context but what have string arrangements got to do with it all?"

The Godin-Cummings Cold War showed no signs of thawing. Dave's enthusiastic prose on behalf of the Northern scene cut no ice with Tony Cummings. And the week Godin's article about his trip to Blackpool appeared in *Blues & Soul*, Tony Cummings' "Black Hits – No Soul" piece in the 11th

September edition of *Record Mirror* put the relationship back in the freezer. Cummings was concerned that pop fans who ventured to ask the question "What Is Soul?" would look to the charts for their answer. Their assumption would be that for a soul record to be successful it would almost certainly be an old record originally recorded in the mid-Sixties and be "monotonously, insiduously ordinary". The finger of blame was pointed to the North.

Record companies had spotted the commercial potential of unobtainable discs being played regularly in the clubs. If sufficient demand could be created, then it would be a straightforward process to reissue them and wait for the money to pour in. The Northern DJs were even buying the records and doing the promotion on their behalf. Cummings recognised the merit of the oldies being re-released but felt that, although they were good dance pop, they were sadly lacking in the soul department. Lovers of other music styles such as progressive rock and country 'n' western, regularly criticised soul music and Tony felt that the exposure given to pop soul like the Northern reissues helped to reinforce their opinions. His insistence that this argument was not just to satisfy the soul purists, amongst who he numbered Mike Booth, Charlie Gillett and James Hamilton, fell on stony ground as it was Hamilton who later recommended to United Artists particular tracks which would hit with the Northern crowd. It was the criticism of Northern fans as an "unsophisticated audience" which caused the inevitable backlash in following issues of *Record Mirror*. An indignant Francisco O'Brien was one of many. "What a small minded person you are…you mean to tell me your view is right and everybody else's wrong?"

Early Seventies soul recordings had absorbed psychedelic and progressive rock techniques into their structure, and Cummings was adamant – "play

Funkadelic in a Lancashire club and they'll hate it!". To rub salt into the wounds, he rubbished "Baby Reconsider", "In Orbit", and other sounds by Barbara Randolph, the Invitations and Chuck Jackson and recommended his own selection of oldies which could be resurrected for the scene. Tony's apparent misunderstanding of the type of record that filled the dancefloors in the North led to some strange recommendations. These included Willie Parker's "You've Got Your Finger In My Eye", Van & Titus' "I Need Your Lovin'", Dorothy Morrison's "Spirit In The Sky", Gladys Knight & The Pips' "The Nitty Gritty" and Carolyn Sullivan's "Dead". The latter, co-written and arranged by Moses Dillard, was issued on Philips in 1968. Although a brilliant record, it was not the type of soul that would appeal to the dancers in the North. Two replies in reaction to the article probably confused Tony even more.

A letter from Brian "Boz" Bosworth from Stoke-in-Trent asked "do you dance differently in London?". Like many soul fans in the North, he enjoyed listening to Curtis Mayfield, Parliament, Doris Duke and even thanked Tony Cummings for introducing him to Charlie Hodges' "I'll Never Fall In Love Again". Brian explained that you simply couldn't dance to them. On the same page, one A. J. Rimshaw from Blackburn, whilst agreeing that some of the oldies fell short on production values and were corny, felt they still had a magic appeal, although possibly only in the North. A. J. described the accompanying floor movements as almost a "tribal dance routine", and stated that it was possible to accurately tell where somebody came from by the way they dance. He rounded off his letter with the view that: "Soul in the North is old danceable stuff, ageless rhythms, more often than not sung by black Americans, but the Negro bit's just a coincidence".

The sparring continued with Dave Godin taking on Tony Cummings in the next issue of *Blues & Soul*. Over two thousand words, Godin jabbed away at each of Cummings' points, firstly accusing him of being ambiguous, then elitist, and delivering a passing blow for being dogmatic. With Tony seemingly up against the ropes, Dave concluded with details of the record that he had intended to open the column, ironically the B-side of the Willie Parker track that Cummings had recommended: "Tony asks for Soul with involvement, and this has got it and then some. "I Live The Life I Love, And Love The Life I Live" somehow has a more profound and meaningful ring to me than "You Got Your Finger In My Eye", and the whole record is involved in the excitement of living, loving and bringing it all on home."

With no sign of a towel being thrown into the ring, Tony and his seconds – *Shout* magazine's Clive Richardson and Roy Stanton, Lou McDermott of the London Blues Society, and Mike Booth of Record Centre – hired a coach, filled it with R&B fans and set forth to the Blackpool Mecca. As Cummings had received shoals of criticism, he felt it was necessary to experience the records in the environment of a Northern club, and hear '...the hidden depths of musical magic spill out from the amplifiers blasting out "In Orbit" or "Darkest Days". Having been to the Mecca with Dave Godin a few weeks before, DJ Terry Davis was now invited by Tony Cummings to repeat the trip. Davis had enjoyed the first weekend and was looking forward to a return visit. However, this time, things would be different.

"There was a certain mood on the coach going up. Tony had always had this thing about the huge amounts of money that changed hands for what he considered to be poor records, even though it had always been a part of the scene. Tony had brought with him a pile of records and a Discotron, and was playing things like Willie Hatcher on Ric-Tic and joking that it was for sale at three shillings, when up North it was fetching thirty bob. There were mixed feelings about Tony's attitude on the coach; in a way we were bemused and at the same time pleased we were able to get good records at good prices! When we arrived we checked into our digs and arranged to meet at the Mecca at around eight o'clock. There were about fifteen of us in the queue and there were lots of comments along the lines of 'Londoners coming up to criticise and slag off the Northern scene'. Having previously enjoyed the Mecca this could have only been because of Cummings' attitude. I'm sure that Ian Levine being close to the manager had had a word in his ear, as I was told my hair was too long and turned away. We ended up having quite an unpleasant evening walking around the pubs in Blackpool, being told we looked like women!"

A few gained entry to the Highland Room including Mike Booth, who although pleased at hearing Paul Humphrey & His Cool Aid Chemists' recent hit "Cool Aid", a James Brown instrumental and an introduction to Accrington's Tubby, he returned to the coach party to tell them "it was like being in a crowd of lunatics all telling you how mad you are".

The spat between the two soul writers continued, and although Godin tried to calm things down, in his next column T.C. would regularly come back for more. Ian Levine had proffered a list of the top Mecca favourites which Cummings summarily dismissed: Mamie Galore was a "thumpety-thump Supremes take-off", the Du-Ettes was a "dreary Andre Williams dancer". However, he did concede that Denise LaSalle's "A Love Reputation" was a good record. In praising soul items from Wade Flemons, Lee Dorsey and James Carr, he could not resist the dig that these discs contained "righteous wailing a million miles from the Blackpool Mecca", and to top it off, he shared a get-rich-quick plan with his readers: "Say, I've got a pretty sneaky idea. I'll get hold of a recently released record by Johnny Williams on Bashie 103 and I'll stick white labels over it, take it up North and persuade the deejays it's the original version of "Just A Little Misunderstanding" on a Ric-Tic pressing. I'll pocket my £50 and return to find more of the dreary, thud, thud sounds". By January 1972, Tony seemed to have tired of the Northern soul scene and stated in *Record Mirror* that one good soul record was worth considerably more than any of the "mush" written by either Godin or himself. And due to "certain views expressed by the Mecca and Northern boogalooers", a planned second trip to the Mecca was considered not worth the trouble and cancelled. When he next stepped back into the fray, it would be when he became a staff writer at IPC's monthly *Black Music* in the summer of 1974.

Today, Tony Cummings feels that the "war" was bizarre. "I became aware of the Northern Soul scene after some trips to the North. I once lived briefly

**Terry Davis
at The Fountain 1971**

133

**En route to Blackpool
October 1971**

in Derby. Yes, I was very serious-minded about Northern Soul, wasn't I? I suppose I was part of an earlier era of soul buffs who'd come immersed in soul music yet wasn't particularly comfortable with club culture. I didn't dance. I went to clubs to see live music. I had more records than most DJs. So I brought all my preconceptions and prejudices to a culture I didn't fully understand. In fairness, I suppose they were right to be miffed by someone coming up from London telling some of their 'classics' were crap. But Godin's pieces were absurdly OTT and exercises in pomposity."

Being turned away at the doors of the Blackpool Mecca, made one coach party member even more determined to get in the club. Tony Rounce had first met Ian Levine at the Soul City shop. "I was still at school, running a fanzine called the Motortown Review, and Levine, who was a big Motown collector, asked Dave Godin to introduce me to him. So, I met Ian, and went to stay with him at his family home in Blackpool. This was in the pre-Mecca days when Bob Stevens was playing the records at the Lemon Tree – which was owned by Ian's dad. Well, I stayed in touch, on and off, from '69 until the

Northern thing started." In 1970, Ian Levine came down to stay with Tony in Essex. This was a big soul area, and Chris Hill deejayed at a pub called the Orsett Cock. "I took Ian there, and Chris, being Chris, ripped the shit out of Ian mercilessly all night, because Ian was going up to him and saying 'Why are you playing all this crap for, put on "You're Ready Now' by Frankie Valli, or whatever, and Ian gave, what I believe is, the first demonstration of Northern Soul dancing to the bemused Essex multitude. Nobody knew where to look, but there was Ian being Ian – a man without fear.

"I was working in Record Corner at Balham, and all sorts of bits and pieces would come in, ones-and-twos of this and that, and one of the things I found that had been sent there, was a 'Will you stock our record?' promo, by Eddie Parker called "Love You Baby". Of course, I was absolutely gobsmacked by it, fantastic, wonderful, brilliant! And around this time, I was meeting people who were coming down from the North like Stevie Appleby, Alfie they used to call him, and Ian was bringing odd people down to the shop, and we were starting to look for odds-and sods of rarities. Ian said, 'Well you must come up to the Mecca, you've got fantastic records, bring them up, you must have lots of things we haven't heard. Well I didn't go up at first, because I was working in the shop on a Saturday, so it was difficult to go, but I used to send records up via Alfie. And some of the other early records I had first, were things like "I'm In A World Of Trouble" by the Sweet Things and "Baby Boy" by Fred Hughes."

Levine saw Tony outside the Mecca, on the day of the ill-fated coach trip, and told Rounce to come to the front of the queue. As he was with his friends, Tony stayed put. "I didn't twig at the time what he was trying to say to me. But he'd obviously been tipped off by Bill Pye, the manager of the Mecca, that there were a bunch of Londoners coming up and they weren't going to get in at any price. Not getting in made me very angry, made us all very angry, but it strengthened my resolve to go, and I was up there the following week, and it was like an epiphany – that's all I can say."

Tony's experience of the Mecca was a turning point. "I experienced my own personal *Quadrophenia*, when I went up one weekend and didn't come

135

home. Blessed, dear Janet Thompson and her parents had a guest house on Kirby Road on the South Shore – she was going out with Boogaloo, but she liked me and I liked her, but that was as far as it got…but they let me live in their attic room. I had no money, no job, and I just lived for about three months by phoning my grandmother saying, 'Can you send me a fiver, nan?, I'm not coming back'. But I got sick, I got ill, I realised it wasn't working out. I had a wonderful time up there, but Blackpool in the winter is not as hospitable and welcoming as Blackpool in the summer, and eventually, I sort of wore out my welcome with Blackpool, and I sold Tony Jebb, my copy of Willy Kendrick's "Change Your Ways" for a fiver to get the bus fare home."

Rounce continued to take records up North – Wendy Rene's "Bar-B-Q", the Vibrations' "Cause You're Mine" and Philip Mitchell's "Free For All". Even when he had stopped going to the Mecca, Tony sold Levine records by Ray Paige, Lorraine Chandler and Sharon Scott – all RCA label 45s which he got from Dave McAleer, who then worked for the company.

What Cummings had headlined in *Record Mirror*, as the "Soul Civil War", now transferred itself to the pages of *Blues & Soul*. The debate continued, fuelled by a combination of editorial comment and readers' letters. Editor John Abbey, as a long time champion of R&B and soul music, was determined to avoid division amongst his hard-earned readership and placed equal prominence in his magazine to the contemporary soul scene and to the demands of the many enthusiasts north of the capital who were listening to and buying soul from the previous decade. Adopting the role of soul music's peacemaker and go-between, he tried to convince both sides to try and see things from each other's viewpoint. Abbey's fair mindedness, and no doubt keen business acumen honed by the prospect of mail-order record sales through the magazine's Contempo Oldies, was ignored by devotees of both camps and letters poured in condemning one or other of the favoured styles. Abbey's stance was all the more determined because of the relative lack of interest by music fans in soul music. Progressive rock was far more popular amongst the majority of record buyers, and what had started as "underground" had now become definitely mainstream. The only DJs on Radio One who were playing Black American music were Mike Raven, hidden away in a weekend evening slot, and Emperor Rosko, who featured soul music prominently on his show. It was not unusual to hear him spin new imports from artistes such as Marvin Gaye, Honey Cone and the Dramatics. In January

1972, David Simmons took over from Mike Raven to become Radio One's soul DJ. After serving in the Second World War, Raven had had a variety of jobs including photographer, conjurer, ballet and flamenco dancer, Shakespearean actor and interior decorator. His filming commitments in horror movies such as *Crucible Of Terror*, where he was cast as a psychotic sculptor, created the opening for Simmons. Many felt that Raven's soul had deserted him and the change was seen as a positive step. Simmons was definitely a Southern soul fan in the sense that he concentrated on new releases, and rarely played discs aimed at the Northern market. This was mostly because of limited airtime and his decision to extend his perceived remit as an R&B disc-jockey to encompass African music – Simmons' record selections often reflected the period he had spent in Senegal. Another criticism levelled at Dave concerned his playing of B-sides when his show was quite often the only opportunity soul fans had to hear the official A-side.

Tony Jebb, the DJ at the Blackpool Mecca, had written to Dave Godin listing the Highland Room's current favourites; Robert Banks' slice of gospel soul "Mighty Good Way", Little Richard's rousing OKeh 45 "I Don't Wanna Discuss It", Detroit star Rose Batiste's "Hit And Run", Mamie Galore's gritty "It Ain't Necessary" and Nella Dodds' polished "Come Back Baby". Jebb had put a lot of work into building the reputation of the Mecca, and within the Northern soul scene, coach trips to the seaside meant more than candy floss and fun fairs. When the Wheel closed, Blackpool really took off. By the time Godin had made his visit to the Blackpool Mecca on New Year's Eve, Ian Levine was also deejaying.

The visit was reported in February of 1972 and by this time, Godin noticed a mellowing in the sounds with a move to a mellow-funk ingredient as distinct from the sharp, clean cut Uptown style. The biggest sound at the time was Johnny Jones & The King Casuals' version of Jimi Hendrix' "Purple Haze", which had been issued on Brunswick and produced by William Bell for his Peachtree Productions. Godin recalled that when it was new, Soul City had overstocked on it and copies were easily available. Other Mecca jewels included Bobby Hebb's celebratory "Love Love Love" which had languished on the flip of the follow-up to "Sunny", and the Young Folk's Mar-V-Lus outing "Lonely Girl".

LONDON
AMERICAN RECORDINGS
45 R.P.M.
MADE IN ENGLAND
THE DECCA RECORD CO. LTD.
RECORDING FIRST
PUBLISHED 1964
Recorded by
HI,
New York
BIEM NCB
Jewel Music
K/T
S
HLU
9925

LITTLE QUEENIE
(Berry)
BILL BLACK'S COMBO

FOUR
BROTHERS
45 RPM
45 RPM
VOCAL
4-Bros-10467
45-452
Pub., Fairshake,
BMI
Time: 2:29

I'VE GOT SOMETHING
GOOD
(Dandridge - Weems)
SAM & KITTY
A Wee Dan Production
Distributed by ATCO RECORD SALES
1841 BROADWAY, N.Y. N.Y.

Verve
SPECIAL DISC JOCKEY RECO
CLARA
WARD
Orch. Arr. And
Cond. By
Charles Calello
A Jack Lewis-
Monte Kay Prod.
(Schroe
VK-10412
(66-VK-293)
Acorn Music
(BMI)
2:32
MGM RECORDS—A DIVISION OF METRO-GOLDWYN-MAYER INC.—MADE IN

Verve
SPECIAL DISC JOCKEY RECORD
THE
SUPERIORS
WHAT WOULD
I DO
★
Produced by
Hy Mizrahi
(Williams-Wood)
Arr. by: Sal Ditroia
Tender Tunes Music
BMI
2:05
A Kama Sutra
Production
VK-10370
(65-VK-511)
MGM RECORDS—A DIVISION OF METRO-GOLDWYN-MAYER INC.—MADE IN U.S.A.

Stateside
STATESIDE IS THE TRADEMARK OF THE GRAMOPHONE CO. LTD.

I'M STANDING (2.24)
RUFUS LUMLEY

LIZARD
45-1010
(1010-A)
PROMOTION COPY
Vul
T
NOT

KEEP ON KEEPING ON
(Richard Flowers)
N. F. PORTER
Prod. by Gabriel Mekler
LIZARD RECORDS · 8913 SUN
LOS ANG

perception
RECORDS
Popdraw Music
Corp.
ASCAP
Time: 2:47
P-4
Z4KM-0041
PRODUCED BY
PERCEPTION
PROD.

"LET HER GO"
(Konyon-Curtiss)
OTIS SMITH
PERCEPTION RECORDS SUBSIDIARY OF PERCEPTION VENTURES INC. N. Y.

CONSTELLATION
RECORDS, INC.
C-65-279
VOCAL
A' Bill Sheppard
Production
Costoma
Music-BMI
Time: 2:25
Arr. By:
Richard Evans

JUST LIKE THE WEATHER
(Richard Parker)
NOLAN CHANCE
C-161

date
45 RPM
2-1
ZSP
2:

I WORSHIP YOU BABY
- J. Hirschorn - A. Kasha -
THE GLORIES
Arranged by T. Wiltshire
Produced by Bob Yorey
"DATE" MARCA REG. MADE IN U.S.A.

St. Lawrence
Arc Music,
Cragvee Music,
BMI
Time 2:31
15394
Produced by
Pinchback,
Henderson &
Hagood

I CAN'T GET ENOUGH
(OF YOUR LOVE)
(Monk Higgins & Johnny Sayles)
Arr. & Supv. by M. Higgins
JOHNNY SAYLES

KAREN
Distributed by Karen Record Sales Co.
1841 B'Way. N.Y. N.Y.
45-1533
K-11440-PL
VOCAL
Pub., McLaughlin
-Aneece, BMI
Time: 2:18

1193
A(1)

QUICK CHANGE ARTIST
(Greene - Griffith)
THE SOUL TWINS
Arr. by Mike Terry
Produced by Ollie McLaughlin

DET. MICH.
GOLDEN WORLD
RECORDS INC
DISC JOCKEY
NOT F
Myto Music
BMI
ZTSC-107588
G'
Time

I LOVE THE LIFE I LIVE
(AND LIVE THE LIFE I LOVE)
(A. Hamilton, J. Bratton, B. Hamilton)
TONY MICHAELS

CHAPTER 10

The Beautiful Night

THE FIRST ALL-NIGHTER at The Torch took place on 11th March 1972 and the DJs were Keith Minshull, Johnny Beggs, Colin Curtis and Alan Day – Chris Burton paying them ten pounds each. Keith and Colin had been friends ever since they discovered their mutual interest in soul music through the electrical shop, Steel Brothers. Together they frequented soul clubs including the Twisted Wheel and the Golden Torch. They began deejaying at a local club The Magic Roundabout, and to subsidise their soul addiction, often resorted to undertaking more commercial bookings. Curtis managed to avoid the later controversies that surrounded the Northern circuit, and with his long hair stood out on the scene as a rather enigmatic individual, but who was, at the same time, an approachable and popular character on the scene.

"My first visit to the Torch came when I'd just been grounded by my parents, for doing something ridiculous no doubt." remembers Curtis. "We lived in this pub and I was allowed to go out on this particular evening, so I caught the bus. I went into Tunstall and thought I'd go to the Torch. It was a mid-week night, and I was wearing purple flares and a yellow jacket. And I went into this club, and Stringfellow was playing that night, and it just freaked me out. I was late back from this session, so I was completely grounded again. I was desperate to go again, but I had to escape from the pub this time, through the window, across the yard. A guy picked me up on a scooter, but said he couldn't take me all the way. He took me about a mile, and then I walked all the way to the Torch, and the fucking place was shut. I didn't even think they'd have an itinerary. I thought they'd just be open on the night. Why would anybody want to close this fucking dream place?"

Dave Burton, who introduced many rare 45s to the Northern scene in the early Seventies, was a regular visitor to the club. "The Torch was great for an all-nighter. It was this huge derelict cinema, with balconies around three quarters of it, looking down onto this massive wooden dance floor. There were huge speakers on the stage that were crap, but they just used to turn it up to full power and it would sound brilliant. The walls were painted black, and there were these large portraits of soul singers behind the stage, and, of course, these huge black power fists." The paintings were by Torch regular Tony Benbow.

Throughout 1972, Jay Boy reissued many acknowledged Northern classics including Keni Lewis & The Dreams' raucous "Jess James", Philip Mitchell's "Free For All (Winner Takes All)", the Mirettes' "He's Alright With Me", Jackie Lee's "Oh My Darlin'" and others by Jimmy Thomas, Furys, Fi-dels, Watts 103rd Street Rhythm Band, Bob & Earl and Bobby Womack. These were taken from the Mirwood/Mira, Shout and Keymen catalogues which had previously been released through Fontana, Action and London. A three volume set called "Keep The Faith" was issued, which included 36 of the finest Jay Boy and President releases. Included were tracks from Jackie Lee, the Olympics, Viola Wills, Richard Temple, Bob & Earl, Willie Parker and many others. Jay Boy had been started in 1968 as a subsidiary of President Records – and its first release had been Doris Willingham's "You Can't Do That". As Doris Duke, she would later record the R&B hit "To The Other Woman (I'm The Other Woman)" with Jerry "Swamp Dogg" Williams. After this initial soul release, Jay Boy issued a mixture of pop, reggae and, bizarrely, the Detroit rock band the MC5's "Kick Out The Jams". When the Invitations appeared in the UK as the "Original Drifters" in 1970, they recorded for Jay Boy "How'd We Ever Get This Way", and from then on the label concentrated on soul music. George McCrae's "Rock Your Baby" was a deserved later hit.

Other companies with an ear to the Northern scene reactivated club favourites which they dug out from their back catalogues – in some cases achieving healthy sales in return. EMI issued the Sapphires' "Gotta Have Your

Archie Bell and the Drells

Love", now one of the most highly prized UK collectors' items on its original HMV label. Tony Blackburn picked up on this one and played the track heavily. On the recommendation of Dave Godin, Philips reissued Bobby Hebb's "Love, Love, Love" which made it to number thirty two in the charts. Capitol were slow to react and missed the boat with Bobby Sheen's "Doctor Love", which was by then played-out. They were chided by reviewer John Abbey, who wondered what the record's chances might have been, if it had been reissued when they first realised its popularity. After much prodding by *Record Mirror's* record reviewer and DJ James Hamilton, United Artists reissued Little Anthony & The Imperials' "Gonna Fix You Good", the O'Jays' "Working On Your Case" and Timmy Willis' "Mr Soul Satisfaction". Atlantic blew the cobwebs off oldies by the Soul Brothers Six, Johnny Copeland, Mary Wells, Esther Phillips, the Capitols and were rewarded with a top twenty hit for Archie Bell & The Drells' "Here I Go Again". Tamla-Motown remembered that it owned the rights to the Ric-Tic catalogue and the San Remo Strings' instrumental "Festival Time" broke into the top forty, although Laura Lee's vocal of the same track, "To Win Your Heart", flopped. Wand put out two in-demand tracks, Ronnie Milsap's "Ain't No Soul" and Roscoe

141

Robinson's "That's Enough", another of the 45s which had been bootlegged by Jeff King. It had been gospel singer Robinson's first secular hit in 1966 and sold a million copies. And Phonogram, who had acquired the rights to Chess, finally put out one of the most sought after items; Joy Lovejoy's "In Orbit".

This flurry of activity surprised many, not least the poor collector who had paid £80 for a Mirwood copy of Jimmy Conwell's "Cigarette Ashes" which Jay Boy issued in March 1972. This was the backing track to another Mirwood production, Richard Temple's "That Beatin' Rhythm", Temple and Conwell being one and the same person.

The vocal version was a popular sound at the Catacombs in Wolverhampton when the club's DJ Allan S heard that an instrumental version existed.

"I'd had "That Beatin' Rhythm" for ages, in fact I got it the same day I bought Johnny Sayles' "I Can't Get Enough" off a list, for next to nothing. "That Beatin' Rhythm" became a massive sound at the Catacombs, in fact I got a bit of a name for it. Anyway, I heard that Billy Butler, who was the DJ at the Mardi Gras in Liverpool, had an instrumental version. So I drove up to Liverpool with this guy called Pete Sylvester who used to be a local DJ at the Royal Walsall on Sunday nights. I used to do the odd

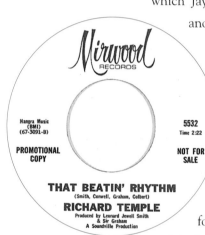

spot there every now and then. We met Billy Butler in the office upstairs, and I asked him to sell the record to me, which I'd now discovered was called "Cigarette Ashes". He wouldn't sell it at first, but after a while he gave in and I bought it off him. I know I paid far more than I usually would. The record was just lying on the floor behind the turntables. Anybody could have taken it." The record became well known

The Royalettes

Danny White

on the circuit and Ian Levine recalled later that he made the journey to Wolverhampton specifically to hear it.

At Contempo Soul Source in London, the top three sellers were the JBs' "Gimme Some More", Betty Wright's "Clean Up Woman" and Joe Simon's "Drowning In The Sea Of Love". The chart from Sinfonia in Blackpool was topped by Philip Mitchell's "Free For All" and other retailers across the North reflected the widening chasm between the tastes of soul fans in the North and those from the South. Yet small outposts of rare soul could be found away from the heart of the scene. DJ Barry Kingston was spinning the type of records more typical of a Northern club at Boo Boo's in Hove, near Brighton, and Torch regular Dave Rivers had an oldies night at The Shack Disco in London's

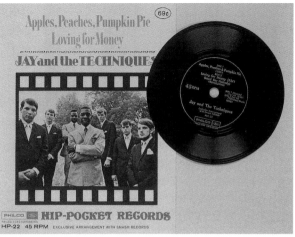

Swiss Cottage. Classic oldies such as Bettye Swann's "Make Me Yours" and Dean Parrish's "Determination" were played alongside rarer items like Joy Lovejoy's "In Orbit". Mick Smith and Clive Everitt from Stevenage had already visited the Pendulum and the Cromwellian in Manchester and, on spotting Dave's night advertised in *Blues & Soul,* went along. Mick Smith now sells soul records from Hitchin, and DJs at various venues around the country.

"We went along to this place in Swiss Cottage, just like a church hall , and there was Dave deejaying from this slot in the wall. I don't think there was anyone else in the place! In July '72, he'd started doing a thing with Dave Burton at the Bird's Nest in West Hampstead. That was a bit more popular, and you could hear the same records as they were playing at the Torch. We also used to go the Shades of Green in Camberley, that was around 1971."

Mick remembers hearing "(At The) Discotheque", "Follow Your Heart" and "Just A Little Misunderstanding" at the Stevenage Locarno. "There was a guy there called Danny Leno, we used to call him the fastest DJ on the Floor. We used to go to Fred Moore's house in Leighton Buzzard, and he had one room racked out with singles. He'd only sell you one copy of any record, he'd always say 'You'll only go and sell it up North.' We went up to the Torch and I remember hearing Major Lance's "You Don't Want Me No More" and

145

Archie Bell & The Drells' "Here I Go Again", and before long we'd starting dealing, selling to the DJs.I think the first record we sold was George Carrow's "Angel Baby", which we got from a shop in Hemel Hempstead. We started selling to Richard Watt in Carlisle, and we tried to sell Tony Jebb, Jimmy "Soul" Clark's "Sweet Darlin", but Jebby took it off after fifteen seconds because of the slow start. He bought it in the end though.

Mick Smith and Clive Everitt in the USA with Bernie Binnick, who discovered Mickey Lee Lane, 3 Degrees, George Woods, Norman Johnson and Gamble & Huff

"Clive and I used to go everywhere to sell; Up The Junction, Hanley, the Catacombs, and then in '73 we went to the States. We flew to New York, and went everywhere by Greyhound bus. Nothing was planned, we just rolled into a town and had a look around to see what we could get. As we were over there, we went to see Martin Koppell in Canada, but he'd gone home to England! So we went down to Detroit and Chicago. We got a cabbie to take us into the Southside to a record store, and he couldn't rest until he knew we were safe – he ended up waiting for two hours! It was a good trip though, and we came back with some great stuff. Jack Montgomery "Dearly Beloved", Butch Baker "Workin At The Go-Go", Bob Relf, Tempos, and the Invitations' "Ski-ing In The Snow" which we sold for £25. And I don't care what Ian Levine says, we discovered Lee David out there."

Although the Soul Sounds pressings that Jeff King had made were clearly bootlegs, and were accepted by everybody as a cheap alternative to the original copies, collectors were becoming annoyed at counterfeit copies which looked identical to the original. Paul Rudzetis from Leicester wrote to *Blues & Soul* in March 1972 about a fake copy of Laura Lee's Ric Tic release "To Win Your Heart" which he had recently bought. Paul's fears that this could be just the start of a flood of similar counterfeits were well founded.

By the summer of 1972 the rare soul scene was thriving: 45s like Johnny Sayles' sublime "I Can't Get Enough", Danny White's rough-and-tumble "Cracked

Up Over You", and jewels by Nella Dodds, Jerry Cook, the Carstairs, Johnny Jones, Sounds Of Lane, Younghearts, Roy Hamilton, Triumphs and James Bounty, were echoing throughout clubs and dancehalls in the North of England. The Torch was now running monthly all-nighters with DJs Keith Minshull and Alan Day; Day was also deejaying the Sunday all-dayer at the 76 Club in Burton-on-Trent and Up The Junction in South Street, Crewe; Allan S, Blue Max and Oscar Michael at the Catacombs were laying claim to the Wolverhampton venue being "The Country's Leading R&B And Soul Discotheque".

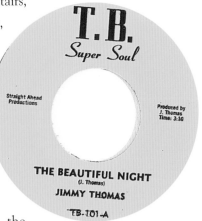

Following a deal with Bell Records, Mojo announced the forthcoming reissues of further club classics: The O'Jays' "I Dig Your Act"; James Carr's "Freedom Train" coupled with "That's What I Want To Know"; Moses & Joshua Dillard's two long since deleted 45s "My Elusive Dreams" and "Get Out Of My Heart"; the Invitations' "What's Wrong With Me Baby" and the Incredibles' "There's Nothing Else To Say Baby". After Mojo's closure the latter was not issued until 1974 when John Abbey's next venture, Contempo, put it out.

In November 1972, Tony Banks, who had been deejaying at the Bali Hai at Wakefield, went to the States to hunt for records. Banks had been planning to go with Julian Bentley, but as Bentley had been busted for drugs and refused a visa, Banks went alone. He returned with discoveries such as the Fabulous Downbeats' "Life Goes On", Tari Stevens' "False Alarm" and over five hundred bootleg copies of Jimmy Thomas' "The Beautiful Night".

Jimmy Thomas' break came at the bottom of the bill of the Ike & Tina Turner Revue. He toured Britain with them in 1966, and whilst Ikette P. P. Arnold stayed, Jimmy returned home. He recorded "Where There's A Will" for Mirwood, which later went on to become a Northern favourite, but quit the States in 1968 to return to the UK. Jimmy's first recording for Parlophone, "The Beautiful Night" was never officially released although a few demos got out and became popular on the scene fetching £50 a copy.

Banks took a copy with him to New York, had the metal master manufactured on Broadway and five hundred and fifty copies pressed in Newark on his own TB Soul Sounds label. Because he had two suitcases packed with records, he paid £90 in excise to customs on arrival. Booked to

THE DRAMATICS
Sport Record Artists

SUPER SONIC SOUND PRODUCTIONS
Detroit, Michigan

DJ at the Torch, he sold one hundred copies off the stage the night Major Lance returned to the club after having recorded his live album. One of the copies sold ended up in the hands of Selecta Disc in Nottingham and was subsequently bootlegged again.

Jimmy Thomas was sent a copy of the pirated disc, and contacted Essex, the publishers who had recorded the song and leased it to EMI. They were not that interested in reissuing the track, so Thomas tried to buy the master tape. Despite having written and produced the song, the asking price was way beyond Jimmy's means.

Tony Banks was born Anthony Newton, but took his DJ name from soul singer Darrell Banks. At the invitation of the manager Jimmy Savile, Tony had started deejaying lunchtimes at the Leeds Mecca in County Arcade. Soon after Banks featured what he called a "total black music spot – the first pure soul, but then it was called R&B, because even the labels which were around at the time, the red and yellow Pye International singles had "R&B Series" stamped in the centre. Such stuff as Tommy Tucker's "Hi-Heel Sneakers" and Timmy Shaw's "Gonna Send You Back To Georgia". I used to play R&B at the

Locarno on Manning Wood Lane in Bradford in amongst the pop stuff. Then there was the Three Coins just off Albion Street in Leeds. And then the old Mecca, where I'd started, became the Spinning Disc. There was also the Earl Seaton Youth Club, where the biggest sounds were Homer Banks' "Hooked By Love" and Darrell Banks' "Open The Door To Your Heart". I deejayed at the Bin Lid at Dewsbury and the Esquire in Sheffield. In the late Sixties there was a club in Bradford called the String O' Beads where there was a record shop run by a chap called Pearson and he used to stock everything. Literally. I used to go and sit on his floor upstairs and go through all the stuff that I found. And that's where a lot of stuff came from. For instance, if he had ten copies of Los Canarios "Get On Your Knees", I used to buy them all. Keep one myself, keep a spare if they were cheap enough, say 50p, and then sell the rest on to Jumbo Records in Leeds. I used to play Bud Harper's "Mr Soul" at the String O' Beads and Pearson gave me "Mr Soul" as a handle."

The Pendulum had been one of the longest running clubs in Manchester since the Twisted Wheel closed. Originally in Hardman Street, in 1972 it moved into the basement of the Manchester Sports Guild Building in Long Millgate. Consistently popular every Friday night, the doors would regularly close once the legal limit had been reached. The regular DJs, Dave White and Barry Tasker, both progressed from R&B to soul. Dave via John Lee Hooker's "Dimples" and Barry when he witnessed one of the American Folk Blues Festival concerts – Sonny Boy Williamson, Willie Dixon and other blues greats at the Free Trade Hall in Manchester. the Pendulum made a great impression on the future Wigan Casino DJ Richard Searling.

"I thought the music there was great. I still do actually now, even over twenty years later. It's just sort of come back to me. What they were playing was a logical progression from the deep Soul that I'd first loved into what became known as Northern Soul. The fact that the music they played had a dance beat was nice, but there was something more. The Pendulum was in a first floor Seventies building, fairly modern, right behind the Law Courts in Manchester, off Deansgate, behind the Manchester Evening News Building on Hartman Street. I can remember guys walking round in there with like Bobby Bland EPs on Vacalion, things like that, you know. I suddenly became aware of this sort of magical world…it didn't alienate me because to me it was still deep Soul, and I can remember the record that stands out more than anything was, ironically, by a white group – the Prophets' "I've Got The Fever". And that sort of tied in, because of Tesco stocking all the Mercury and Phonogram deletions at the time and all these junk shops." Richard was not alone in discovering that many of the in-demand oldies could be found, if one was prepared to put in the work.

"I remember trawling the Tescos and finding these things. I worked in Salford, just up the road from where I work now at Jazz FM, actually. I remember one Monday morning – I don't know what made me do it – a guy still reminds me. I just blew out of the place, I had forgotten to go to loads of Tescos. He said 'I'll try to cover for you as long as I can'. And I got about eight copies of Bobby Paris' "Personally" out of the bin and got them back. Took them to the Mecca on the Saturday night, and I can remember Tony Jebb coming across – I don't know what I did, but I must have transgressed some unwritten law there, because I was trying to sell them from a little box. I'd never tried to sell records, but I had "Love On A Mountain Top", several

copies from Ralph's Records. And all these copies of Bobby Paris. I remember Tony Jebb coming across in the nicest possible way, and saying 'For Christ's sake, stop it!' I don't even think there was anybody selling records in the place that would have objected, but there must have been something about me selling records, and Stuart Cunliffe still reminds me to this day, of how he stuck up for me and kept me my job at that place.

"I also remember going to a shop, it was either a Co-op or a Tesco, in Levenshulme with a guy called Arthur who'd never been on the scene really. He used to have this flat above a bank in Prestwich, and he'd found Lou Johnson's "Unsatisfied", Jeanette White's "Music", The Gospel Classics' "More Love". I can remember finding Prince Harold on Mercury "Baby You've Got Me". But the best thing was the Inspirations' "Touch Me, Hold Me, Kiss Me". I remember we found two copies for like 10p each. By then I thought Christ, Tesco, they've got everything! I remember going to the Wigan branch and finding loads of copies of "What A Wonderful Night For Love" by Bobby Patterson. It was just absolutely amazing. It was fascinating.

"And then there were the junk shops in Moss Side. I was at Didsbury Teacher Training College studying art and drama as a day student, which is bad news if you go to those sort of colleges. My friends left, so I eventually left as well. But in the year that I was there, I can remember a junk shop in Didsbury which, for some bizarre reason had demos of the whole Jay Boy catalogue. But also we crossed to Moss Side. And on two separate occasions and on two separate weeks, I found Patrice Holloway's "Love and Desire". One copy was there one week, and the week after, another. Now, it makes me reflect on

Richard & Judith Searling

what Moss Side might have been playing at the time. Maybe that was a record that was quite influential. And then the other most influential person to me is a guy called Bob Stevens. Bob ran Star Pick Studios, next to the Empire. He was quite a short guy only about five foot two. And as you walked in this place, he had like a 45 degree rack of singles with things like the Chi-lites' "Love Bandit" on Beacon. All the Pama stuff. Loads of President. I'm sure that fantastic thing from Chicago, Jimmy Robbins' "I Can't Please You" that everyone now wants on British, would have been there. This guy opened up a whole new world to me. They weren't deleted. The shops in Manchester just weren't stocking them, but this guy had them all and they were all there. I remember Bob, all you could see was the top of his bloody head as he walked past the back of the rack. We used to see him at the Mecca. I've said to Ian Levine that I remember "Every Beat Of My Heart" and "Hit And Run" and all that stuff. But Bob Stevens was the man, because he sort of linked us with buying the records.

"Before Judith and I got married, we used to go to Blackpool for weekends, as did many people at the time. The fact that the Mecca was there was

151

BRENDA & the TABULATIONS

Dionn
Records

Personal Managers
Gilda Woods & James Ross
421 W. Ellet St.
Phila., Pa. 19114

fantastic. But there was a bit more to Blackpool than just that, you know. It was a bit of an in crowd. And this shop was a real focal point. I can even remember the most bizarre thing of all. On a Wednesday afternoon in Blackpool, we ended up down a street quite close to where that shop was, and don't ask me why, but they had stacks and stacks of Stateside issues in the packets for about 10p each. And it was like racks and racks of them. And I remember buying "West Coast" by Ketty Lester on Capitol, James Carr "A Losing Game" on Stateside. God knows what was there that I didn,t take. I remember it was midweek, and going back to Bob Stevens, and he said 'I don,t believe you,ve got all these things. It,s down the bloody road'.

"When you went to Bob Steven's house, it wasn't that big. But all you could see were these blue Stateside packets and Capitol packets and everything. I remember he wanted "Love And Desire" which I had a spare copy of. And he said I,ve got a spare copy of Al Wilson's "Now I Know What Love Is", so I let him have it. And when we got married and moved to Bolton, he came to our house warming party. It was about the time of Bobby Womack's "That,s How I feel About 'Cha" came out. He had yellow high heeled boots on. Bob Stevens was a major, major factor."

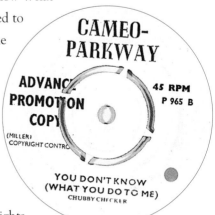

The Torch in Tunstall had successfully filled the vacuum left by the Twisted Wheel and by 1972, could rightly claim to be the number one all-nighter in the country. Manager Chris Burton has fond memories of the converted former cinema.

"We regularly had attendances of over a thousand on Saturday nights, it wasn't that big, but when we had fifteen or sixteen hundred in there, it was just hell. All the drinks' labels would peel off the bottles on the bar due to the heat. We couldn't have coped with that every week, but I think it had it's part to play in the Northern soul thing. For a time it carried the torch I suppose – the Northern flame".

Burton had run his first promotion at the Borough Hall, Stafford, coming out with a £50 profit. After an initial partnership which failed, he joined forces with Keith Fisher, who had a small entertainment agency, and together they started running dances at the King's Hall in Stoke. Chris bought the Regent Cinema in Tunstall and turned it into a dance hall. In an article written for a local magazine, Burton pointed with pride to an architect's drawing on the wall: "That's our latest baby…The Golden Torch."

"We have been through this plan so many times," he continued. "We are building for five hundred people. To make sure they would get in we had a scale model built and then bought five hundred toy soldiers of the same scale. They went in all right. Tunstall has been a neglected end of the city and I'm sure we are going to give them something they want."

The first attraction to the club, on 31st January 1965, was Billy J. Kramer & the Dakotas and it was not until 1967 that the first soul music act played

Major Lance

live – Inez and Charlie Foxx. The early DJs at the club were more like entertainers, as Burton recalls: "Peter Stringfellow, from the Mojo in Sheffield, would deejay on Sundays and another guy called the Red Baron. There was "Barmy Barry", Dave Plumb, Tony Teret. The DJs were very much in the Jimmy Savile mould, silly on stage, that type of thing. Until Keith Minshull came along in 1969 and did a soul night."

Martyn Ellis and Alan Day joined him, and as the word spread the crowds began to flock to the club. Although Burton flirted with progressive rock, blues nights and reggae, the club eventually adopted a 100% soul music policy. The transition to a rare soul club surprised Burton.

"I must say that the first Northern night we did was incredible, just the sheer energy that the people had. You could feel the energy that they created enjoying themselves. Those early DJs like Minshull, Colin Curtis, Alan Day were not the image I had of a DJ in my mind. They hardly said a word, just grunting and putting records on, and everybody thinking this is a great scene."

Martyn Ellis from Manchester and Alan Day from Burton-on-Trent were brought in, and when the Twisted Wheel was closed in 1971, despite the efforts of other clubs to replace the it's place in the heart of the growing soul scene's fans affections, the Torch quickly became the number one club.

In August 1972, Tony Jebb was poached by Chris Burton from the Blackpool Mecca leaving Ian Levine and Les Cockell. Three months later, Levine would join the more successful Torch set-up, and the Highland Room closed.

Artists welcomed to the Torch for the end-of-year festivities, included Bob & Earl, Otis Leaville, Oscar Toney Jr, and Edwin Starr – whose tour itinerary in 1972, featured such famed soul havens as Whitchurch Civic Hall, Stafford's Top Of The World, the Lafayette in Wolverhampton and the Wigan Casino. Yet it was the appearance by Chicago soul star Major Lance, on December 9th 1972 that would be best remembered. Supported that night by fellow Windy City artist Otis Leaville and UK soul act Mac & Katie Kissoon, Lance's performance would be recorded for John Abbey's new Contempo label due to be launched in the coming year.

"It got closed down because of the residents, who were rightly up in arms. There was a hay merchant next door to the Torch and they had a horse in the stables. The headline was something like "The Horse Can't Get To Sleep At Night Because Of The Music"! So this poor old horse that used to sleep to the left hand side of the stage got it in the ear all night."

Chris Burton

THE TORCH

The Country's only...
ALL-NIGHTER

Twelve So-Full-Soulful-Hours

8-30 p.m. — 8-30 a.m.

Members 50p—Guests 60p (before midnight

ON THE WAY IN ... Major Lance

"Va-Va's was a bit of a fluke really. I got asked to do it by a guy called Rick Barrett. Rick was a very cool Jamaican who lived in Bolton, who happened to be into Soul music."

Richard Searling

VA-VA
GREAT MOOR STREET
BOLTON

Presents *EVERY FRIDAY*

THE MOST SENSATIONAL ALL NIGHT SOUL SESSION IN THE NORTH

with D. J. RICHARD 'S'

Hear the Country's Top Soul Sounds between 1 a.m. and 7-30 a.m.
Sound like: "CAN IT BE"– Mel Williams, "I CAN'T HOLD ON"– Lorraine Chadler, "WHAT SHALL I DO"– Frankie & The Classicals, "I'VE GOT TO HAVE YOUR LOVE" – The Volcanoes, "YOU'RE A PUZZLE"– Jive Five, "HEARTS DESIRE"– Billy Joe Royal, "ONCE UPON A TIME"– Orlons.
Plus: Little Jimmy Scott, Sharon Soul, Johnny Howard, Adventurers, Roy Thompson, Thrills, Carl Jackson, Jerry Cook, Vel-Vets, Linda Jones, Debbie Dean, Amazers, Diplomats, Sapphires, Gladys Knight, and various other obscurities

ALL-NIGHTERS EVERY FRIDAY OF THE YEAR

Admission £1.00

Bars Open 'Til 2

★ WE ALSO CATER FOR TRENDY WEDDINGS

TUNSTALL C
DRUG CENT
JUSTICES
TOLD

**YOUNG PEOPLE FROM ALL PARTS OF ENGLAND HAD
N FLOCKING TO STOKE-ON-TRENT — TO A TUNSTALL
B THAT HAD BECOME A DRUG CENTRE, IT WAS
IMED TO-DAY.**

And Mr. David McEvoy told the City Licensing Justices: " The
en Torch has a national reputation as a place where drugs can

be obtained and for trafficking in drugs."

Mr. McEvoy was representing the police, who were objecting to an application by Mr. Christopher Burton, owner of the Golden Torch, for the renewal of the club's liquor and entertainment licences.

Since July, 1972. 40 people had been involved in drug offences in connection with the Golden Torch, he told the Justices.

"Many of these were cases where the individual had packets of tablets ready for distribution on the premises— they were to be sold at the Golden Torch," he alleged.

The club's "Torch All Nighter" on Saturdays had attracted people from a wide area — from the south coast to the North of England. Some came from Scotland, he said.

Students from the Stok picketing outside the

STU
STI

CHAPTER 11

Blowing Up My Mind!

IN JANUARY 1973, *Blues & Soul* magazine launched its new label Contempo, which was to be distributed through Decca. Whereas John Abbey's previous label, Mojo, had concentrated on releasing American recordings mixed with a steady flow of in-demand oldies to sate collectors' demand, he emphasised that Contempo would be predominately geared towards creating its own product. In reality, many original US recordings were released. The first single, issued on 26th January 1973, was Major Lance's reworking of Billy Butler's club classic "The Right Track". Produced by former OKeh label boss Carl Davis, and employing the services of foremost Chicago arranger Tom "Tom" Washington, it was clearly intended to have all the necessary credentials to appeal to Northern fans. The flip side was a reworking of Major's 1964 hit 'Um, Um, Um, Um, Um, Um', although this was a British recording arranged by Gerry Shury and produced by Lance himself.

Other recording artists signed to the label were Otis Leaville, Bob & Earl, Jimmy Thomas and ex-Fantastics vocalist Ritchie Pitts. Contempo would also be handling the Mirwood/Mira catalogue. It was patently clear that the label's new product would be produced by artists respected on the Northern circuit and aimed squarely at this growing market.

Chris Burton, the manager of the Torch, who would later produce bootlegs in partnership with Abbey on the Out Of The Past label, had also recognised the strength of the Torch brand. In conjunction with Top Rank, he formed the International Soul Club, which effectively meant that Torch events could be promoted at their clubs and ballrooms. The club would run all-nighters every

Saturday at its flagship in Tunstall, the Torch, and at Top Rank clubs in Watford, Hanley, Reading and Doncaster.

Big sounds at the time included: Clara Ward's "The Right Direction", a single taken from her "Hang My Tears Out To Dry" album on Verve; P. P. Arnold's UK-Immediate release "Everything's Gonna Be Alright"; Eddie Parker's frantic powerhouse "Love You Baby"; Lenis Guess' "Just Ask Me"; the Invitations' monster "Skiing In The Snow"; the Glories' sing-a-long "I Worship You Baby"; Johnny Moore's strident "Walk Like A Man"; Sam & Kitty's stacatto "I Got Something Good" and Fathers Angels' "Bok To Bach".

This last 45 had been discovered by Tony Banks, then DJ at the Central in Leeds. "I had received the demo from MGM in 1968 – I used to get them all. I used to play the A-side, the Sam & Dave song "Don't Knock It" and the flip side was too fast when it was issued. But in 1973 I was going through my record collection at the time when instrumentals were popular. And I found this and thought that it was brilliant. I lent the copy to Julian Bentley, who took it to the Mecca. I'd already played the disc at the Central in Leeds on the Friday night soul night and then Ian Levine played it at the Highland Room." The zippy string and harp instrumental originated from Heritage Records and is said to feature session musicians Earl Young, Bobby Eli, Bobby Martin and Vince Montana, stalwarts of the famed Sigma Studios in Philadelphia.

Other instrumentals which gathered momentum on the scene included the Righteous Brothers Band's storming rendition of Leonard Bernstein's "Rat Race". Featured as the final track on the Rightous Brothers' 1966 Verve album "Soul & Inspiration", the single was heavily bootlegged. Then there was Earl Wright's driving "Thumb A Ride", tailor-made for the scene with its perfect rhythm and raucous jazz sax solo. Another was Bob Wilson's "Suzy Serenade" from the US Sound Stage 7 set-up. Not all the records played were oldies though, and the Niteliters' instrumental "K-Jee" was a new release on RCA in 1971. This slice of early jazz funk featured Wes Montgomery-style guitar over a strutting beat that was way too fast for the Southern clubs. Produced by Harvey Fuqua, the Niteliters were the backing band behind the groups New Birth and Love, Peace & Happiness.

Tony Petherbridge, who as Tony Windsor had been responsible for organising soul events at the Up The Junction Club in Crewe, reappeared on the scene. He was now running a club in a hotel near Whitchurch called The Beefeater, although it would change its name a few months later to the Raven. With resident DJ Soul Sam, it attracted a large following from all round the country. Petherbridge also ran Nantwich Cricket Club on Sundays, and occasional functions at the Warrington Co-op and Whitchurch Civic Centre.

Dancing competitions became common at different venues and at the Torch, Ian Clowrie from Rotherham, better known as Matchy, together with Valerie Finlayson, were voted Number One Soul Dancers in the Country. Their prize was £25 each. Frank Booper and Janet Leech from Blackpool were second.

Frank Elson began his regular column for *Blues & Soul* magazine in February 1973. Taking the bull by the horns, it was titled "Check Out The North". A diary of Elson's visits to clubs around the country, it included interviews with DJs, visiting artists, record collectors, but more often than not, soul fans simply out having a good time. Lists of DJs' current rarities were interspersed with soul tracks seemingly picked at random from Frank's own collection, and he would

163

Frank Elson

regularly touch upon relevant issues such as drug problems, the threatened closure of clubs, bootlegging and his own views on the state of Northern Soul. As a local journalist he had eagerly reviewed Edwin Starr's appearance at the Torch. Sadly, by Frank's second column, ominous publicity began to appear about the club in the *Evening Sentinel*.

Three girls celebrating a birthday at the club were given tablets by a stranger and told that they would keep them awake all night. They took three each, but were spotted by a member of the Staffordshire Drug Squad on duty in the discotheque. The two eldest girls, aged seventeen, were fined £30 and the youngest, only sixteen, was placed under a supervision order for two years. The Drug Squad had been regular visitors to the Torch since September 1972 when at Burton's invitation, they convened at the club to discuss ways of ironing out the drugs problem. At this meeting it was arranged that Chris would point out drug pushers in the Torch to Drug Squad members on duty within the club. As reported at the final hearing, Burton had not done this.

Drug related arrests were reported prominently by the *Sentinel*. Dave Rivers, from London, who together with Dave Burton had introduced many rare sounds to the DJs at the club, was fined £50 and sentenced to six months' imprisonment suspended for two years. Peter Rhodes, prosecuting at the City Stipendiary Court, told the court that Rivers had been taken from the club and searched by officers of the Drug Squad and was found to be in possession of three tablets containing amphetamine and amylobarbitone. Dave Burton remembers "Dave went missing at around two o'clock, but it was usually to take some girl out to the back of a borrowed Transit van. It was only later that I was told he'd been busted." Chris Burton had to apply to the City Licensing Justices for the renewal of the liquor and entertainment licenses, and the head of the Drug Squad, Detective Sergeant Ernest Gardiner, gave evidence at the hearing.

"Using information from neighbouring drug squads, as well as my own officers, I would say that seventy per cent of the people going to the club are involved in drug abuses." He went on to explain that many youngsters visiting the club had to travel great distances. "They leave home early Saturday and return late Sunday – they need a stimulant." In February, roadblocks were set up at the slip road from the M6 at Barthomley which resulted in sixteen people being charged with drug offences. They were all going to the Torch. The only non-police witness called during the hearing lived directly opposite the entrance to the club in Phoenix Street. He described what it was like living so near to the club. "The noise of people departing from the premises is very bad. I have had to get up at 2 or 3am on Sunday morning to go downstairs. Once someone was strumming a guitar in the street." He added that Chris Burton had tried to solve the problem by supplying "No Parking" signs in the street and had placed somebody on the entrance of the club to stop the disturbance.

Following the police's estimate of the volume of drug abuse at the Torch, Chris Burton defended the behaviour of his customers. "We are very proud of the people we deal with in the club. They are a wonderful set who love their music – they are not junkies." Burton explained that he had done everything in his power to ban drugs from the Torch. He had withdrawn memberships and taken photographs of those banned, which were placed in the pay-box so that the cashiers could identify them. Since it had opened, the club had half-a-million

"They leave home early Saturday and return late Sunday – they need a stimulant."

Detective Sergeant Ernest Gardiner, Evening Sentinel, Stoke-on-Trent 1973 visitors and in 1972 over 62,000 customers from a membership base of 12,500. "This is a specialised form of music that has its devotees and they are very passionately involved with their music."

On Friday 16th March, the Stoke-on-Trent Licensing Justices refused to renew the licences. The chairman said the reasons for the decision were the widely reported drug problems and evidence of after-hours drinking. Burton was criticised for not showing responsibility and for insufficient supervision at the club. He added that there was clearly a demand for this type of club but that the all-night sessions should be discontinued.

John Abbey and Frank Elson from *Blues & Soul* gave evidence. Abbey told the hearing that the Torch was one of the best venues in the country for soul music and insisted that "Soul music and drugs do not go hand in hand." Elson stated that he had occasionally overheard conversations about "gear" and maintained that this was a national problem and not one confined to the Torch. Acting for Burton, John Loyd told the justices that if the Torch was closed then the problem would simply go elsewhere. Despite the reported figure of seventy per cent of the club being involved in drugs, the actual total of convictions was only nine with three further cases due to be heard. Edwin Starr, promoter David Daniels, Melvin Harrowby and Trevor Harley the doorman were all in court and gave evidence.

Chris Burton appealed, but to no avail. Frank Elson wrote: "So, all those pill-heads can cut another notch on their guns. To a trophy with the words

Major Lance on stage at the Torch

"Twisted Wheel" they can add one with "Torch". They can start looking around for another club to defile and ruin. They make me SICK!"

Looking back, Burton feels that it simply made better headlines. "The drugs thing was what attracted the press and the politicians, and certainly to attract the magistrates attention it was there, but no more than when you look

167

at the scene nowadays. By comparison, it wasn't socially acceptable at all. The real issue was the noise. When the police want to close you down, they'll find a reason. We were licensed for six hundred and eighty but when they click-in twelve, thirteen, fourteen hundred…what can you do? I was told at the time to get back to the normal figures or we'll close you, but at the time it was so good and financially it was right. It got closed down because of the residents, who were rightly up in arms. There was a hay merchant next door to the Torch and they had a horse in the stables. The headline was something like "The Horse Can't Get To Sleep At Night Because Of The Music"! So this poor old horse that used to sleep to the left hand side of the stage got it in the ear all night."

Neil Rushton, a Wolverhampton Chronicle journalist and soul fan, started a regular Northern soul feature in Roy Stanton's *Black Wax Magazine*, which had started in January 1973. The first "Northern Lights" feature entitled "Torch Parade", covered the unsavoury publicity surrounding the Tunstall club. By the time the fanzine had been produced, the club's fate had already been decided. A promised appearance by the O'Jays had to be cancelled because of illness and their manager, Jeff Davey, made a flying visit to the club to apologise in person to Chris Burton. Rushton's next report in May, headed "Lights Out!", mentioned the Torch closure, but it was now old news. Neil visited the Catacombs, which was undergoing a face-lift, and felt that the club had lost some of its magic. The club's top sounds were the Autographs' frantic "I Can Do It", Bob Relf's "Blowin' My Mind To Pieces", Lou Johnson's "Unstaisfied", P.P.Arnold's "Everything's Gonna Be Alright", Jimmy Bee's "Wanting You", Emile Griffith's "Going, Going, Gone" and Carolyn Franklin's "Reality". Advertising in the fanzine was John Anderson, one of the foremost suppliers of rare soul records to Northern soul DJs and collectors, then operating a mail-order service from Glasgow.

When the problems started at the Torch, Keith Minshull ("Mr. Soul Man Himself") and Colin Curtis moved to Tiffany's in Newcastle-under-Lyne. Advertised as the "Adult Nitespot With The South Seas Atmosphere", the Sunday night scene promised a house full of soul for the princely sum of 20p. Live acts scheduled to appear at Tiffany's over the coming months included Doris Troy, Billy Preston and Sam &

Dave. Tom West, the manager of the club and instigator of the original scene at the Blackpool Mecca, invited Keith and Colin to return with him to the Highland Room. Ironically, Ian Levine and Tony Jebb, the previous DJs at Blackpool, were now deejaying for Chris Burton at the Top Rank in Hanley. Frank Elson wondered whether they waved to each other across the motorway.

The 76 Club in Burton-on-Trent was the only club open in the Midlands for soul on Sundays. After ex-Torch DJ Alan Day left, Carl Dene from the Catacombs took over behind the decks and the club's membership grew to over sixteen hundred souls. Neil Rushton stepped behind the decks at the 76 Club in the summer.

Neil Rushton rubbished John Abbey in *Black Wax Magazine* over his remarks that most worthwhile Northern sounds had already been issued in the UK, and provided a list of tracks that could profitably be released. Brunswick took him at his word and issued the Cooperettes' "Shing-A-Ling" and Phonogram released the Dells' 1966 oldie "Run For Cover". He also updated readers on the latest activity from Nottingham- based company Selecta Disc. Their list of pressings included legitimate re-releases arranged through the American labels Brunswick and Columbia and future titles were promised from more dubious sources. Counterfeit copies of Rose Battiste's "Hit And Run" and Sam & Kitty's "I Got Something Good" were on their way, together with Johnny Moore's "Walk Like A Man", which although originally issued on the Columbia distributed label Date, would appear on a fake Soultown marque. In fact, it would not be long before Selecta Disc would be fined in court for pirating Homer Banks and Little Anthony discs.

Other top sounds on the circuit included the Trips' "There's A Mountain", the Tempos' "Countdown Here I Come", Duke Browner's "Crying Over You", Toni Lamarr's "Just In The Nick Of Time", Clara Ward's "Help", and Bobby

Patterson's "My Baby's Coming Back To Me". Despite earlier reservations about the Catacombs, Rushton reported that it was doing great business on Saturday nights with Alan Day, Blue Max, Pep and Martyn Ellis behind the decks.

In the same issue of Black Wax, Tony Cummings, who had kept a lower profile since his earlier series of articles in *Record Mirror*, could not resist a barbed review of "Ain't No Soul", the single taken from the forthcoming album "Major Lance's Greatest Hits Recorded Live At The Torch". "Confirming all my deep-rooted prejudices about Northern discos, this piece of unbelievable crassness comes from the forthcoming LP. Maniacal drumming, thinnish vocals and 'off' clapping from an ecstatic crowd who even sing along on "Soul" like a grotesque parody of the Cockerel Chorus. Not a nice one, Cyril."

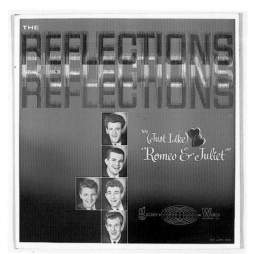

Understandably praised in *Blues & Soul*, the live recording received few good reviews. One of the most amusing came from Clive Richardson at *Shout*. Pulling no punches he wrote: "Without doubt, the worst live LP ever made/issued – unless you want to hear the Torch audience live at the Torch, supported by the lousiest band I've heard in years. I guess Major's in there someplace, chanting 'Hey, hey I feel alright' in response to the audience's incessant, often double-time clapping, while they shout the lyrics of the song at him. Apart from the total absence of musical content, the record's technically poor, badly balanced & fading tracks in the wrong place (I can't remember which tracks – I only played the LP once & wouldn't insult my pickup, or ears, by playing it again). I was going to trade it in for credit at Black Wax, but as a public service gesture I moulded it into a flowerpot instead. Nice sleevepic – write to Contempo, maybe they'll send you a free sleeve!"

Through an introduction from Pendulum DJ Barry Tasker, Richard Searling was offered a job at Global in Manchester, the record importers run by American Eddie Balbier. Searling remembers the turnover in staff at the company was high. "Most people usually only lasted there about nine months because the temptation to steal was too great. We all did a few. We got paid nothing so we ended up knocking a few down our pants and walking out or whatever, so everybody got fired in the end. I was there for a few months before I got to go to Philadelphia where I found quite a bit of in-demand stuff. Half way through my stint at Global, I was approached about doing Va-Va's. By which time I'd managed to get the Shirelles' "Last Minute Miracle", Dotty Cambridge's "Cry Your Eyes Out", the Tymes "What Would I Do", the Adventurers' "Easy Baby" and a few other things. It was a bit of a fluke really. I was asked to do it by a guy called Rick Barrett who called me at Global. Rick was a very cool Jamaican who lived in Bolton, who happened to be into soul music, and he had got wind that this place wanted a Friday all-nighter. I used to walk from where we lived, about a mile outside Bolton with my record box box to Va-Va's and do the all-nighters."

Expensively rigged out with over £10,000 worth of sound equipment and lights, Va-Va's was a smart "pop" discotheque situated in Great Moor Street. Pete Fell, who deejayed at the Keighley OKeh Club, reviewed the club for *Hot Buttered Soul* in October 1973. "Descend the steps, pay your £1 admission, and

MABLE JOHN
ARTIST MANAGEMENT
8469 Sunset Blvd.
Hollywood, Calif. 90069
(213) · 654-1787

WORLD ENTERTAINMENT PRODUCTIONS INC.
54 East Colorado Blvd.
Pasadena California.
(213)   654-1787

171

you can feel the atmosphere immediately. The sounds vibrate around the room from a complex of speakers – and what sounds!…there are plenty of seats for the weary to sit on, many in small alcoves partitioned off from the main area by 'plastic glass' screens. These can seem invisible at 5 in the morning, so look before you walk through them…the dance floor is rather small but adequate and I've not heard too many people complain about it."

At the time, Richard was desperate to get hold of Lynne Randell's "Stranger In My Arms" on CBS, however he had plenty of other great records to keep the Va-Va's crowd happy: Stanley Mitchell's earthy "Popcorn" Wylie production "Get It Baby", Mel Williams' "Can It Be Me", Lee David's "Temptation Is Calling My Name", Linda Jones' "Just Can't Live My Life", Patti Austin's "Take Away The Pain Stain" and the Magnificents' "My Heart Is Calling". Gloria Jones' "Tainted Love" was another Searling discovery which he found in a warehouse on one of his trips to the States.

Pete mentioned that to hear better sounds at Va-Va's, Ian Levine would have to be hijacked from the Highland Room. Richard Searling had been a regular on Saturday nights at the Blackpool Mecca, going by coach with a crowd from Bolton and Levine proved to be a great influence upon Richard when he started to deejay.

"I think it started in about March or April 1973 and we soon started to attract quite a following. I've got to pay homage to Pep and Alan Day for being very supportive of me there. Because, although they weren't deejaying, they used to bring me acetates down and encourage me to play things. Because I was just a novice, I didn't know. And I'd got a few things from America. But, basically, we were playing Herbie Goins' "Number One In Your Heart", "Under My Thumb". I mean, things that probably now people would say, how the hell did he get away with it. But we did at the time. And my naivety was legendary. We started Wednesday nights at Va-Va's because the all-nighters were going well and because of transport or whatever, I left my records at the club on the Wednesday and expected to go in on a Friday and pick them up. And I can remember Jimmy Muirhead from Bolton asking me to play Jo Armstead "I Feel An Urge Coming On". All my records were filed by title

172

order and I remember going to "I Feel..." and the whole bloody lot had gone. So there was no "I Hurt On The Other Side" or "I Gotta Find Me Somebody" – they'd gone. Not all the records, but just a handful. But I had only myself to blame. Strangely enough, about ten years later they all turned up in a house in Bolton and I got them all back. It was one of the DJs at the club who had done it, through jealousy or whatever. So Va-Va's was a strange one. I first met Russ Winstanley there. I was aware of him as he used to come down early on selling records. But I remember

MAJOR LANCE

Pep more than anybody, and the lads from Doncaster. They were the most loyal supporters. It closed in June and then it re-opened, but it was never the same. The magic somehow went and I remember dead, awful nights there. Really poor."

The management clearly thought the same and, without warning, they pulled the plug on the all-nighter. But it was too late to stop people travelling. "I remember the last night we had two coach loads from Cheltenham. They had to sit in a bloody car park in Bolton all night just wondering what had happened. And I remember, I had finally got my hands on a copy of Lynne Randell..."

WIGAN
Casino Club
1973 ALL NIGHTER 1980

RICHARD

MIKE

GERRY

RUSS

HARRY

JENNY

EVELYN

BETTY

SHEILA

HILDA

THE HEART of SOUL

CHAPTER 12

Casino Royale

THE SUMMER OF 1973 was a golden era for new discoveries, and Frank Elson's "Check Out The North" featured endless lists of 45s that have since become acknowledged Northern Soul classics. At the Pendulum, Barry Tasker recommended the Charades' "Key To My Happiness", the Sapphires' "The Slow Fizz" and Lenis Guess' "Just Ask Me", a disc unearthed at Moondogs' rock 'n' roll record store in the East End of London. At Tony Petherbridge's Whitchurch Civic Centre All-dayer, Pep was spinning Bobby Treetop's "Wait Till I Get To Know Ya", and reporting to Elson the theft from his collection of the Invitations' "Skiing In The Snow" and the Glories' "I Worship You Baby". At Duckinfield Rugby Club, Dave Evison was raving about the Superlatives' "I Still Love You", featuring the lead vocals of the improbably titled St. Julian Bonaparte and Ian Levine

at the Carlton Club mentioned Damita Jo's answer to the Drifters' hit "I'll Save The Last Dance For You", Joan Moody's "We Must Be Doing Something Right" and Christine Cooper's "Heartaches Away My Boy". Apart from Simon Soussans appalling discovery of L. A. Power & Light Company's "Let's Spend The Night Together", Soul Sam was playing Sandra Phillips' "World Of Sunshine", Thelma Houston's "Baby Mine", the Steinways' "My Heart's Not In It Anymore", and Lee Andrews' "I've Had It". Keith Minshull at the Top Rank in Hanley was pushing Jerry Cook's "Love Man".

Tony Petherbridge's Northern Soul Club promotion at the Whitchurch Civic Centre, on August Bank Holiday Monday, was temporarily held up when a bomb scare brought proceedings to an abrupt halt. With most of the leading DJs of the day present – Soul Sam, Colin Curtis, Tony Jebb, Martyn

Ellis, the Soul Quins, Andy Hanley and Pep – Ian Levines' set was stopped half-way through whilst he was spinning Linda Jones' "I Can't Live My Life Without You".

There was no respite from the cause for the dedicated Northern fan and even on holiday it was possible to meet like-minded souls in the resorts of the West Country. In Devon there was the Compass Club in Torquay and in Cornwall the Coral-A-Go-Go in Newquay, where DJ Ivan kept the soul fires burning. This was a tradition going back to the Sixties, as John Knight from West Yorkshire recalls. "We would go down to the West Coast, and on scooter runs to places like Scarborough and Blackpool. There was a good scene then at the Mecca and the Blackpool Twisted Wheel, which had the same cartwheels as the Manchester one. All over the country you could tell by the clothes, the hair cut and by the music they loved. There would always be odd records that you had never heard of, which they would play in the clubs down there."

HOT BUTTERED SOUL

The word was slowly beginning to spread on the grapevine. Frank Elson was beginning to meet more and more devotees from around the UK. At the Catacombs he met David Batts, who had travelled to Wolverhampton all the way from Cardiff, and Colin Jackson and Terry Chamberlain from Cheltenham, who told him about the local Spa Lounge and Max's Club in Gloucester. And DJ Soulful Sid was playing Bob Relf, the Tymes, Jerry Cook, the Sweets, the Tempos, Sam & Kitty, Rex Garvin and the Dramatics at the Greyhound in Dunstable, Bedfordshire, advertised as the "Biggest Soul Cry In The South".

In the September issue of *Hot Buttered Soul*, Chris Bloor from St. Helens contributed the first of a regular Northern page entitled "Talk Of The North". The Blackpool Mecca was featured as the "UK's No.1 soul discotheque" and on the same page he was particularly complimentary about Russ Winstanley, who Chris reckoned was doing great work for soul in Wigan. Russ told him that he had plans to run an all-nighter in the area soon, a news item confirmed in *Blues & Soul*.

Frank Elson had been informed by Dave Swift that the venue would be the Wigan Casino and the first night was scheduled for 22nd September 1973.

Elson advised fans that if they anticipated arriving at the club before midnight, they should take a tie along because of the door policy.

Russ Winstanley, who had been deejaying regularly at venues in and around the Wigan area, was not highly rated by the more die-hard fans – in fact, many questioned whether the venture would last beyond the first few nights. Nevertheless, until its last night in 1982, Wigan Casino would prove to be one of the most successful and longest running all-nighters in the North, at one point boasting a membership in excess of 100,000. Northern Soul would became a household name and sufficient media interest was generated by 1977, that Granada TV's documentary on the Casino, *This England*, would be watched by almost 20 million viewers. However, at the same time, a combination of events almost became the death knell of Northern Soul. The music policy promoted by the club's DJs, a tendency to play stomping pop records that fitted the bill and the division created by the new direction being forged at the Blackpool Mecca by Ian Levine and Colin Curtis, meant many fans became disillusioned and disgruntled, turning their backs on the scene altogether.

Although many record companies had raided their back catalogues for in-demand Northern 45s with little expense or risk, the chance to further cash in on this newly discovered phenomenon was too great an opportunity to miss. Russ Winstanley's involvement in the dreadful reworking of the Invitations' 'Skiing in the Snow' by the hastily formed Wigan's Ovation in early 1975 led to dozens of torrid cover versions of classic tracks, which did little to convey to the uninitiated the magic and appeal of the scene. In some quarters Russ was blamed for all of this, but he was not the only guilty party.

Born in Wigan, Russ Winstanley left the local grammar school in 1969 after completing his A-levels, and much to the horror of his parents, abandoned plans for a high profile career in personnel management to take a job as a salesman. After a short spell as a roadie and occasional backing singer in the band Rainbow Cottage, which had been formed by fellow pupils at Wigan Grammar, Winstanley decided to pursue a part-time career as a DJ with another local lad John Lowe. The attraction of the saleman's job to Russ was that it came with the added benefit of a van, obviously making his life as a DJ considerably easier.

"I called and wrote to almost every bar and club in Wigan to try and get a regular DJ spot but the only reply was from the Bier Keller. They said I could have a Monday night as it wasn't doing anything special, which I turned into an oldies night. It was a bit of a mod's night really; I'd feature the Four Tops, the Small Faces, the Who, the Beatles, whatever. And as it began to pick up they gave me Saturday nights as well. Then I decided to look for somewhere out of town, so on Thursday nights when I got offered Newtown British Legion, I thought that I'd try and do something a bit different.

"By then I'd started going to the Highland Room at the Blackpool Mecca. There was the big dance hall downstairs with hundreds of people, which was where the majority of people used to go. And when you got a bit fed-up you'd go for a look to see what was going on upstairs. That's where I first went, and if they're honest, that's what nearly everybody did. I remember hearing Chubby Checker's "You Just Don't Know", Barbara Mills' "Queen Of Fools", Dobie Gray's "Out On The Floor" and the Crusaders' "Put It Where You Want It". From Wigan you could get a free coach to the Mecca. I started going there regularly, and occasionally to the Torch but that was a bit further away. I started to play Northern soul records.

"People were asking me where they could get these records I was playing at the Wigan Rugby League Club, which I did on Friday nights, so I got a list of imports from Selecta Disc in Nottingham, opened an account with them and started selling copies at the Rugby Club and other gigs until I began selling them on Wigan market. My job was bringing in about twenty quid a week or something, which was pretty good in the early Seventies, but the first Saturday of selling records I made sixty pounds. So after a few months I got enough money to get another vehicle together and I packed my job in."

Winstanley thought that there was a possibility of creating a new venue. "When I heard that The Torch was closing I thought the Casino would make a great venue for an all-nighter. I didn't then know Mike Walker or anybody else at the club, even though I'd been to the Casino many times, so I just went in off the street. Luckily he'd heard of me through my work locally as a DJ. I said to him that there was a demand for another soul all-nighter and I'd like to use the club."

The Wigan Casino in Station Road was originally known as The Empress Hall and had consisted of a huge dance hall with a balcony on the first floor, and a billiard and snooker hall on the ground floor that was large enough to take over thirty full size tables. There was also an annex, the Palais de Danse – a miniature version of the main dance hall, which was used exclusively for private functions. From the late Forties, and right up to the beginning of the Sixties, the Empress was very popular locally, open six nights a week with its own dance band. The name was changed to The Casino in the Sixties when it was bought by a local brewery, and as popular tastes in music changed, so did the club, and it played host to many stars from the early beat groups as well as top cabaret acts. The

Wigan Dancers

179

**Behind the decks
at the Casino**

club's manager at the time of Russ Winstanley's approach, was Gerry Marshall, a local businessman who had been at the club since the late Sixties. When Russ and Mike Walker mooted the idea of an all-nighter, Russ recalls a rather less than enthusiastic response.

"Gerry said something like 'You must be out of your head, we're not doing all-nighters'. But the fact was they weren't doing that well at the time. In '73 cabaret was coming to a dead-end and they were having to pay a grand a week rent – a hell of a lot of money; so Mike Walker sat down with Gerry and convinced him to give it a try. I proposed a fifty-fifty split and took out a whole page ad in *Blues & Soul*."

Although many felt that Winstanley was all wrong for the job, begrudgingly, they had to admit that he was now the DJ of the biggest all-nighter on the scene, and other DJs were begging to play there. Not by asking Russ of course, who had pulled the whole thing off, but by going behind his back and asking Mike Walker. Everybody went, although they complained about the crowds, the flooded toilets, the drugs and the white pop records. They also reckoned that Winstanley was coining it. He didn't do badly, but the original fifty-fifty split agreed with Casino manager Gerry Marshall did not last five minutes.

"On the first night we had over six hundred and fifty people at 75p each, which I reckoned with my deal would get me about £200 on the Monday morning. Gerry Marshall thought differently and gave me £50. He came up with dozens of excuses: 'A thousand people didn't have eight pints each and flipping heck, I've got to pay more staff wages, and minus this and minus that so I'm losing money', and I thought here we go, the usual thing. But because it was such a big adventure I thought, well 50 quid wasn't bad considering an average DJ only got twelve quid a night…and it was just so great, it was like our own all-nighter in Wigan. Everyone was saying it would never continue, the police'll shut it. So we just went along with it then. I got him to agree that I could sell my records free of charge which was really the master stroke, as that was what made up my money."

The first three records played at the Casino were the Sherrys' "Put Your Arms Around Me", a record which used the same backing track as their father Little Joe Cook used on "I'm Falling In Love With You Baby"; Detroit Sound's "Jumping At The Go-Go" and Mike Post's "Afternoon At The Rhino", an instrumental written and arranged by a twenty six year old who later wrote the theme music to "The Rockford Files" and "NYPD".

After his initial two paragraph announcement in *Blues & Soul*, Frank Elson devoted two whole columns to his visit to the Casino on its opening night. As usual in his reports of club visits, he recorded all the characters present and predicted that the Casino stood every chance of filling the hole left by the demise of the Torch. Despite some early problems with membership cards being held up in the post and delays getting into the building, everybody seemed pleased. Especially the previously reluctant Casino manager, Gerry Marshall.

As Russ Winstanley remembers "It was all cash on the door. Even in the Granada TV documentary you can see all the money being handed over. At the fifth anniversary all-nighter in '78, I remember it being a fiver to get in and we had three thousand people in that night. We used to get ten thousand people a week over Monday, Wednesday, Friday and Saturday nights and Gerry used to stash the money in his greenhouse with these green tomatoes –

you can imagine them all with the Queen's head on! But the rotten thing was he had this tax investigation and I think he had quite a large tax bill at the end of it."

The Casino had seen better days; the wooden panelling in the entrance hall needed repairing, the seats on the balcony were well-worn and the windows were cracked. Yet even though the ballroom was in serious neglect, as soon as the lights were dimmed and the sound system fired up, it was second to none. As regular Tim Ashibende will never forget. "The atmosphere was incredible, the sheer scale of the place, the balcony overlooking the dancefloor and the smell of Brut in the toilets – nothing comes close to it."

Lester Wardell, from Halifax, was a regular at the Casino, and remembers going to the club for the first time. "I was too young to go, so I had to sneak out the bedroom window on to the porch and down the drainpipe. When I got back in the morning, my mum was waiting there and I got a good hiding. She said 'You're not going again!', but that didn't stop me, as it was fantastic!"

Although Russ started the all-nighter with just Ian Fishwick helping on the turntables, it was not long before other DJs joined, with aspirations of playing at what was fast becoming one of the big nights on the Northern circuit. The first to arrive was Kev Roberts, promoter of the successful Togetherness events and partner in Goldmine Records – one of the most prolific of the Northern Soul reissue labels. Roberts was not that impressed by the records he heard on his first visit to the Casino, and felt he could do better. Kev had started deejaying at the Britannia Boat Club, on Trent Bridge in Nottingham. Like many of the lesser-known DJs, Kev relied on Selecta Disc's imports and pressings. He befriended Alan Day, DJ at Up the Junction in Crewe, who worked behind the counter at Selecta Disc. A visit to the Torch in December

183

The Masqueraders

1972 was Kev's introduction to what he called the "real scene", hearing records that he had never heard of such as the Younghearts "A Little Togetherness", the Just Brothers' "Sliced Tomatoes" and J. J. Barnes' "Please Let Me In".

"Whatever had come out at Selecta Disc I bought, and played them one after another. It was a great play list at the time. But one night, this little French Moroccan guy came up, looked through my record box, and was not too impressed, although I'd got a few British singles in there. He wanted to buy the British singles, but I told him they were not for sale. He asked 'Do you know who I am?' I quickly found out he was Simon Soussan."

He took the records from Roberts and gave him in exchange a handful of, then unknown, US imports. Amongst these were Sandra Phillips' "World Without Sunshine", Patti Austin's "Take Away The Pain Stain", the Masqueraders' "Do You Love Me Babe", Darryl Stewart's "Name It And Claim It". He took these along to the Mecca where Roberts remembers Ian Levine raising a quizzical eyebrow at this new kid on the block.

Kev did not make it to the first night at the Casino but entered the cavernous ballroom the second week. His friends gave Russ Winstanley a hard time, requesting records that they knew he did not have. Urged on by his friends, he convinced Russ to let him DJ and soon became a regular fixture. Winstanley was happy for the extra help as he realised that the outside DJs would not only bring rare records, but also their own local support which, in turn, could only help to increase the club's popularity. Another DJ who would later join and further enhance the reputation of the Casino was Richard Searling.

Black Wax Magazine folded after six issues, and the planned launch by IPC of the glossy monthly *Black Music* was eagerly anticipated by Clive Richardson at *Shout*. Tony Cummings was lined-up to be a staff writer on the forthcoming publication and Richardson hoped that it would go some way to knocking *Blues & Soul* off its throne!

By the Autumn, Ian Levine was starting to work at more clubs; The Peacock Room at the Welcome Inn every Wednesday and Friday; Saturday nights at the Blackpool Mecca; and Sale Mecca with Andy Hanley on Tuesdays. An advertisement for the Peacock Room venture in *Blues & Soul* included an overwhelming list of current discoveries including Sons of Moses, Susan Barrett, Edward Hamilton, Fuzz, Tina Mason, Sam Moultrie, Dave Love, Morris Chestnut, Braceros, Mel Wynn, Estelle Levitt, Larry Laster, Frank Beverley, Sissie Houston, Lee David, Jessica James & the Outlaws, Len Jewell, United Four, Larry Atkins, Gems, Genies, Ambers, Barbara Lynn, Masqueraders, Jack Hammer and R. Dean Taylor. Included were two cover-ups, one credited to the Righteous Brothers Band and the other to the Johnny Jackson Experience. Their fictional "Let's Shingaling At The Go Go" was Mel Carter's "Strange Brew". In the same issue a quarter-page strip for the Blackpool Mecca exclaimed "The Place That's Established Beyond Any Shadow Of Doubt As The Country's No.1 Soul Place".

Ian Levine was clear in his mind that this was no idle boast: "Despite the heavy competition on Saturday nights, there is nowhere at all which has records even half as good as ours. We've already proven ourselves as being the undisputed Top Soul Club in the country and we'll stay there. There is nowhere to touch the Mecca for atmosphere, people or records. It's the place to be every Saturday."

J.J. BARNES

The Detroit-based Ric-Tic label had an affinity with Northern soul collectors. Formed in 1964 by LeBaron Taylor, a DJ at the Detroit radio station WCHB, it quickly became part of local club owner Ed Wingate's Solid Hitbound Productions, a collection of small labels that did their best to steal some of the thunder from their mighty neighbour, the Motown Corporation. By craftily employing the moonlighting Hitsville USA's Funk Brothers legendary studio band, Solid Hitbound became the closest threat to the Detroit giant. So much so that Gordy bought the company in 1966 for a reputed one million dollars. Although Ric-Tic's most successful artist was Edwin Starr, rare soul fans held fellow label mate J. J. Barnes in greater esteem. His discs such as "Please Let Me In" and "Real Humdinger" had long been

J. J. Barnes and Mike Ritson 1973

popular in the Northern clubs and news of his first visit to the UK in the autumn of 1973 was eagerly anticipated. As far back as 1970, Ian Levine had written a letter to *Blues & Soul* asking for the magazine to feature an article on J. J. Barnes when his name had cropped up in the review of a Mavis Staples single.

Promoter Ron Watts had originally booked William Bell but this had been cancelled by the booking agency. Cult artist J. J.Barnes was hastily drafted in to kick-off the season of soul acts at the 100 Club in London's Oxford Street. The capital had more than its fair share of Northern soul enthusiasts, many of whom regularly made the trip up North to visit soul all-nighters. One of these was Terry Davis, who had previously deejayed at The Fountain and who now ran regular soul nights at The Wheatsheaf in London's Kings Road. This was a well respected venue gaining plaudits from the likes of *Hot Buttered Soul* editor Chris Savory, who considered it to be the only place that had successfully married Southern soul sounds with Northern favourites, and Dave Godin, who went to the pub on several occasions. Watts visited the Wheatsheaf and asked Terry if he was interested in deejaying at the 100 Club gigs. Terry agreed and was the DJ on the night of Barnes' British debut.

The evening was reviewed by Clive Richardson in *Shout*, and once again the soul clapping of the audience came close to ruining the evening for him.

Storming into "Please Let Me In", J. J. followed this with a version of "Close To You" which gained Clive's approval. As did a "really impressive" rendition of "Real Humdinger" and a great performance of "Stormy Monday Blues", although some of the rare soul fans retreated to the bar as Barnes' slowed the tempo. The single black gloves worn by some of the crowd were mocked by Richardson, who questioned whether the wearers were aware of the social significance of such an act. In 1968, at the Mexico Olympics, the black American athletes Tommie Smith and John Carlos each raised a black-gloved fist on the podium at the medal ceremony. The soul fans' imitation was perhaps naïve but well intended.

Other appearances by Barnes at the Top Rank in Hanley and Warrington's Lion Hotel were witnessed by Chris Bloor in *Hot Buttered Soul.* The enthusiastic audience at the Lion Hotel pulled J. J. on to the floor where he danced amongst the crowd. The Northern coverage in the fanzine began to grow, with Pete Fell writing about Ginger & Eddie deejaying at the Ukranian

The Fashions

188

Club in Todmorden, Wigan DJ Kev Roberts raving about Rubin's "You've Been Away" – a track that had first been spun by Soul Sam at the Top Rank in Hanley – June Edwards' "Heaven Help Me" and the Volcanoes' "The Laws Of Love", and Bloor's "Talk Of The North" was extended to two pages. Mentions were given to Ken Rigby's Leyland Village Hall night where the Fashions' "Lover's Stand", Del Capris' "Hey Little Girl", Phil Flowers' "Discontented" and Kenny Chandler's "Beyond Love" were the floor fillers. The Pendulum was still going strong at the MSG in Manchester where Barry Tasker shared the turntable action with Richard Searling after the closure of Va-Va's. Top sound here, as at many other venues was Tony Clarke's "Landslide". Power plays at the Wigan Casino included Lee David's "Temptation Is Calling My Name", Joe Hicks' "Don't It Make You Feel Funky", Arnold Bryant's "House In Order", Larry Laster's "Go For Yourself" and the Fuzz' "I'm So Glad". Soul Sam, Andy Hanley and Keith Minshull were doing the honours at the Top Rank in Hanley, and the industrious Pep was working at the Catacombs, Tiffany's, The Raven, and Max's Lounge.

COME GO WITH ME
(C. E. Quick)

Fee Bee Music/
Gil Music
BMI - 1:53
732
(45-67091)

Produced by
Ed Cobb for
Greengrass
Productions

UPTOWN

GLORIA JONES
Arranged by Lincoln Mayorga
Engineer: Tom May

On a wet and windy afternoon in late 1977, Nigel Caulfield was working in Norfolk, close to the Wash. At around 3 o'clock his boss decided to call it a day, and so they packed their tools into the van and headed home to Cambridge. After a while travelling along narrow Norfolk lanes they found themselves lost and low on petrol. Fifteen minutes later they came upon a small hamlet which consisted of a few houses and a run-down garage. They parked at the garage and whilst his boss filled-up with petrol, Nigel wandered off for a cigarette. An adjoining barn was full of old furniture, one item which his boss was interested in. As the proprietor showed him round Nigel noticed a box of records. Unbelievably, they were all US imports on labels such as Golden World, Goldwax, Revilot, Ric-Tic, Brunswick. "Are these records for sale, mate?" was answered with "Yes 10p each". Nigel knew that some were worth between £5-10 each. He managed to borrow £20 off his boss and ended up buying 300 singles. He sold a few for between £3-5 each but kept some of the special ones. Rita Dacosta "Don't Bring Me Down" (Mohawk white DJ), Gloria Jones "Come Go With Me" (Uptown whiteDJ) plus a few copies of Barbara Jean & The Lyrics "Any Two Can Play" on Big Hit, but he had trouble getting rid of those. This recently sold for £300. They returned to Norfolk the next week but just could not find the place. It was almost as if the place had disappeared. He went back on his own, but still no joy. (Could be a case for the X-Files!)

"Our list number one was, and still is, the most talked about and highly successful list ever put out in the Northern scene. It has been criticised by some ignorant half wits as being too good to be true. Well, the people who have been serviced by us, will no doubt correct these innuendos, and shut up these vain cretins who make a questionable living selling EMI-discs and found us to be a sudden threat to their obscure activities.
If we happen to have 10 or 15 copies of any title well so does the outlet in King's Lynn, Suffolk (sic).
As for even mentioning pressings or bootlegs, nobody in his right mind would bootleg 15 copies of a record, because they will cost him 25 dollars a piece, and nobody in his right mind would ever consider bootlegging in the US since the passage of very stiff laws against bootlegging, all of which stipulate 5 years imprisonment and $20,000 dollars fines at the least.

Furthermore, if any of the records we have sold were bootlegs well they would have (ended at) some wholesalers' warehouse already. Finally for those of you (some very few incorrigable twits) who believe the scene is going bad let us laugh please. If you believe that is the case take the first train to the Mecca, where you will be welcomed by an unterminable cacophany of pure G-A-R-B-A-G-E and 1976 computerised T-R-A-S-H and <u>stay there.</u>

We have been highly complemented for the variety of sounds, the availability of these very sounds, and unquestionably the knack to discover Northern Super Gems. With your support we'll endeavour to provide you always with what you want. This is the time now, to make this unique scene just what it is UNIQUE.

Northern Soul Records
PO Box 3813 Beverly Hills California

"There's too much backstabbing going on between fans who talk about peace and love and soul but who in reality are blindly intolerant of the other person's point of view. And it's not just a racial thing. Our Northern Soul feature last month revealed the trivial but bitter prejudices that can exist within the same social group."

Black Music, July 1974

CHAPTER 13

Shake 'n' Bump

IN DECEMBER 1973, IPC, which published the established music magazines *Melody Maker*, *New Musical Express* and *Disc*, launched a new monthly magazine, *Black Music*. On its front cover, was the boast that this was the "first *complete* black music magazine!", covering not only soul music but also reggae, jazz and blues. Editor Alan Lewis had also brought together Tony Cummings and Dave Godin. Godin had left *Blues & Soul* in August 1972 and this was his return to the soul world after a much needed sabbatical.

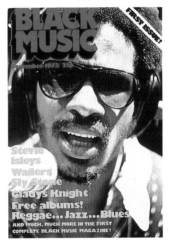

Turning up the heat on the debate that Blues & Soul had chaired in recent months, the magazine included a regular column "Hey Mr DJ!" which aimed to reflect the divide between the clubs and discos in the North and those in the South. In one corner, representing the views of the Southern fans, was Mo Claridge, who ran his Mojo Sound System in clubs, at parties and U.S. Airforce Bases across the South of England and in the other corner, defending the Northern scene, was Blackpool Mecca DJ Ian Levine. In his first column, Levine extolled the virtues of Linda Jones' "I Just Can't Live My Life (Without You Babe)", Terrible Tom's "We Were Made For Each Other" and David & the Giants' "Ten Miles High", and bemoaned the activities of the bootleggers. Wigan Casino was noticeable by its absence – the Blackpool Mecca was seen as the new temple of Northern Soul, even though Frank Elson in *Blues & Soul* had reported that the all-nighter at Wigan was starting to effect the attendances at many of the leading soul venues including Catacombs and the Mecca.

The decision to invite Dave Godin to join their new baby was a coup for *Black Music*, as he was certain to bring with him much of his large and loyal readership. Dave's second column recounted a visit to an old stomping ground, the Highland Room at the Mecca. Records recommended in the column by Highland Room DJ Colin Curtis included Johnny Caswell's "You Don't Love Me Anymore" (Decca); Wally Cox's "This Man" (Wand); Susan Barrett's "What's it gonna be"(RCA), a song which was covered in the UK by Dusty Springfield. Her version would be reissued a year later, due to Northern demand created by those who had been unable to get the more coveted US original. And the track that would become the final record played each night at the Mecca, Young Holt Unlimited's "California Montage": an instrumental taken from the soundtrack to the 1971 Paul Newman film *Winning*.

Despite some misgivings about the slight drop in quality of the records being played since an earlier visit, Godin went on to put the blame at the feet of the DJs, commenting that their relentless search for rarer and more esoteric releases would be to the detriment of the scene.

Colin Curtis, in an interview given some years later to *Manifesto* magazine, thought that this view was unfair. "We were often criticised at the Mecca for turning music over too quickly, and I suppose if you only came to the Mecca once every month or two, then the change could be unacceptable. But when you're there every week, you just changed it as the new stuff came out. We used to sit in Levine's house for eight, ten, sixteen hours at a time playing through piles of new records that he'd brought back from America, putting them all into different categories."

Ian Levine's favourite at the time was Freddie Chavez's "They'll Never Know Why", which he had listed in his debut column as one of three discs he was searching for. The turnover was staggering, records were being discovered at a phenomenal rate. Frank Elson

raised this issue at an all-dayer at the Blackpool Mecca. Levine commented: "People come to the Mecca for the rare sounds, that's how it got it's name around the soul scene. If I play pressings then people may get to like them so much that they'll go out and buy the pressings. The fact that I'm playing new releases all the time can be blamed on the people who press all our big sounds mercilessly without any regard to the welfare of the scene."

The seeds of change were being sown. In February 1974, Ian Levine was spinning new tracks such as Total Eclipse's "You Took A Heart (That Was Torn To Pieces)". It was a recent release on the Roulette label, then enjoying success on the soul charts with Ecstasy, Passion & Pain's "I Wouldn't Give You Up". Although many new releases had been played on the Northern scene, it was usually because they had the same stacatto beat as the much loved Sixties soul. What made Total Eclipse different, was that it featured a shuffling, slower rhythm, as did another of Levine's plays at the time – the Carstairs' "It Really Hurts Me Girl".

On Gene Redd's Red Coach label, the record had never been released, and a handful of white label demos had found their way into a cheap box at John Anderson's import operation in King's Lynn, Groove City. John remembers Levine as a particularly good customer. "He'd visit our office regularly, perhaps every two weeks, and would buy anything if it was a bit unusual or out of the ordinary. He would grab a pile of records and just play through them. He bought the Carstairs' record for 50p, although I must admit I couldn't see what he saw in the record."

Originally from Detroit, the Carstairs were known on the Northern circuit through a cover of the Motown track "He Who Picks A Rose", recorded with Sandy Linzer for the OKeh label. In 1972, the group had met up with Gene Redd, owner of Red Coach, and Cleveland Horne, who had sung with the Prophets and the Fantastic Four. Cleveland had co-written "It Really Hurts Me Girl" with the late Raymond Evans. The group liked the song, but the disc never received sufficient airplay to warrant progressing beyond promotional copies. The record was pirated by Bob Catteneo's Soul Odyssey operation in San Francisco, but legitimate copies from Red Coach stemmed the flood of

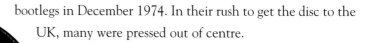

bootlegs in December 1974. In their rush to get the disc to the UK, many were pressed out of centre.

Sounding unlike any other record played at the Mecca, it was slow to take-off. After a ponderous introduction, the drummer launches into a tricky rhythm that stops and starts, over a melody full of unusual key changes. But with consistent plays, the dancers overcame the tempo, a new shuffling-style of dancing was developed, and it grew in popularity, to the point where it would regularly fill the Mecca floor. Ian Levine recalls the disc's impact.

"The Carstairs had a trigger effect. Once the crowd had taken to the rhythm, it was possible to play a completely different style of music. It was then that tracks like Larry Sanders' "On The Real Side", Oscar Perry's "I Got What You Need", Bill House' "Common Thief", Pat Lundy's "Party Music", and what to me epitomises the later Mecca sound, Crown Heights Affair's "Dreaming A Dream" took off."

Ian thought the acceptance of modern soul releases – replacing the Sixties sounds, which he perceived as a tired formula – would be a logical progression. Contemporary releases did infiltrate other club's playlists, but the older sounds stayed stubbornly on the turntables. The fast turnover at the Mecca, meant that many of the overlooked 45s were given a second chance at other clubs, where DJs did not have Levine's financial resources. In fact, some of the Mecca's also-rans became popular years later.

Selecta Disc, the soul mail order service and shop in Canal Street, Nottingham, was often berated by Northern soul fans for its continued sale of bootlegs. It advertised ten new titles in *Black Music* including Tony Clark's "Landslide", which would eventually be released in the UK by Chess, Christine Cooper's rare US-Parkway 45 "Heartaches away my boy" and others by Patti Austin, Sweet Three, Thelma Houston, Didi Noel, the Gems and P. P. Arnold.

Managing director Brian Selby and sales director John Bratton, had started Selecta Disc in 1971 as a retail outlet for progressive music after having first started selling records on a stall in Mansfield Market. As the soul scene grew, and customers began asking for more obscure soul records, they started a basement in their Nottingham branch, specialising in soul music, together with the mail order service selling UK releases and American imports.

Jeff King's success with the Soul Sounds bootlegs, encouraged Selecta Disc to emulate him. They had an established distribution set-up and with their BJD and Greenlight labels, soon pushed King off the scene. Keith Minshull, who was then occasionally deejaying at the Twisted Wheel, recalls the rivalry between John Bratton and Jeff King.

"There was fierce competition between King and Bratton, to see who could get the rare imports in first. Soul Sounds had pressed Chubby Checker's "(At The) Discotheque", and then a week later the BJD version appeared. Same thing happened with Leon Haywood. That came out on Selecta Disc's Greenlight label. I supplied the records to Jeff King, but when I'd finished with him, I supplied John Bratton. The Fuller Brothers' "Times A Wasting" was one of them. And then, it was Chris Burton and his International Soul Club pressings – "Ski-ing In The Snow" was mine."

Selecta Disc also negotiated with the US owners of the rights to the in-demand records, and arranged for them to re-press copies. OKeh label stormers from the Autographs, Williams & Watson, Triumphs, Sandi Sheldon, Major Lance and others were imported; the only discernible difference from the original issues, was the smaller "45" on the purple label. MGM put out Northern favourites from, amongst others, Dottie Cambridge, the Velours and Clara Ward on their reissue label, as did RCA. The Northern scene had created a retail demand that was clearly too good an opportunity to miss, and so what started as a trickle soon became a torrent. As well as the legal reissues, discs of dubious origin began to appear on Select Disc's lists. Having organised the OKeh re-releases with Columbia, it was odd that other releases originally issued on Date, a label distributed by in the States by Columbia, were made available on the unconnected Soultown label. Two Date recordings – Johnny Moore's "Walk Like A Man" and the Sweet Things' "I'm In A World Of Trouble" – came out on Soultown, as did Cindy Scott's "I Love You Baby", a disc originally released on Veep, a subsidiary of United Artists.

In April 1974, *Black Music's* editorial focused for the first time on the Northern soul scene. The bootleggers were an easy target: "As you dance to that rare Northern sound, does it make you feel good to think that the guy who poured his soul into it may be penniless and forgotten?" However, the perpetrators were only successful because clubgoers bought the pressings. The majority of soul fans were probably grateful to the pirating operations for giving them access to records well beyond the means of their pockets. It was one thing to write letters to soul magazines condemning the pressers, but if you wanted a copy of Christine Cooper or David & The Giants or Patti Austin, they could be yours for 85p each. There was always the possibility that the legitimate owners of the recordings would release the track, but it was a toss up between whether to give your money to a company like Selecta Disc, for an illegal pressing unbeknown to the actual owners, or to a private individual selling an imported copy for considerably more than the few cents he had paid for it from a cut-out store in the States. Either way, the original artiste would not benefit. There was no guarantee of remuneration if the record was legitimately re-released; in many cases, the singers and musicians only received a one-off fee for their endeavours. Also the rights to the publishing and recording may well have been sold on.

Black Music declared that the Northern scene was receiving so much publicity, it was as if they were actually making the music up there. This was rather an overblown statement, as the scene's coverage was still confined to soul music publications and the odd reference in the music press. In fact, it would not be until manufactured dance records were produced, that the national papers would become interested.

While the Mecca was advertising itself as the number one club in the country, Chris Burton claimed that the International Soul Club was "The World's Number One Soul Club". Now that Colin Curtis was deejaying with Ian Levine at the Highland Room, Keith Minshull's new sparring partner was Soul Sam. Their title was "The Country's No.1 Soul Spinners". In amongst all these bloated claims were listed the new pressings from Burton's Out Of The Past label.

In partnership with *Blues & Soul's* John Abbey, Burton had decided to bootleg many of the top rarities. The venture was successful, but Ian Levine reported the operation to the copyright protection agencies and Burton was heavily fined. His stock of over thirty six thousand records was confiscated. Chris is happy to put his hands up, and admits that it was done purely for financial reasons.

"I asked Keith Minshull to sort me out some records that we should press up. At first it was 'Well, how do we get the rights for them?' We were trying

I LOVE YOU BABY
CINDY SCOTT

I'M GONNA
PICK UP MY TOYS
(AND GO HOME)
(Knight - Allen)
DEVONNES

Legacy Music
BMI
Time 3:30
Arranged by
Joe Renzetti

COLOSSUS

SOUL BANDIT

Speedball
Pub.
(B.M.I.)

SB 003

SKIING IN THE SNOW
(Linzer / Randell)
THE INVITATIONS

SOUL SOUNDS

SS 1013   Side A

45 r.p.m.

DETERMINATION
(Klinger, Feldman)
DEAN PARRISH

DISTRIBUTED BY SOUL-WISE INC. N.Y. U.S.A.

CHE-706

Satellite Music
Arranged by
Andre Williams
Produced by
Monk Higgins

CHERUB
Records

Time 2:43

THE JOCKER
(Miles Grayson)
BUTCH BAKER

INKY DINKY W
(N. Teney-A.

OOTP-033

THE DRAMATICS
MV-70 MUSIC - BMI
Produced by Andre Williams and
Dave Hamilton

Soultown
RECORDS

Produced by
KaprAlk./McCoy
Time 2:35

S-138-A
45 RPM

M IN A WORLD OF TROUBLE
(V. McCoy)
THE SWEET THINGS
Art. & Cond. by Van McCoy
A Daedalus Production

TRANS
RECORDS

TA-8010-B
213-385-9334
A RUSH BROS.
PRODUCTION

Rush-Juni
BMI - 1:55

BLOWING MY MIND TO PIECES
(Leo Baxter)
BOB RELF

S-139-A
Time 2:25

Soultown
RECO

WALK LIKE A MAN
(L. Gaines-J. Moore)
JOHNNY MOORE
Produced by Jack Daniels

TANDING
(us Lumley)

SIDE A

RUFUS LUMLEY
OUTHERN MUSIC - NCB

Real Soul
Productions

RS-703 A

BMI
Time 2:35

A Bradley-Bridges
Production

YOU CAN'T TELL THE GOOD GUYS
FROM THE BAD
(Dianne Smith)
PATIENCE VALENTINE

LIBERTY BELL

45 RPM
Arranged by
Joe Renzetti
& B. Martin

LB-506-A
A Gamble - Huff
Production

IF THAT'S WHAT YOU WANTED
(F. Beverly)
FRANK BEVERLY
& THE BUTLERS

A LIL
OMETIMES
th)

DI STATO

UNITY
RECORD
```
```

THE
```
```

to do it right. I spoke to John Abbey and I think the first ones we got were the Funky Sisters' "Do It To It", and he actually got them shipped over. The first ones came to Contempo's office just off Oxford Street. They were delivered there and paid for."

Through Major Lance, Burton knew singer Otis Leaville who arranged for the records to be pressed in Chicago. Chris went to the States and met up with Leaville, Chi-Lite Eugene Record and famed producer Carl Davis in the Brunswick Studios. "I gave them this pile of records, Major was sitting there in a brown leather coat with this horrible knotted synthetic fur collar, smoking away. They made the shellacs and sent me over to a place in Little Springs to have them pressed up. These cost 10p each and there were fifty six thousand of them." Until the authorities stopped them, dozens were bootlegged including the Invitations, Patti Young, Milton Wright, Ben Aiken, Steinways, Ambers, Mob, Rozetta Johnson, Roy Redmond, J.J.Barnes and Jerry Williams.

An advertisement in *Black Music* boasted that the Casino was the only place in the world where you could hear instrumentals of many of the scene's favourite vocals – "Hit And Run", "Our Love's In The Pocket", "I Can't Get Enough" and "Landslide" amongst a list of eighteen titles. Richard Pack wrote to *Black Music* declaring the practice "another nail in the Northern Soul coffin", which Casino DJ Russ Winstanley strenuously denied. Russ maintained that none of the listed instrumentals were backing tracks, because in fact, they had been recorded by Soussan in a Los Angeles studio. One memorable night at the Casino, Soussan deejayed and played a succession of his creations much to the bemusement of the all-nighter crowd. Soussan later convinced Randy Wood, to supply him with the master tapes of the Keyman and Mirwood catalogue. The original vocals were wiped off, and another lucrative source of bootleg material was created.

After only a few months, Wigan Casino was starting to hit other venues including the Mecca and the Catacombs. The attendances were also down at many of the smaller clubs, as the all-nighter became more and more popular. However, Wigan Police had threatened to close the club if the drug problem did not improve, and manager Gerry Marshall appealed to the soul crowd through Frank Elson's column in *Blues & Soul*.

203

"They call it the 'Northern Soul Sound', and it isn't the Northern States but the North of England they're talking about."

Roger St. Pierre New Musical Express June 1974

CHAPTER 14

The Strange World Of Northern Soul

"THE TIME HAS come, my friends, to talk about Northern Soul. If you've never heard of this type of music before, then may we suggest you pay close attention to what we have to say. Because, without doubt, Northern Soul is the most dramatic and most exciting thing to happen to British music in the past ten years. And we're not exaggerating." This was how a breathless Beverley Legge disclosed the "new phenomenon" that was sweeping across the country (to *Disc* readers in December 1974). Like other popular music journalists, Legge could not resist the opportunity to reveal to his less well informed readers the inside track on the Northern scene. Wigan was described as the soul centre of the North and Russ Winstanley bestowed with the title of "Mr Northern Soul". A Northern Soul Top Ten was printed which included the current favourites Keanya Collins "Love Bandit", Towanda Barnes "You Don't Mean It" and Larry Santos "You Got Me Where You Want Me". Inevitably the article was accompanied by large photographs of Wayne Gibson and R. Dean Taylor, whose 1967 single "There's A Ghost In My House" had been a Top Ten hit in the summer.

1974 was the year that the spotlight fell on Northern Soul. The scene had always resisted the wrong kind of attention, but as more and more teenagers began to attend all-nighters, the temptation to cash-in by promoters, record dealers, bootleggers and anybody with an eye on a quick buck, became too great. This had not escaped the attention of long-term soul fans, who considered that the promoters were beginning to take the scene away from the fans. John Bollen, who had been a regular at the Twisted Wheel had noticed this on his first visit to the Torch.

"It had the right atmosphere – the club was dark, with condensation running down the walls and there was nothing wrong with the music. But the DJ was elevated up on the stage, and it seemed to me that they were becoming more important than the music. Nobody knew, or cared, who the DJs were at the Wheel. It was becoming too commercialised with badges and suchlike, and worse still, the promoters seemed to be trying to take control." Chris Burton's International Soul Club (ISC) had progressed from badges to bootleg records, from promotions at different venues across the country to key-fobs and car stickers – even the possibility of a weekend festival in Majorca. Criticism would soon be levelled at the ISC for a major soul festival held in Leeds.

On Saturday 6th April 1974, the International Soul Club organised a star studded all-nighter at the Queen's Hall. Heavily promoted through *Blues & Soul*, the advertisements promised live appearances from Major Lance, J. J.

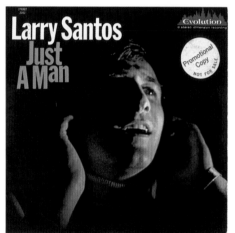

Barnes, The Funky Sisters, Mel & Tim, Willie Henderson and the Hearts of Soul. Early advertisements even included the news that other live acts awaiting confirmation included the Chi-Lites, Detroit Emeralds and Limmie & Family Cookin'.

Expectations were naturally high, but the event turned out to be a terrible disappointment for the seven thousand present. The former tramshed and exhibition hall echoed badly, and the concrete floor made dancing difficult. The Exciters were first on the stage and performed well, although Major Lance, who followed them, played an indifferent, though professional set. Mel & Tim were ill-suited to a Northern soul event, the highlight of the short set being a gospel-style version of their 1972 hit "Starting All Over Again". Hearts of Soul were just bad. The only saving grace came in the form of J. J. Barnes who was excellent, despite coming on stage at five o'clock in the morning.

Frank Elson gave Burton the chance to defend himself against the barrage of complaints, and he promised to make amends with future ISC promotions. Chris was also forced to take legal action against rival promoters who spread a rumour that the all-nighter would be an all-seat event. Many believed the story and stayed away. Competition was becoming fierce.

A new contender came in the shape of the Inter-City Soul Club (ICSC). Launched on 19th July 1974, the club came with promises of no rip-offs, discounts on soul records and even package holidays. The ICSC was determined to unite all soul fans – there was no reason why Northern soul fans could not get together with funk fans. Respected soul collector John Farrell gave the proceedings credibility, when he was brought in to oversee the deejaying side of things. The brains behind this venture was the shaven-headed John Harvey, nicknamed "Kojak".

Starting his working life as an apprentice engineer, he joined the RAF and soon began broadcasting on camp sites with old broadcasting equipment. On leaving the airforce he worked as an MC before becoming a DJ. He worked predominately in the Midlands at venues such as the Wolves Sports & Social, The Nautical William at Kidderminster, The Winter Gardens at Malvern, and The Punch Bowl at Bridgenorth, one of the most popular soul venues in the area.

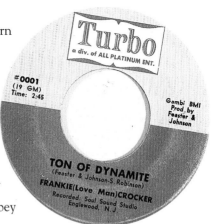

The first night at the New 67 Club in Wolverhampton, started off on the wrong foot. The promised all-nighter was advertised as ending at 4.00am, but this was quickly changed to 2.30am. Leaflets were handed out at the door explaining that, the application for the all-night extension had not been granted.

Also the club allowed its regular members in, creating a strange mixture of *Top Of The Pops* and Northern dancing on the floor. The general view was that the ICSC was patronising, talking down to its members. From the off, nobody believed that half of the venues would be forthcoming; the promised July 26th all-nighter was not an all-nighter; the Weston Super Mare festival was called off; the ISCS and Northern Soul Club fell out after one joint venture; gigs at Sheffield, Aberystwyth, Hereford and Newtown were cancelled, Cambridge was doubtful, and the nights at Luton and Telford were changed to Swindon, and Shrewsbury!

However, the ISCS did have ambitious plans, and Northern Soul events were held all over the country, though these were often poorly attended, with only a handful of soul fans present. A major soul festival was scheduled in December 1975, at the Norbreck Castle Hotel in Blackpool. This was to have included Bessie Banks, Tamiko Jones, Chris Bartley, Oliver Sain, Ultrafunk and the Fantastic Four. The promotion was so disorganised that when Harvey was suddenly hospitalised, the event was cancelled. *Blues & Soul's* John Abbey

and Dave Godin, radio DJs Andy Peebles and John Hallam, and journalist Roger St. Pierre had all made sterling efforts in the promotion of the eventual fiasco, and what credibility Harvey had had before the event, was lost in an instant.

With Gary Glitter at number one with "Always Yours", and David Bowie, Sparks and Bad Company riding high in the album chart, *New Musical Express* dipped its toe into the unknown waters of the Northern scene. Soul correspondent Roger St Pierre, reported on the "Big Scene of the 70s. That is the Northern Soul Scene". Quite why the article was titled, "The Funky Freaks Of The Far North", was particularly odd, considering the concerted efforts of sister publication *Black Music* to reinforce the musical differences that were supposed to exist between Northern and Southern soul fans. St Pierre's Northern article had followed on from a previous article surveying the Southern soul circuit.

It gave a fair overview of the scene, although it did give prominence to the three clubs that had bought advertising space around the article – Tony Petherbridge's Northern Soul Club, John Harvey's Inter-City Club and Chris Burton's International Soul Club. Andy Peeble's Piccadilly Radio show "Soul Train" was recommended listening, and a list of the top clubs told you where to go to experience the "funky phenomenon to end them all".

Richard Searling, DJ at the Pendulum, Manchester, selected some typical rare sounds including Ila Vann, Lee Andrews, the Carstairs, Sam Ward and Connie Clark. He also listed "Golden Oldies" which reflected the English label collectors' favourites – Jerry Jackson "It's Rough Out There", Gene McDaniels' "Walk With A Winner", Derek Martin's "You Better Go" and Linda Jones' "Hypnotised". To appease the regular readers of *NME*, St Pierre mentioned John Peel's recent interest in the scene and his view that it was the "real underground of the 70s". Peel had visited a few clubs in the North and had prepared a Radio One special.

Roger St Pierre was particularly astute in his closing paragraphs. "One thing's for certain, if a cult of such epidemic proportions was happening in London, rather than far-off Blackpool, Keighley, Warrington and Manchester, the pop press would be full of it and the record industry would be rushing out

209

Cody Black

the records like peas from a pod. As it is, the fanatics feel unjustly neglected, yet at the same time fear massive recognition of the kind which would make their scene readily available and accepted by everyone, thus removing its current elitist attractions.

"How long it will last nobody knows. Nor can anyone predict whether

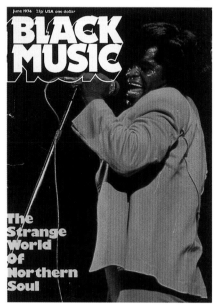

these kids will evolve their tastes with the development of soul music, or one day drop it as a passe fad, just as the mods did in '67 when they suddenly ditched soul for flower-power, swopped pork-pie hats and mohair for beads and kaftans and became hippies."

In June 1974, *Black Music's* Alan Lewis stated in his editorial, that the only hope for the future of Northern Soul was the replacement of the bootleggers and exploiters that dominated the scene, by a system whereby records were released legally to the benefit of the original recording artists. The same issue featured a seven page investigation into the rare soul scene, entitled "The Strange World Of Northern Soul". Apart from a small section written by Dave Godin, the majority of the in-depth article was penned by staff writer Tony Cummings. The introduction by Cummings was an imaginary story about singer and guitarist Eddie Foster. Foster is walking back to his car after finishing a jazz set at Mini's Can Do nightclub in downtown San Francisco. He thinks back over the last twenty years…his early Baptist church days, the start of his recording career in the early Fifties in a local doo-wop group, the Five Stars, and how he had cut a record for a tiny record label. "The producer swore it had the beat the kids wanted and would make him into a big star. Never did happen! In fact he only caught it on the radio twice. What was that damn record called! It was on In Records. "I Never Knew", yeah, that was it."

As he falls asleep in his car, Foster's spirit rises from his body and soars over land and sea towards England, before landing in the queue pushing into an Easter All-dayer at Tiffany's in Newcastle. The spirit makes its way on to the dance floor, where the fans are dancing to Eddie's long forgotten track. After this wistful introduction, Cummings switched to his more robust style.

Apart from positive comments about the high standard of dancing, Tony's article emphasised…"the beat, the beat, always THE BEAT smashes its hypnotic way into mass consciousness."

Although Cumming was not too disparaging about Colin Curtis, Ian Levine or Pep, Soul Sam was taken to task for playing a new secret sound which Cummings recognised as the Packers' "Go Head On", the flip to the 1965 R&B hit "Hole In The Wall". Sam wrote to the magazine and explained that the disc he had played was in fact the B-side to "Sign Of The Crab", which had come out on Action in 1969.

The next day Cummings spent at the Northern Soul Club's All-dayer at the Community Hall in Whitchurch, Shropshire. Almost seven hundred were present to listen to Levine and Curtis spinning tracks like the Velvet Satins' "Nothing Can Compare To You", Joe Hicks' "Don't It Make You Feel Funky", Morris Chestnut's "Too Darn Soulful", Les McCann's "River Deep, Mountain High", Van McCoy's "Soul Improvisions", and Thelma Lindsay's "Prepared To Love You". Also played was the Carstairs' "It Really Hurts Me Girl"which Cummings was interested in buying, but Curtis explained to him that it was one of only three copies in the UK. Tony asked Pep to explain the appeal of the scene. "It's like a club, almost like a secret society. Kids know they'll hear the best sounds here."

The final venue visited was the Blackpool Mecca's Highland Rooms – "The 'stronghold of the connossieurs of the Northern scene, those who look at their 'black bombing, bootleg playing, dull brained brothers from Wigan' with almost as much contempt as the teeny bopper masses." Somebody tried to request "I Never Knew", but the DJs would not play it, as it had been bootlegged.

211

The all-nighter crowd at Wigan

Cummings imagined black spirit, rose once again and flew back home. As Eddie Foster woke up, he recalled his dream: "Man, what a funny dream…where the hell is Wigan?" A fancy conceit, considering Foster's spirit had been to Newcastle, Whitchurch and Blackpool. It was a self indulgent and cheap dig at the Casino, guaranteed to set the sparks flying. The next month's issue featured two pages of letters in response, the first from Russ Winstanley.

"The worst thing about your article was the fact that eighty per cent of your readers, who haven't attended the Mecca or Wigan Casino, might believe it. I also write reports on acts and places I've visited – which appear in *Hot Buttered Soul*, but like most writers, I make sure they are my opinions – first hand – and not hearsay from other people. I certainly wouldn't visit Wigan for opinions about Blackpool, or vice-versa, as Mr. Cummings seems to have done – it's like asking Liverpool supporters for their opinion of Everton! One of the worst results of the article is that it seems to enjoy bringing out the bad points of the Northern Scene, yet one quote stands out – 'No one person makes the Northern Scene. It is a collective thing which makes every person as important as the next. It's the best there is.' Every club on the scene is as important as the next – PLEASE don't try to create a feud between the Casino and the Mecca."

Winstanley's final thoughts were reserved for the bootleg issue. Russ was all for the record companies releasing the big sounds, but felt that they were not interested. He asked what was wrong with making records available for 85p instead of £8 or more. "Where would Major Lance, Robert Knight, J. J. Barnes etc. be without pressings – probably just surviving like Eddie Foster." A view that Alf Billingham didn't share, in a letter to *Black Music*, a month later: "Russ obviously doesn't credit soul fans with any principles and integrity if he thinks this is so. He argues that because an artist like J. J. Barnes received little financial reward from Ric-Tic then the bootleggers are justified in pressing records. It just doesn't wash Russ."

Frank Elson claimed that much of the article was completely inaccurate. Blackpool Mecca DJs, Ian Levine and Colin Curtis, had received such favourable comments, that many readers suspected they had led Cummings astray. Levine issued a statement, which appeared in *Blues & Soul*, denying this and repeated that the last thing they wanted to do was cause any enmity between the Mecca and Wigan Casino.

Tony Cummings' terse descriptions of the leading DJs, had annoyed those mentioned. Alan Rhodes rushed to defend Richard Searling – who was accused of playing Soussan's bootlegs – and Rick Cooper, for his supposed lack of knowledge about soul music. Cooper himself, laid out his soul credentials, and suggested that Cummings had taken too much notice of more voluble interviewees. Soul Sam was viewed by Tony, as the "joker in the pack", and he retaliated, understandably, with a lengthy response, putting Cummings right about his alleged "pop" playlist, the "evil pressing exploitation", and asking who exactly were Simon Soussan's customers. Following Russ Winstanley's lead, Sam asked how the kids were expected to get the sounds if the record companies did not release them. The answer came in the form of Pye Records, and their head of A&R, Dave McAleer.

"A note from Dave McAleer reveals that Pye are to launch a series of 45s devoted to reissues of 'in-demand' northern discotheque sounds. Oh dear. They join Probe, Contempo & Phonogram in the field of catering for the idiosyncratic (lack of taste) of that minority clique who spend their time belting around dancefloors to the accompaniment of largely poor mid '60s soul flops, who usually don't give a damn about the musical quality of a disc so long as it has a fast beat."

Clive Richardson, Shout, May 1974

CHAPTER 15

Temptation 'Bout To Get Me

DAVE MCALEER, WITH Ian Levine's assistance, had put together a compilation of Northern soul favourites from the Scepter and Wand catalogues, which Pye International held the rights to. Much to Dave's surprise, the album sold over six thousand copies. After Dave had seen Levine's vast collection of over sixty thousand records, and witnessed the scene for himself, he became taken with the idea of establishing a label specifically to cater for the Northern fans. McAleer does not forget the impact of that first visit.

"My initial port of call was the Blackpool Mecca with Ian Levine. I was stunned by the dancing, which was unbelievable, and loved the fact that the records being played were so obscure. I felt at home with the one-upmanship and understood immediately its appeal. Ian influenced the first few releases, but after a trip to Wigan Casino, it became apparent that the scene there was much more commercial, and closer to what I was all about – which, of course, was selling records."

The unimaginatively titled Disco Demand label, was launched in June 1974, with three releases: Frankie & the Classicals "What Shall I do", the only one of the discs to have been issued in the UK before – surfacing briefly on Philips in 1967 – it transpired that there were eight different versions of the same song, and many were played in the clubs; Jerry Williams' "If You Ask Me (Because I Love You)", which originally came out in the States on Calla, but had been released in Europe on the Spanish Exit label; and "I'm So Glad" by Washington girl trio the Fuzz, was not particularly rare, having reached number thirty five on the R&B charts in October 1971, but had been ignored by the Northern soul crowd at the time. The label's first major seller was the Casualeers' "Dance, Dance, Dance", which sold over 15,000 copies. Andy Peebles, on Manchester's Piccadilly Radio, probably giving it the biggest boost on his "Soul Train" show. Other black American releases followed from Wally Cox, Little Johnny Blair, Al Wilson, Ila Van, and the Vel-vets. A separate Disco Demand series was established, to cater for British productions, and the first hit came with Wayne Gibson's "Under My Thumb". This cover of a Rolling Stones' song had come out on Columbia in 1966, and had been played on the scene for a few years.

McAleer contacted Gibson's manager, Terry King, who owned the master tapes. Arrangements were made for the disc to be reissued. Dave told King about the song's popularity in the clubs, and the incredulous King received a £1,000 advance against future sales. Gibson's track made it into the charts, and he appeared on *Top Of The Pops*.

The buzz about the Northern scene affected everybody at Pye, as Dave recalls. "A guy in the office had taken a pile of singles home, and had waded through them, to try and find something interesting. He came in one morning and played this B-side that we had issued eighteen months before. That was "Goodbye Nothing To Say"."

Steve Jameson, a white singer from London, had recorded the stomping pop record, and it was distributed to Pye's usual contacts on the Northern scene. Everybody was told that it was by a black American act, the Javells, and originally released on US-Roulette. When the truth came out, many were displeased. Dave Godin admitted that he might have been gullible to believe Pye, but criticised the company for pulling what amounted to a confidence trick. Dave McAleer took the bemused Jameson out for lunch, and told him that he had a hit record. He made a personal appearance at Wigan Casino, singing with two black girl session singers to add a little belated credibility. The disc entered the charts in November 1974 eventually selling 90,000 copies, and after attempts at a follow-up, Jameson disappeared from the Northern scene. He later turned up on television as a comedian, and according to Dave McAleer, can be spotted in commercials for Curly Wurlies and peanut butter.

Disco Demand's biggest hit came in January 1975, with the music from an American toy advertisement, and in the process, Dave McAleer managed to put bootlegger Simon Soussan's nose out of joint. In an interview with Dave Godin in *Blues & Soul*, Soussan described how his "creation" had been stolen. "I found this record in a New York basement on the Roulette label, and I took it home and re-edited it, added the car horns and other sound effects and asked Roulette if they'd license it to me to issue on one of my labels. I'd sent some tapes over of my version to various DJs I knew and before long it was an enormous hit in the North. Then Dave McAleer copied all my creative concept and produced his own legit version which was a hit. Now I don't claim I had any right to alter somebody's record, but then on the other hand what right had McAleer to steal my ideas and concepts which had developed from trying to make something good out of an otherwise indifferent recording?"

Dave McAleer recognised that "Footsee", or "The Sound Of Soul" as Russ had christened it, had the makings of another crossover hit, and stepped in to steal Soussan's thunder. "I discovered that we owned the rights to the original track. I went into the studio, with an engineer, and copied the effects that Soussan had overlaid on the original, even adding crowd noise from the 1966 Cup Final. You can hear the Sheffield supporters shouting 'Wednesday, Wednesday' in the background. At least, they were a Northern team! It was our biggest seller by far, selling 188,000 copies. We did our best to find the artists, but we never did trace anybody to give the royalties to." A few copies came out credited to the Chosen Few, but to avoid problems with Island's reggae act, the prefix "Wigan" was added. Chuck Wood's club favourite "Seven Days Too Long" was put on the flip, Russ Winstanley stuck a Lancashire rose on the sleeve, and the monstrosity climbed into the Top Ten. The nation's pop fans were treated to an athletic display by the Casino dancers, drafted into action for the spot on *Top Of The Pops*.

In January 1975, *Black Music's* Tony Cummings returned to the North, this time, making it to Wigan. He still treated the Mecca with deference, implying that there was a hardcore at Blackpool who were as happy to listen as they were to dance, "Dancing is what the Casino is all about…here in the cavernous, comfortable tattiness of the Casino there's no such nonsense. Peering over the balcony surrounding three sides of the dance floor, your eyes fall upon a packed mass of writhing limbs and bobbing heads. Many youths are dressed in singlets allowing sweat to flow freely. The atmosphere is stuffy."

Selecta Disc who had been the major outlet for Soussan's pressings, and would wholesale the discs to other shops specialising in Northern Soul. The British Phonographic Industry investigated the Nottingham-based company,

Simon Soussan and wife in Ike and Tina Turner's Studio

and as a result of their enquiries, pirated copies of 45s by Sheila Anthony, Bobby Paris and Ann Perry were returned to source. They were probably under the impression that the discs supplied by him were the genuine article – Soussan had a reputation as a formidable salesman.

In an interview in *Black Music*, Soussan told Tony Cummings that he was born in Casablanca in 1944 to Spanish parents. He came to Britain in 1968 and worked for the Burton group, and first encountered the Northern soul scene at the Twisted Wheel. Realising that he owned many of the records being played, he began selling spare copies. Colin Curtis remembers meeting him at the Torch. "I was floating around that night, and obviously you would be a target for the guys with the little fifty boxes. Whether the records they'd got were good or bad, it didn't seem to bother them. In fact it got worse, it got to the point where if you wanted it, they didn't want to sell it to you. They wanted to sell it to somebody else, saying that you wanted it and they could charge them more. And that would just be to another punter, and the record wouldn't get played. I couldn't quite understand that. Everybody had one of these little Woolworth's boxes made out of cardboard and plastic, and there's this guy whose got these long wooden boxes. And he's got the wrong clothes on. He's got his hair done just so. So there's a few people around him. I wait patiently and I get a chance to look in the box. The average box, you'd find three or four things that you might be interested in, maybe one or two that you're very interested in. But this fucking box had everything. Everything, that even if you'd got it, you thought well, where'd he get that from. Then it just got insane. There was stuff in there that you would die for – all original records, original *major* records.

"I went to see Soussan in Leeds, when he was living in a flat there. I walked in, it was a middle class sort of flat from the outside. No big deal. But inside everything was white. The carpet, the piano, were white. He couldn't play the piano, but there was a piano. And then he pulled back the cupboard doors and there was just rows and rows of singles in this cabinet. It was unbelievable."

Soussan would often turn up at clubs to sell rare 45s, and Richard Watt remembers on one occasion that he had a lucky escape. "He had put out a list from his flat in Leeds, and he nearly got rolled at the Catacombs – there were one or two heavies at the Cats!" Ian Dewhirst, DJ Frank, remembers how he inadvertently saved Soussan's life at the Blackpool Mecca. "Simon had arrived with Richard Searling at the Highland Room, and word spread like wild fire that he was in the building. As usual, I was at the right hand bar of the Mecca with my box of records, and I heard that Simon was here. The word was, that he'd brought some real goodies with him, and he was looking for swaps. So he actually came up and asked if he could look through my box. I always remember, I had a really bad record by Shona Springfield called "I Need A Rest" on a Philadelphia label. There were a few of them around at the time, and Simon pulled that out of the box, along with something else, and said 'I must have these two records, I don't know them.' So I said 'Fine, what do you want to do? Do you want to buy them?', Simon goes 'I need them, we will do a swap.' Of course, he never had the records with him, he said that they were at the hotel.

"While all this was going on, quite a crowd had accumulated. I was trying to consolidate the deal with Simon, when people started to crowd him, and started to push and nudge him, and a couple of people were saying, 'Oi, Soussan, I sent you a hundred quid last May, and I never got any fucking records!'. The

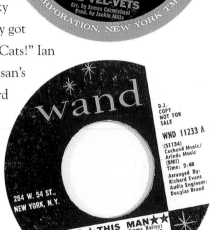

219

situation was beginning to get a bit ugly, and I remember Richard saying 'Simon, I think we had better leave.' All I was aware of is people starting to push, and I got so annoyed about it, that I lent against the bar and sorted of pushed the crowd back. That was the catalyst that set it off, because a couple of people fell down at the back, and then out of nowhere somebody hit me with one of those dimpled pint glasses full on in the face. It broke my nose, chipped my two front teeth, and I went down, In the melee that followed Simon and Richard got out. When I later spoke to him, I reminded him of the incident and he said 'You saved my life!', and in America he would always introduce me to people with 'This is Ian Dewhirst, he saved my life'."

Soussan left Britain to live in New Mexico, before settling in California, and his early lists are a snapshot of the rare sounds being played at the time. One from early 1973, contains Bob Relf "Blowin' My Mind To Pieces", Wendy Rene "Bar-B-Q", Cindy Scott "I Love You Baby", the Sweets "You Satisfy Me Baby", Tempos "Countdown (Here I Come)", Trips "There Is That Mountain", Vel-vets "I Got To Find Me Somebody" and dozens more. DJ Pep was given as a reference to vouch for his honesty, but it was soon after this that he first started pressing bootlegs.

Ian Dewhirst worked with Soussan in the States not long after the bootlegger had, once again, fallen out with Selecta Disc. "I formed a company with Neil Rushton called Interdisc, and the idea was, that I would go out to the States, find rare records to send back to the UK, and at the same time, pursue legitimate licences for records. I hadn't exactly been schooled in what New York was like, so my mother told me to stay in the YMCA, which was a nightmare. I stayed about two days in New York and decided to go up to Los Angeles. When I got there, the only contact I had was Simon Soussan who I'd only met briefly when he came to the Blackpool Mecca. I met him at the airport with my bags and Soussan said 'Follow me, follow me Ian, and I'll show you around.' Of course, he gets about five yards and there's a woman approaching and he's instantly all over her. 'Ah, baby, baby, please, please, I must have your number.' And within one minute, he got her number. This had all happened within the first minute. The girl was drop dead gorgeous, and as he walked ahead, I asked him if it was as easy as that to pick up girls. Soussan just ripped the card up, threw it away and said 'There's thousands Baby Boy.' That was my introduction to LA and Simon Soussan.

"We had this secret Northern Soul language which he used to love because nobody knew what he was talking about. I'd just sit there cracking up with laughter. One night, he wanted to hit every club in town. And his main thing was, as soon as we got to a club, he would head straight for the women's toilet, on the basis that it was the first place that women going into a club would go to look at themselves. He said 'Look at this, Baby Boy, tonight we are going to pull anybody you want. It's easy.' This girl suddenly appeared, and Simon said to her, 'Allow me to introduce myself, my name is Michel Soussan, that's his real name, I am from the Revilot Design Company – a dress design company – and we use quite a few designers, J. J. Barnes you may have heard of? In fact we have a brand new dress, it has a pocket on the front, and we are thinking of calling it "Our Love Is In The Pocket". He was a guy on a roll, everything he said was connected to Northern Soul, so that was his sense of humour – if he was in the mood. He hated funk records, and would swear at his car radio 'That fucking funk, why can't they play Northern Soul!'.

"Selecta Disc had been operating with Simon for years up to that point. He'd fallen out with them. Whatever happened, something went wrong. Neil and I didn't want to get into the whole bootlegging thing, our plan was to put out records legitimately. I found a couple of market stalls and stated turning up some good stuff, and Simon began to get a bit paranoid that I was going to pick up records he didn't have. He said that he was going to get the rights to records and get approval to put things out. Of course, I now know that was dodgy. We went through this 4-6 week period, when he was trying to convince me how straight he was. At the time, there had been some dodgy copies of Kenny Smith's "Lord What's Happening To Your People" which had come over to Britain on the GRA label. I asked him about these, and he said 'I know Kenny Smith, I'll ring him for you now.' He'd get on the 'phone and say 'Hi Kenny, how are you? You've got a huge record in England.' He was so convincing.

"Soussan was fantastic. He was magician-like in his ability to convince people. It was only after years of experience that I realised that he was the king

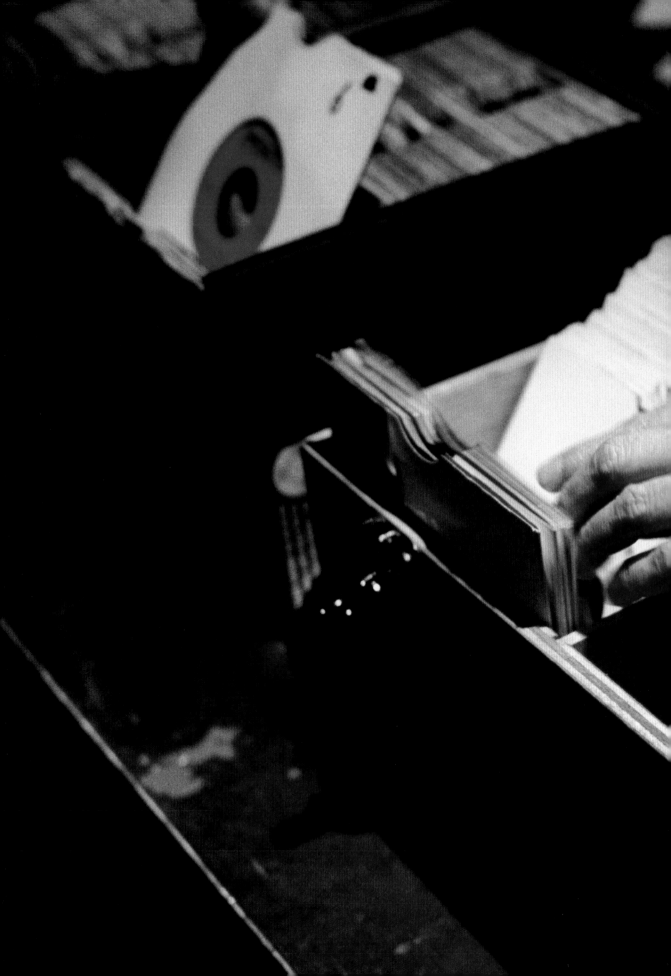

bullshitter of all time. But sometimes you get seduced by these things."

Dewhirst would call round to Soussan's office each morning where he would always find him hard at work, surrounded by a huge pile of papers on the desk. Anytime that Ian questioned the legitimacy of one of the releases, Soussan would produce the necessary proof from the pile. "We did 'Love Factory' by Eloise Laws, which I can't think in a million years that he had the rights to."

Dewhirst and Soussan were in a Beverley Hills club called Chez Nous, when they heard the Ritchie Family's hit "The Best Disco In Town". Dewhirst recalls: "We were listening to it and Simon says 'You know, Baby Boy, we should do a Northern Soul medley...with "Nothing's Too Good For My Baby", something like that.' I told him that nobody would know the tunes, and said to him that Motown would be better."

Dewhirst's partner, Neil Rushton, recalled that they had put twenty per cent of the money up to pay for the production. "It was going to be a twelve inch, and when Simon still had the idea of a Northern Soul medley, he wanted to put a picture of Russ Winstanley on the label. I remember taking this 'phone call from the States, and going 'No, no, I can't sell it!'."

The song, "Uptown Festival", was recorded in Ike & Tina Turner's studio, using session musicians including Motown's Eddie "Bongo" Brown and Jack Ashford. The medley of "Going To A Go-Go", "I Can't Help Myself", "Uptight", "Stop! In The Name Of Love" and "The Same Old Song" was issued on TV host Don Cornelius' Soul Train label. Jody Watley, Jeffrey Daniels and Gerald Brown, were singers and dancers on the show, and after the record was a hit, they became the public face of Shalamar. Soussan could not resist a Northern Soul reference, taking their name from Sari & The Shalimars, whose "Stop And Take A Look At Yourself" had been a Torch favourite.

As well as the bootleggers who produced discs in massive quantities, there were also individuals who supplied Emidiscs of the rare sounds. Pete Lawson and Keith Bradley were the two most well known, and even Wigan DJ Kev

SARI AND THE SHALIMARS / exclusively on
A DIVISION OF UNITED ARTISTS

Roberts admitted to Tony Cummings, that he taped his rarest 45s and had a few copies cut as acetates for sale. Tony was prepared to believe that Roberts' action was justified, when he wrote in *Black Music*: "Kev is motivated by a continual desire to expose and promote superb discs savagely ignored with the too-many-releases situation of the American record business, but distracted from such a noble path by the wheeling and dealing always surrounding situations where young people with their free spending habits are involved."

By the time of the article, Kev had left, or depending on your view of the situation, been sacked from the Casino. In *Blues & Soul*, Frank Elson revealed that Roberts had been fired by Russ Winstanley for allegedly taping and pressing rare vinyl. The two records in question, Billy Prophet's "What Can I Do" and Jeanette Williams' "All Of A Sudden". Russ Winstanley is adamant about this, but Kev's memory of the circumstances surrounding his departure are less controversial.

"I think it was a number of things. I think Russ felt that I was on Blackpool's side, played a lot of their records. The Mecca was going through a change, they were playing the funkier stuff, "Shake And Bump" by Snoopy Dean, "Music Maker" by King Sporty. I was playing them at Wigan and I don't think Russ liked that one little bit. Started to look daggers at each other, bad vibes. There were many other issues, but I think that, suddenly, I didn't fit into Russ's jigsaw whatsoever."

Roberts' exit did not make a great difference to his fortunes as a DJ. Kev began working with Chris Burton at the Top Rank, Hanley, The Heavy Steam Machine and at Tiffany's, Coventry with Pete Waterman.

The future member of the Stock, Aitken & Waterman production team was a long term soul fan, and Northern Soul DJ, regularly appearing at Mr George's in Coventry. He gained much of his recording experience working in Philadelphia, and the mention of Hoagy Lands' "The Next In Line" is guaranteed to put a smile on his face. In fact, he was going to get Rick Astley to record a version of the song, but it never materialised. "I learned a lot from Pete" says Kev Roberts "he was a very smart guy. When the whole Kylie and Jason thing broke for him, it didn't surprise me one bit, because he was like that as a DJ. Very good at sussing people out. I'd go on with the Salvadors, Mel Britt and other big sounds of the day, and I'd have sixty or seventy dancers on the floor. People would come up and say 'Brilliant stuff, Kev.' Pete would stick on "Love On A Mountain Top" and have five hundred dancing. He just knew I was too hard core to be playing that."

Waterman started working as a Mecca DJ in 1964, and his interest in the Northern Soul scene was kindled by hearing Mitch Ryder & The Detroit Wheel's "Breakout". He opened a shop in Coventry called Soul Hole, and remembers searching for rare soul records in Philadelphia. "I was in a

AIN'T IT BABY
(J. Bishop - K. Gamble)

ARCTIC

Blackbuster-Stilran
Music (BMI)
A-KGA2A
Time: 2:15

National Dist.
Jamie /Guyden
Dist. Corp.

Vocal
A Dynodynamics
Production

D. J. COPY
NOT FOR SALE

KENNY GAMBLE
& THE ROMEOS
114
ARCTIC RECORD CO., PHILA. PA.

warehouse, and I heard this noise coming from behind these records. I thought that there couldn't possibly be anybody else daft enough to be looking, so I moved through and there's Ian Levine. He must have been surrounded by about forty five thousand records, and I think he probably played every one. He had a bloody 'plane and he was bringing thousands back at a time. We were all guided by the label credits in those days, I mean if you liked the look of them, and knew the label, there was a good chance that out of three hundred records you might get one decent one. For twenty cents you could take a chance – something like Gamble and Huff on Artic. A couple of days in a warehouse was all part of the fun."

The Casino went from strength to strength. Following the growing publicity, many teenagers turned up at the all-nighter to see what all the fuss was about. Through television exposure, hearing the odd track at the local youth club, or being told about Wigan by an older brother, the Casino became the Northern scene's focal point. The Mecca may have been perceived by journalists as the cooler option, and many of the Wigan sounds may well have been played first at Blackpool, but the humid, stifling ballroom packed with kids dancing to the Flirtations' "Stronger Than Her Love" or Johnny Bragg's

"They're Talking About Me" or Lorraine Chandler's "I Can't Change", was the big draw. By April 1975, Mike Walker had been forced to suspend membership, due to complaints about overcrowding and trouble at the entrance.

Tailor-made Northern Soul productions may have embarrassed the faithful, but they would never have bought them anyway. The scene had finally become mainstream, but none of the pop hits had done anything to convince the disbelievers. Critics continued to ridicule the scene and the Goodies rubbed salt into the faithful's wounds with their dire 1975 hit "Black Pudding Bertha (The Queen Of Northern Soul)".

Wigan's Ovations' hit cover "Ski-ing In The Snow" was contrived by John Smith and Barry Kingston at Spark Records, and although Russ Winstanley and Mike Walker had introduced the previously unknown Sparkle to the London record company, the group, thankfully, never appeared at the Casino. Covers of David & the Giants and Bobby Paris tracks struggled into the lower reaches of the charts and Spark turned their attention to Tommy Hunt. Ruth

Swann covered Gloria Jones' "Tainted Love", but pop fans had to wait until Soft Cell's version became a worldwide hit in 1981. Ian Dewhirst remembers giving a copy of the disc to Mark Almond when he was working as a cloakroom attendant in a club in Leeds. Almond and fellow Soft Cell member Dave Ball had both been to the Casino.

Selecta Disc made the logical move, and set up their own Black Magic label. Dobie Gray's "Out On The Floor", which had gained popularity through the Casino's oldies room Mr. M's, entered the Top Fifty. But it was Simon Soussan's productions for the company that became more successful, most notably the Sharonettes' "Papa Oom Mow Mow". Selecta Disc continued a strained working relationship with Soussan, and his antics continued to be reported in the soul magazines.

In *Black Music*, Phil Holmes, promotion man for the label, admitted that although the company had "been a bit naughty in the past", they were anxious to become legitimate. Selecta Disc's releases were now distributed in the UK by CBS, and they were keen that nothing should jeopardise this arrangement; when they signed an exclusive contract with Simon Soussan's Soul Fox Productions to release his new US recordings, they insisted that he sign an agreement only to supply material that was completely legal. However, Simon Soussan could not keep things totally above board.

Previously, he had often changed label credits on bootlegs to increase their appeal to his Northern Soul audience, so it was not surprising Soussan should suggest that the line-up of the Sharonettes comprised of Paula Roussell, Clydie King, Patrice Holloway and Shirley Matthews. Ex-Raelette Clydie King's duets with Jimmy Holiday had been early Northern favourites, as had Patrice Holloway's "Love And Desire". Mirwood label composer Shirley Matthews added an extra touch of credibility to the line-up. Despite the presence of Matthews on the original recording, the other two members of the group were in fact the unknowns Carolyn Willis and Becky Louis.

At the Blackpool Mecca, Tony Cummings interviewed one soul fan who declared that "the sounds have never been better." They had

229

certainly never been so diverse. Sixties-style stormers like "The Larue" from blonde go-go dancer Lada Edmund Jr, and Rita Dacosta's infectious "Don't Bring Me Down" were mixed with Seventies releases such as Boby Franklin's wah-wah guitar and vibes' strut "The Ladies Choice", Snoopy Dean's "Shake And Bump", King Sporty's "Music Maker" and Eula Cooper's frantic "Let Our Love Grow Higher". Without Ian Levine's change of direction, classics like James Fountain's "Seven Day Lover", would never have seen the light of day.

The media lost interest in the Northern scene and everything got back to normal. Mike Walker went on stage at the Casino to ask the crowd if they wanted a television crew from the *Nationwide* programme to do a report on the club. He received an emphatic 'no', yet at the time researchers from Granada TV were already planning a documentary on the club. This again was voted upon with a show of hands at the club, and rejected by its members, but filming *This England* would start a few months later.

"Then he landed, did a spine-breaking backward bend, came up and bobbed for a while. Then went into a spin, arms held tight across his chest like an ice-skater. He looked triumphant after that. The scene's his."

Geoff Brown, Melody Maker, January 1975

CHAPTER 16

Baby Make Your Own Sweet Music

IN FEBRUARY 1975, Les Cokell returned to DJ at the Blackpool Mecca, as temporary replacement for the absent Ian Levine. The Highland Room's supremo had swapped turntables for the mixing desk, and was busy at work in a New York recording studio. Levine had heard the efforts of Simon Soussan, and confident that he could do better, approached Dave McAleer, by then at 20th Century Records, to organise the session. Ian had befriended the Exciters' Herb Rooney, when the group had toured the UK, and Rooney had agreed to assist, if the studio costs could be met. McAleer persuaded music publisher Craig Baguley to fund Levine's first session to the tune of £600. Dave's superiors had not been excited by the prospect of a Northern club DJ, with no previous experience, being let loose in an expensive studio.

Dick Watt, Les Cokell and Shelvo

Assisted by Herb Rooney, four tracks were cut; two Northern favourites – Sandi Sheldon's "You're Gonna Make Me Love You" and Eddie Parker's "Love You Baby" – together with two new compositions, "Suffering" and "Reaching For The Best". This last title had been poached from one of Soussan's sales lists, where it had been catalogued as being by Bob Relf – in fact the record did not even exist.

Such was the furore caused by Levine's debut as a producer, that even before the tracks had been released, *Blues & Soul* were forced to publish an apology to Baguley's company Horse Music Publishing, over suggestions that the recordings might have been sub-standard. Dave Godin was threatened with legal action, for comments made about an interview Levine had given

233

SPECIAL DISC JOCKEY PROMOTION LIMITED ISSUE ONLY

LE001A

LEVIATHIAN/HORSE MUSIC

DOOMSDAY
(Levine-Leake)
EVELYN THOMAS

Melody Maker. Godin was not intimidated by Levine's tactics and in the same *Blues & Soul* replied: "Not one penny, my old son! Ian would do well to remember that this 'reputation' which is obviously so precious to him, was in part created for him by writers like myself who he used to constantly accost, badger, sycophantize and cajole for repeated name-checks and mentions when he was an ingenue DJ on the up-and-up. In those days, people like myself were constantly embarrassed by the way he constantly fawned over us, and it seems sad now that Ian Levine has such an overblown and high opinion of the importance of his contribution to the British Soul Scene that he confuses valid criticism with libel, and regards Her Majesty's Courts as mere handmaidens with no more pressing function than to assuage his childish tantrums. Freedom of speech is worth defending and worth a bit of inconvenience to preserve, and frankly, I'd rather drink muddy water than pay one penny to soothe such infantile petulance. So, Ian, let's see the colour of your writ!"

The Exciters' "Love You Baby" came out first, but was a disappointing retread of the Parker classic. At the same time, Selecta Disc's Black Magic issued Simon Soussan's version of the same song – allegedly by Northern Soul heroine Lorraine Chandler, although she has no recollection of ever recording the song. Soussan's treatment was inferior to Levine's, but came with the added bonus of a flip-side featuring the genuine Chandler, singing the in-demand "What Can I Do", which probably explains its slightly greater sales.

The follow-up, "Reaching For The Best" was much better, and the record entered the charts, justifying McAleer's faith in Levine. The record was Radio Luxembourg's "Power Play", but stopped at number thirty one, missing out on the all important *Top Of The Pops* appearance.

Levine's father financed a record production company, Voltafine, and Ian teamed up with Danny Leake from the soul group 100% Pure Poison. In August 1975, Levine flew to Chicago, auditioned singers and further hits emerged from the session; Evelyn Thomas' "Weakspot" and "Doomsday", and

L.J.Johnson's "Your Magic Put A Spell On Me" were chart entries. The Exciters toured Britain on the strength of "Reaching For The Best", but in interviews, Herb Rooney maintained that he had been the sole composer of the song, and that Levine had contributed nothing to the production. This led to a terrible row and the former partners fell out. Rooney apologised and Levine flew out to the States to work on a new batch of songs. After some disastrous auditions that Herb Rooney had set up; a wino who sang "Crying In The Chapel", a junkie, a plumber who just happened to be in the building they eventually found Doris Jones, who was an old girlfriend of Rooney's. A singer from New Jersey, Tyrone Ashley, saved the day when he was persuaded to sign for the company. The hits eluded Levine, but he persevered, and it would only be a matter of time before he would get lucky.

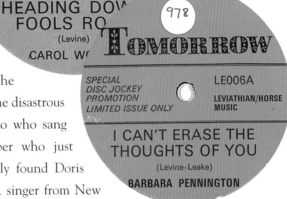

By September 1976, Levine was despondent about the reception he had received from his old stomping ground, declaring that he did not want to be associated with Northern Soul anymore. Ian's focus became the American disco market, and his persistence finally paid off. Barbara Pennington's "24 Hours A Day" became a massive hit on the *Billboard* Disco chart, selling 100,000 copies and James Wells' album "My Claim To Fame" became another disco hit in 1978.

Following Pye's entry into the Northern Soul arena, a deluge of 45s were issued by almost every record company in the country. In the December 1975 issue of *Black Music*, Tony Cummings compiled an exhaustive list of discs that were directly, or indirectly, connected to the Northern Soul world. Amongst the familiar labels were a couple of new names, Right On and Swan.

On 8th August 1975, Pye had launched Right On!, with Dave Godin overseeing the label's product. Although not specifically aimed at the Northern audience, the first release by the Crow, the haunting "Your Autumn Of Tomorrow" gained many plays in the clubs, as did other 45s by the Jelly Beans, Chris Bartley and the Fantastic Puzzles. It was a short-lived venture with just seven releases, and the label closed after only a year.

The other newcomer, Swan, was run by Ed Balbier, the owner of Manchester-based importers Global Records. He had purchased the master tapes of the famed Philadelphia label when Swan went bankrupt in 1966. The only two releases on the label were the Guys From UNCLE's "The Spy" and another Northern favourite, the Modern Redcaps "Never Too Young (To Fall In Love)". A sister label, Cream, was created to issue material from other US outlets, but difficulties in arranging distribution hampered the planned release of James Fountain's "Seven Day Lover". After exhaustive negotiations with William Bell, the owner of the rights, the disc finally appeared in February 1976. The other launch 45, Eddie Carlton's "It Will Be Done", had been found by Rick Cooper at Global when sifting through the Swan tapes.

Another Cooper discovery was unearthed in the garage of a Bradford record shop owner. The Jaywalkers' "Can't Live Without You", was played by Ian Levine, and proclaimed a classic. Promotional copies were sent to Northern DJs, but knowing that the record would eventually be released, it was not deemed an exclusive enough sound. The fourth release was Johnny Jones & The King Casuals' "Purple Haze", and once again, disaster struck for the company when Brunswick issued the disc at the same time. The Showstoppers' "Ain't Nothing But A Houseparty" was the fourth, and final, outing for Cream, and through discussions with the US owners, it was discovered that they owned the rights to the Four Perfections' "I'm Not Strong Enough". The copies that were being played by DJs, were acetates supplied by

Jackey Beavers

I'M NOT STRONG ENOUGH
(Steals-Thomas-Steals)
THE FOUR PERFECTIONS
PT-1001

Simon Soussan, which he had covered up as by the Exceptions. Nobody was aware that the disc had come out on the same label as the Showstoppers' record, and Cream immediately set about obtaining the rights. Rick Cooper left Global, and for whatever reason, the disc never appeared in the shops.

Neil Rushton ran Inferno, from Walsall, which opened its account with the Ad Libs' "New York In The Dark". Neil was beginning to get fed up with the arrangement with Simon Soussan. "He'd tell me stuff was legal, and when it arrived it was bootlegged. If I'd known what I was doing it would have been a lot better. I've always been a bit of a purist, and I didn't like the idea of selling bootlegs. We could have been his replacement for Selecta Disc, but I wasn't interested. So Ian and I went our separate ways. I was getting records from here, there, and everywhere, and met a guy at Columbia Special Products. I sounded him out about leasing material for a record label, things like the Poppies "Pain In My Heart", Lynne Randell "Stranger In My Arms", and the Vibrations "Cause Your Mine". The price I got for legitimate reissues, was cheaper than the cost of buying bootlegs off Soussan. I thought, as people are snobbish, they would be prepared to pay more because they were legal. So I got them cheaper, and charged an extra 15p. I sold 20,000 copies of the Poppies' "Pain In My Heart", which was unbelievable. It got me thinking about doing it properly.

"Well, I went to see Billy Jackson, the producer, to see about issuing Frank Beverly's "If That's What You Wanted". He said he would help sort it out, and while I was

238

there, I asked him if I could buy some originals he'd got. So I opened this cupboard, and in this water stained box were white demo copies of the record on Sassy. I had one on Gamble, but nobody had seen those before – that paid for the air fare over. There were also things like Patti Austin's "You Didn't Say A Word" and the Tymes' "Here She Comes". So, this seemed better than importing records or worrying about bootlegs, so I thought that I'd go for it."

Rushton picked up the rights to a wealth of the more commercially viable Northern tracks; Johnny Bragg's "They're Talking About Me", Gloria Jones' "Tainted Love", Barbara Mills' "Queen Of Fools", Frankie & Johnny's "I'll Hold You", a different mix of the Carstairs' "It Really Hurts Me Girl", Fi-dels' "Try A Little Harder", and the biggest seller, Freda Payne's "Band Of Gold".

"The best story though, was when I went over to Los Angeles to negotiate the Invictus tracks. I got off the 'plane and met Eddie and Brian Holland. And they must have thought I was mad, because I kept talking about "Candy To Me" and all this stuff. Anyway, we do the deal, give them the money and get the tracks. They played me an unreleased Chairman Of The Board record that they lost the next day. I swear, it's better than "Give Me Just A little More Time", called "What's The Use". So they invited me to come up to the hills where they were recording a thing for Jobete Music. It was going to be called "Yesterday, Today And Forever", and was going to be a double album of all their Motown songs, which they hoped to get covers on. It's worth a lot of money now, about £1,000. So, I'm in the hills having just come from an all-dayer at the Ritz in Manchester, and it's like Paul Riser, McKinlay Jackson, all the guys from Detroit, recreating the Motown sound. It's Beverly Hills, restaurants and I'm thinking this is what it's all about. But after a while you start to get a bit blase about the whole thing. So I'm in the toilet having a pee, and there's a guy next to me, and he starts whistling "I Hear A Symphony". And I looked up and it was Brian Holland. It was absolutely amazing, from the Catacombs to that."

In 1977, Grapevine Records was started by Soul Bowl's John Anderson. A soul collector since the mid Sixties, he began selling records mail-order from Glasgow. "I used to buy imports from Global in Manchester, and from a guy in

Bradford who had a warehouse full of records. I used to go down and swap loads of crap for good stuff. He didn't care, to him they were just a commodity. He used to put them in the market, or off load piles to fun fairs to be used as targets. He had millions of them." Anderson moved down to King's Lynn in November 1972, and set up Groove City with Terry Jones. The partnership was later dissolved, and in January 1973, Anderson changed the name of the company to Soul Bowl. He quickly gained a reputation as one of the key discoverers of rare soul on the Northern scene. With distribution through RCA, the label quickly established itself as a favourite amongst collectors. Although, much to John's annoyance, the label's biggest seller was white singer Judy Street's "What".

The label had somewhat unusual origins, as John recalls. "We were trying to get some tracks re-pressed in the States, but the guy took the money and spent it all at the racetrack. There was no money to get the records pressed, so I was left with all these masters. So that's how Grapevine started."

Richard Searling, who was one of Anderson's customers, worked as an assistant to Derek Brandwood, promotional manager for RCA in Manchester. A distribution and manufacturing deal was set up and the first three releases were issued in July 1977: Richard "Popcorn" Wylie's "Rosemary What Happened", the Soul Twins' "Quick Change Artist" and Stanley Woodruff & The US Trio's "What Took You So Long". The first two releases came from Ollie McLaughlin's Karen label in Detroit. Ollie started out promoting with his brother Maxie in the late Forties, and in 1954 became a DJ on university radio station WHRV in Ann Arbor. One of the first black DJs in the area, McLaughlin was known as "Scooby Doo" and at one time had a fan club with over 25,000 members. His musical discoveries included Barbara Lewis, Deon Jackson, and Del Shannon.

Among the forty or so Grapevine 45s, were many dance floor favourites, many now almost impossible to acquire – such as Jimmy Burns' "I Really Love You". Mark Bicknell, editor of *Soul Underground*, was staying with a musician friend in Chicago in the late Eighties. Thinking it unlikely that his friend would know Burns, Mark asked if he knew him. Within ten minutes, Mark was talking on the 'phone to Burns, and a meeting was arranged at a nearby blues club. In conversation, Bicknell discovered that Jimmy had no knowledge of the Grapevine release, yet he seemed happy that at last he had received approval and recognition for what he had believed to be a good record at the time. Burns later sold Mark a copy of the record, which is still only one of a handful in the country.

Even taking into account the few lacklustre issues, with releases including Lester Tipton's "This Won't Change", Dena Barnes' "If You Ever Walked Out Of My Life", Duke Browner's "Crying Over You", Al Williams' "I Am Nothing", Morris Chestnut's "Too Darn Soulful" and Sam Williams' "Love Slipped Through My Fingers", Grapevine proved to be one of the class acts of the reissue labels of the Seventies.

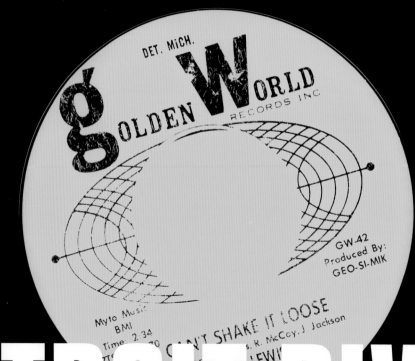

DETROIT DIVAS

Pat Lewis and Rose Batiste are Northern Soul legends. Between them, they recorded some of the best loved dance tracks of the Sixties. While visiting Britain in 1998, they spoke of their early days in Detroit.

Pat Lewis, who was one of Detroit's top session singers during the '70s and '80s, backing everyone from Isaac Hayes to Aretha Franklin, told us of her beginnings in the music business. "My mother used to work with Thelma Gordy – they were both nurses. My brother, who also loved to sing, said that he would take me to her family's studio. That must have been in '61 or '62, and I've been at it ever since. While I was there Richard Street was a writer and producer, as was Norman Whitfield – they were older than me. And it was just "let's hope we can eat tonight". You know, everybody walked everywhere because nobody had money to buy cars. Anyway, I left there and went to start working with Mr. Wingate."

Together with her sister Diane, and two other sisters from their neighbourhood, Betty and Jackie Winston, they formed the Adorables. It was early days for Golden World, as Pat recalls: "Ed Wingate did not have his own studio so we recorded at Correc-Tone, which was owned by Wilbur Golden. Then we moved into Joanne Bratton's basement and rehearsed there. I don't know whether Wingate and Golden fell out or what, but we started going to Chicago to record, that must have been around late '63."

Rose Batiste, who had sat quietly sipping her orange juice suddenly interrupted. "Oh, so you were the Adorables? You sang that song "Deep Freeze"?"

"Yeah, I did the 'little heart, little heart' part and Betty sang the rest of it."

The Adorables recorded a Richard "Popcorn" Wylie and Ronnie Savoy composition "Ooh, Boy", and "School's Over", the flip of which "Be", Pat gave an instant rendition of, much to everyone's surprise in the hotel's bar.

Pat and the girls also sang back-up on other acts on the label such as the Reflections. They were a white group whose most successful 45 was, of course, "(Just Like) Romeo and Juliet". The Golden World act sounded like something out of a Damon Runyan book – Tony 'Spaghetti' Micale, Dan Bennie, Ray 'Razor' Steinberg, John Dean and Phil 'Parrot' Castrodale, who was the group's falsetto tenor.

"Yeah, Phil looked as if he could have been one of the Beach Boys." laughed Pat. Eventually Wingate built his own studio and when the Adorables split, Pat recorded her first solo track "Can't Shake It Loose" which was issued in March 1966.

Prior to her solo debut Pat had been kept busy singing backing vocals at Motown. Her first session was Stevie Wonder's hit "Uptight", when Louvain Demps of the Andantes could not make the session. Pat became a regular at the Motown studios each Monday, and after her next session on Kim Weston's "Take Me In Your Arms (Rock Me A Little While)" she became a regular fixture, eventually joining the Andantes. Although Pat said that it was not easy money.

"We were making five dollars a song and then we got a raise to seven dollars and fifty cents. We were paid by the song but you didn't get any more if the song was a hit, it didn't make a difference. No royalties, nothing. I wasn't in a union then and I didn't know anything about a union then, but we started getting raises and we got up to 15 dollars a song. When I started singing with Aretha Franklin I eventually joined a union because of all the TV appearances.

"In fact, it was because Louvain Demps didn't show up for the Golden World session that George Clinton asked me to do it.

"Can't Shake It Loose" was what we would call a turntable hit, it got a lotta plays and did pretty good with sales. As a matter of fact our family was on vacation and we were driving through Nashville on our way to Alabama when it came on the radio. And my mother said that I should stop and call the DJ, John Richbourg, you know thank him for playing the record. And my Dad says OK, so we did that."

Pat stopped to ask Rose how she first got started.

"Oh, I recorded "I Can't Leave You" when I was about 13 or 14, something like that."

"I Can't Leave You" was issued on Thelma, the label owned by Robert and Hazel Coleman and named after their daughter who was Berry Gordy's first wife. The company was based opposite Rose Batiste's high school and the first person she met when trying to persuade somebody to hear her sing was Emanuel Lasky. Her first song was written by Don Davis, who would later persuade her to move to Solid Hitbound Productions.

"It was really exciting hearing your own song on the radio. I was queen of the neighbourhood. Well the block anyway!"

Rose first met Pat and her sister Diane when she moved to Golden World and recorded "Sweet Heart Darling" which came out in January 1966.

Both Pat and Rose spoke fondly of Ed Wingate, the label's owner.

"Mr. Wingate is still around living in Las Vegas. He returned to the business about 8-9 years ago and did an album with Ronnie McNair. Diane and I met him again and he still remembered us as little girls. He was sitting there looking at us both drinking and smoking. We were not little girls anymore you know, but it was shocking to him. He kept saying 'I can't get over it'."

Rose moved to Revilot and her first release was the double header "Hit & Run" and "I Miss My Baby".

"Hit & Run" written by George McGregor and Cody Black, was also recorded by Martha Reeves, Gwen Owens and the Debonaires but their versions were never released. One other release on Revilot was "I Still Wait For You" backed with "Come Back In A Hurry".

Rose was completely unaware of Doni Burdick's instrumental of "I Miss My Baby", "Bari Track". But given how young she was at the time it's not surprising that she was unaware of what was going on in the Detroit music scene.

Pat moved to Lebaron Taylor's Solid Hit where she recorded "Look At What I Almost Missed" the label's first release in the autumn of 1966, "Warning", "No One To Love" and what became the company's last issue "The Loser". Incidentally, Rose remembered covering "Warning" but it was never put out.

Rose was oblivious to the interest in the UK for her recordings until she ran into former Ric-Tic musician Al Kent in downtown Detroit.

"He said that my music was really popular in England and that everybody was looking for me. I thought he was telling a fib, because I didn't believe he was serious. Then later on I met Emanuel Lasky who gave me Francisco Garcia's number, and the rest is history."

CHAPTER 17

That Beatin' Rhythm

IN A CARDBOARD box, hidden away in his loft, Coventry soul fan Dave Krynski keeps a single coloured light bulb and a battered cloakroom sign. When the Catacombs closed on 14th July 1974, and Walter Jackson's "Where Have All The Flowers Gone" echoed around the bare brick walls of the Midland's foremost soul club, Dave felt compelled to take something to keep as a souvenir. The club had always been fairly primitive, and the light bulbs were simply strung across the walls and ceilings. The police had closed the all-nighter early, halfway through Blue Max's set, and as the crowd clattered down the staircase to the front door, everybody knew that this was the end of an era.

It all started in the summer of 1967. Allan Smith's wife was working at Eve's Boutique, in Wolverhampton's shopping centre, and the owner's husband, Steve Dobson, was about to open a new club. Although Smith had no experience as a DJ, he convinced Dobson to let him work there. "I was with a friend of mine at a party, and we met Steve Dobson and, what can I say, I bullshitted my way in. I collected records and I'd started going to the Twisted Wheel and the Whisky in Birmingham, but I'd never deejayed before. Anyway, he gave me a chance." Allan was joined by "Farmer Carl" Dene, and before long the Catacombs was reverberating to the top sounds of the day – tracks such as the Dynatones' "Fife Piper", Evie Sands' "Picture Me Gone" and Errol Dixon & The Goodtime Band's "I Want".

Graham Warr, who deejayed later at the club, first went to the Catacombs' six months after it had opened. "There were a lot of lads in Wolverhampton, and of course, I was from Parkfields, which is the other side of town, and they didn't sort of get on together very well. I got talking to one guy from

Wolverhampton, and he said that if I went with him, he'd look after me. There'd be no trouble and all the rest of it. And I remember going that night. The Catacombs was in Temple Street, opposite the roller skating rink. There was a little glass door, and you walked up, to the first floor, into the entrance hall. That night there was a queue all the way up the road. The club wasn't very big, but they used to ram everybody in.

"It was an old lead smelting works, and the room that you walked in had the bar, and further down, was where the furnaces used to be. They were arched, and they'd removed the metal doors, painted out all the inside to make little alcoves. In these were tables and chairs, and at the end was the DJ booth. It had a slot, where the DJ could look out, on to the dance floor and the L-shaped stage." In the summer when the club was sweltering, dancers would jam the door open, and go through their moves on the rear fire escape.

Carl Dene was the first DJ to go. There were rumours he went because he played too much reggae, but the truth was far more banal. "Carl got the sack, because at the end of each night he used to announce other venues where he was deejaying" remembers Graham Warr. "He'd say, like 'I'm in Birmingham for the Locomotive on Wednesday, and don't forget to come to so and so on Friday, and the Chateau on Sunday…' Steve Dobson just couldn't stand it. So Carl went, and Bob Crocker came along and he was just amazing."

Like Smith, Bob Crocker had not deejayed before, but he was well in with one of the earliest suppliers of import soul records, F. L. Moore. Smith became known as "Allan S", and changed his name by deed poll. Allan S and Crocker became an irrepressible duo. They were constantly hunting for rare 45s, and did everything in their power to track down the big one. Crocker was not above a little deception. Imports were not that common, and when Honey Cone's "While You're Out Looking For Sugar" was a US soul hit in July 1969, Bob sold a copy to a DJ in Telford for eighty pounds. Hard to believe, but the import copy of Chairmen Of The Board's "Give Me Just A Little More Time" was a cover up at the Cats.

Allan S left his job at British Rail and opened a record shop in Wolverhampton with Crocker, where they sold second hand soul records and the early bootlegs. One night the shop was broken into, and everything was taken. So in March 1971, they set off to Leicester to visit Jeff King to replenish their stock. Bob, being a fast driver, took a corner too fast. They hit a lorry on a bend and the nineteen-year-old Crocker was killed outright. Allan was unconscious for a week, and fractured both legs. It took him three months to recover.

Barry Blakeman, Mick Norton, Chris, Dave Krynski and Rebecca Jones at the Catacombs

Gloucester's Mick Taylor, known as "Froggy", took over while Smith recuperated, and was joined behind the decks by Max Millward, better known as "Blue Max". Allan returned and for a while everything was rosy, until Froggy crashed his car near Worcester. He never returned to the Catacombs.

If a DJ talked too much at the Catacombs, the crowd would start booing. Allan considered the DJs' strength was in knowing what records to put on to keep the dance floor heaving. "The only time we ever spoke in the microphone, was to get people to move a car, or give details about forthcoming attractions. We weren't actually deejaying, we were just record playing. It was all about knowing which one to play next." While still at British Rail, the resourceful Smith would travel around the country searching for vinyl. He had a wants list, and would walk round Gloucester, Cambridge, Oxford and London to find copies of in-demand discs. He bought Jackie Lee's "Temptation Walk" from Soul City, the Dynatones' "Fife Piper" from Poor For Music on the Mile End Road. He would contact all of the mail-order dealers. More often than not, he would get ten terrible records, but there would always be the odd gem.

"Well, I got Sandi Sheldon for four shillings. It was knackered, but it played great. And I got a demo of "Ski-ing In The Snow" for next to nothing off a list, for about 2/6. Bought it blind, just because it was by the Invitations.

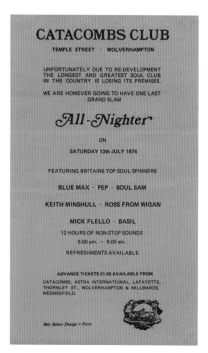

I got Johnny Sayles like that as well. Half the time it was pure luck."

Graham Warr first deejayed at the Ship & Rainbow in the Dudley Road. "There was a guy called Earl St. John, who had all the usual Tamla stuff. I asked him it would be possible to do an hour, or something like that, and he said OK. I used to play things like "Stay" by the Virginia Wolves, that was a massive record, and Chuck Jackson's "Good Things (Come To Those Who Wait)". That was a Tuesday night, and on Wednesdays the Catacombs would be open. Then there was the George at Walsall, and on Friday nights it was the Woolpack, which was under the fruit and vegetable market. Mike Hollis used to do that, he was known as Oscar Michael. And on Sundays, after the Catacombs, we'd all go to the Chateau Impney with, of course, Carl Dene."

In 1972, Steve Dobson sold the Catacombs to Astra Entertainment, the owners of the Lafayette, another Wolverhampton club. After some minor alterations it re-opened, with the DJ line-up of Allan S, Blue Max and Graham Warr. By now, Warr had started to visit the States on record finding expeditions funded by Dave Hastings at London's Record Corner. Graham would return with dozens of unknown 45s, from a warehouse in Upper Darby Philadelphia, that had recently acquired over two million records. These would form the backbone of his collection, and provide spares to sell at other clubs. Suddenly, Graham had records like Johnny Moore's "Walk Like A Man", Dena Barnes' "If You Ever Walked Out Of My Life", Saxie Russell's "Psychedelic Soul", Jimmy Conwell's "Too Much", and Butch Baker's "Working At The Go-Go".

After the Catacombs, Graham and Allan S would go to the Torch and Up The Junction to sell records. Allan remembers: "We had endless copies of things like the Soul Twins' "Quick Change

Artist". I remember going over to Up The Junction – I used to love that place, because it had a lot of atmosphere. In a way, it was like the Catacombs, like being in a cellar. It was one huge room with a bar in the centre, which you could walk all the way round. There was a stage at the top with a dance floor. It was a bit of a dive, not dirty, but dimly lit.

"Graham and I had these shoulder bags with the records in, and we were sitting in the toilet, sorting the money out, when the police raided the club and kicked the door in. They thought we were pushers, but we only had records. And on the motorway services in the morning, while everybody else was coming down, they'd sit and watch us tuck into these great big lorry driver's breakfasts."

With Fridays and Saturdays the soul nights at the Catacombs, the club opened on Mondays to cater for the British Blues revival. Live acts from the States were often backed by British blues bands. Allan remembers the night Bob & Earl turned up. "They'd done another gig somewhere in North Wales, and they had stopped off on the way to the Catacombs and had a curry and a few beers. The club was kept open, as they were late arriving. When they went on stage they were too drunk to sing, they were rolling and staggering about. Steve Dobson went on stage and told them to clear off."

There was never a traditional last record at the Catacombs, all the DJs had their own. Bob Crocker's was Eddie Holman's "(Hey There) Lonely Girl" and Allan S's was the Marketts' "Bella Delana", the flip side to "Out Of Limits".

By 1973, it was never heard again at the Catacombs, when Allan S left and Ian Pereira, a stalwart of the Northern scene better known as Pep, was added to the roster. Alan Day, joined the DJs briefly, but the final months on the Saturday night were overseen by Blue Max and Pep.

When the Torch closed, the Catacombs reigned. Steve Glover introduced items from his large British collection and records like Lou Johnson's "Unsatisfied" became massive. Dave Krynski reckons that

Blue Max's theme at the Catacombs from late '73

251

"Panic" by Reperata & The Delrons was first played at the Catacombs. He remembers asking Richard Searling to play it at Wigan, but Richard did not have it. Other 45s that were massive at the Catacombs included the Yum Yums' "Gonna Be A Big Thing", Jerry Cook's "I Hurt On The Other Side", the Glories' "I Worship You Baby", Mamie Galore's "It Ain't Necessary", Sam & Kitty's "I Got Something Good" and Lou Pride's "Comun' Home In The Mornin". Soul music could be heard on other nights, from other Midlands' names, DJs such as Bill Baker, Phil Simner, Carl Dene, Oscar Michael and Neil Rushton. Neil had the same introduction to the scene as countless others. "I got into it in '69, same as everybody really, through Dave Godin's column in *Blues &*

**Graham Warr,
Brian S and Mick Flello
at the Catacombs**

Soul. And the centre of my universe, when I was at school in the fifth and sixth form, was a place called the George Hotel in Walsall. Carl Dene was the DJ, and he had all the records that nobody else had got, like Jackie Lee's "Darkest Days". I walked in one night, and he was playing Frankie Valli's "You're Ready Now". It's a familiar story, but it was the dancing, the Ben Sherman's, the whole thing really. It was all I cared about. I started deejaying, and could have financed myself through the sixth form by that alone. I even dropped my geography A-Level, because I was too busy deejaying."

Rushton progressed through the smaller venues to the Catacombs on the midweek sessions, and ran promotions at the Queen Mary's Ballroom at Dudley Zoo. Blue Max was selling his record collection at the time, and apart from a few that Pep took like the Salvadors, Neil bought the whole lot. "From having an OK collection, I had the Catacombs' collection. I did alright at the Zoo, and took over promoting the all-dayers at Tiffany's in Coalville. I'd put advertisements in the *Echo*, and didn't have any response at all. I was panicking because I had all these DJs booked, and even though the costings were pretty low, I couldn't afford to have nobody there. People were telling me that they were going, and I went to check the PO Box in Walsall, and there was nothing. I eventually found a guy who'd listen, and he suddenly pulled out this huge sack with eight hundred applications. I had to work that night at a hospital meeting as a reporter, so my Dad filled the membership cards in and sent them off."

In Easter 1975, Rushton held the first of his promotions at the Ritz in Manchester. Two hundred turned up, but Neil could see that the venue would work. Within a few months, there were regular attendances of nine hundred people, and Rushton was earning more at the weekend than he was as an apprentice journalist.

Towards the end of 1975, Barbara Rojan called from a new publication called *Black Echoes*, to ask if Neil was interested in advertising his Heart Of England Soul Club in the newspaper. Neil agreed, and enquired whether they had any vacancies for a staff writer, as his indentures would run out in three weeks. Rushton left the *Western Star*, and started working for the new weekly.

As he walked into the paper's offices, he was greeted by Paul Phillips. Now the managing director, Phillips was then in charge of advertising, and as Neil climbed the rickety stairs, Paul called out. "Do you think this will last long? You haven't packed up a good job for this, have you?" The first issue appeared on Neil's birthday, 31st January.

CHAPTER 18

Northern Lights

ROGER HATCHER'S "We Gonna Make It" was *Black Echoes'* Single Of The Week – a fitting maxim for the fledgling paper. In an informative article, entitled "The Money Spinning Mushroom", Neil Rushton charted the growth of the Northern scene. The only slip up was the date given for the first all-nighter at the Torch – Saturday 14th April 1973. The club had actually closed one month earlier.

At the beginning of '76, the Wigan Casino was still the biggest draw on the circuit. The top sounds being played were Sam Ambrose's "They'll Be Comin", Jeanette Harper's "Put Me In Your Pocket", the Sequins' "He's A Flirt", Oscar Perry's "I Got What You Need" and Bobby Lester's "Hang Up Your Hang Ups". Mr. M's had started concentrating solely on oldies, with

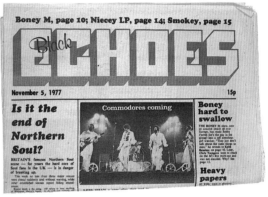

Dave Evison reviving Wheel and Torch sounds. A decision that Steve Whittle, in discussion with Dave Evison on Stoke's Radio Signal, thought was a wrong move. "When the Mecca started playing New York disco, there were certain tracks that were accepted like Kim Tolliver and Black Nasty, but I think the Mecca went too obscure, in that respect, for an all-night scene. The new material started slipping a bit. But when they started the oldies all-nighters, to me that was the downfall of Wigan."

Wigan Casino DJ John Vincent, who started his career deejaying at the Esquire Club in Sheffield, was busy promoting weekly all-nighters at Samantha's. Sharing the turntable action with Ian Dewhirst, John invited guest DJs such as Colin Curtis and John Manship. Jeanette Harper's Wigan favourite, the Yum Yums' "Gonna Be A Big Thing", Al De Lory's "Right On",

Exhausted record dealer at Cleethorpes

Frankie Crocker's "Love Man" and Kim Tolliver's 'I Don't Know What Foot To Dance On" were the Yorkshire club's winners.

Samantha's was formerly known as the Heartbeat. John Vincent became involved with the club in late 1971, and the first all-dayers started. The DJs at the time, included Hector and Steve Elliot from Selecta Disc, and famous Sheffield soul fan Mopsey. It was not long before monthly all-nighters began, and although the first two were rather disastrous with only sixty people turning up, the word spread and the crowd grew to around the two hundred and fifty mark. Kev Roberts and Richard Searling joined the spinning side and before long the all-nighters were fortnightly. Huddersfield's Twink came on board, and when work commitments forced Richard Searling to leave, Ian "Frank" Dewhirst, Paul Curzon and Snowy from Doncaster started deejaying duties. Samantha's regulars will remember the monsters of the day: the Pointer Sisters' "Send Him Back", Willie Mitchell's "The Champion" and the Detroit Executives. Paul Curzon's English label collection was put to great use in the oldies room, the Hallam Suite, and Howard from Sheffield and Wigan's Billy Paul were brought in to help.

Attempts to establish a permanent soul venue in the Midlands had proved difficult since the closure of the Catacombs in the summer of 1974. In *New Musical Express*, Bob Fisher voiced his concern at the prejudice against soul music and its followers in the region. Given that much of the initial impetus

to the Northern soul scene had derived from the Midlands and that most towns in the area had devoted fans who spent heavily in the local record stores, there seemed to be an almost paranoid fear of soul music amongst club managers. Fisher wrote of one large disco-hotel on the A64 between Leicester and Nottingham which displayed a sign stating: 'WE DO NOT PLAY SOUL MUSIC'. Yet the music played was clearly soul and they regularly featured local soul bands like the Hi-Vibrations. Letters had been received by the local newspaper in Leicester from teenagers who had been refused admission to local discotheques for "wearing baggy trousers".

But Fisher held high hopes for a collective that was determined to find a suitable venue which could be home to the legions of soul fans in the area – the West Midlands Soul Club. Run by John Carter, Mick Flello, Steve Russell and Joe Bragg, the club hoped to emulate Chris Burton's International Soul Club, which ran successful one-off promotions around the country. Although Fisher was under the impression that it was a new organisation, the West Midlands Soul Club had been promoting events since the demise of the Catacombs. Mick Flello explained in *Black Echoes*: "We've got four thousand members, and we run a lot of very popular promotions at places like Nottingham Palais. Clubs like ours get on with the job of promoting Northern soul but we never seem to get the attention we deserve. I suppose it's a question of not what we do, but who you know. We try not to clash with other promoters doing the same thing. There's a lot of bitterness between characters on the scene but it's silly. We're all interested in the same thing – the music." The most popular items on the WMSC turntables were the Skullsnaps' "I'm Your Pimp", Rodger Collins' "Sexy Sugar Plum", the Rimshots' "Do What You Feel", Evelyn Thomas' "Doomsday" and Dennis Coffey's "If You Can't Dance To This".

The Blackpool Mecca still featured a blend of old and new. Colin Curtis picked the Rimshots' track popular at the WMSC, Cameos' "Find My Way", Len Jewell's "All My Good Loving", Dobie Gray's "Honey, You Can't Take It Back" and a track from the Smoke Sugar album "I Can't Get Enough".

Rushton's last featured venue was the Lincolnshire Soul Club's fortnightly all-nighters at Cleethorpes Pier. The venue had proved so successful that Wigan Casino had tried to muscle in on the action, by promoting a rival all-nighter at the nearby Winter Gardens. After four disastrous attempts, Casino manager Mike Walker finally pulled out.

Mary Chapman promoted a soul night at Walscott Village Hall in 1972, and from this grew the Lincolnshire Soul Club. An all-dayer held in Cleethorpes gave her the idea of running all-nighters, and on 7th February 1975, the first "Talk Of The North" nighter started on Cleethorpes Pier, the first record played was Frankie Valli's "You're Ready Now". The runaway success of Cleethorpes was such that Mary was forced to find another location to prevent the ballroom at the end of the pier collapsing into the sea. The

Winter Gardens was the ideal site and the two were run in tandem. The DJs, as many as twelve, provided a unique mix of current tracks, rarer '70s releases and older style stompers. The club's most popular tracks included Al De Lory's "Right On", the Anderson Brothers' "I Can See Him Losing You", Kim Tolliver, James Fountain's "Seven Day Lover" and Rain's "Out Of My Mind". DJs were "Poke" aka Blair Aidyn, Soul Sam, Frank, Ginger Taylor, Eddie Antimes, Rick Scott, Rick Todd, Johnny Manship, Pep, John Vincent, Dick Jervis, Dave Appleyard and Chris Dalton. Guests included Richard Searling, Kev Roberts, Tony Dellar, Eric Wood, Graham Coates and Chris Fletcher.

With the competition, from 10th February, *Blues & Soul* went weekly.

By April 1976, Neil Rushton's monthly all-dayers at the Ritz, in Manchester, were attracting crowds of well over fifteen hundred. What made the event such a magnet for dance fans was the broad range of soul on offer. Ian Levine and Colin Curtis were continuing to push out the musical boundaries, Wigan's Richard Searling was mixing '60s stompers with contemporary releases, and DJs like Ian Dewhirst, Dave Evison and Johnny Manship provided a fascinating range of diverse styles. Manship is a well known record dealer on the Northern scene. His elder brother was a mod who introduced John to soul music in the Sixties. One of Johns' earliest experiences of all-nighters was the Lantern in Market Harborough, which to progressive rock fans was better known as the Frollicking Knee Cap.

A newcomer to the Ritz' roster, in late 1976, was Pat Brady. He had heard all about the rare soul scene from older lads who had been to the Twisted Wheel. Pat went to an all-nighter at Va-Va's, and remembers Richard Searling playing sounds such as the Adventurers and Sharon Soul. Aged sixteen, he began to buy soul records from Soul Bowl and made the occasional visit to the Blackpool Mecca. With his collection growing, he was given an opportunity to DJ, by John Vincent, at an all-dayer at Samantha's in Sheffield. Pat spoke to Neil Rushton, who had just returned from the States and, making a good impression, was given the chance to DJ at the Ritz.

"I remember following on from Ian Levine at the Ritz, who was playing what we'd now call Seventies' disco – and the floor was absolutely empty. And all the collectors crowded round, and I remember playing the Twans, Bernie Williams, Don Varner and everything that was pretty big then. And I was off and running." His next step on the DJ ladder was at Terry Samson's all-nighters at the Kay Gee Bee, in Sheffield. At a time when the Northern circuit was going back underground, Samson identified a resurgence in the Yorkshire soul scene, and for the next couple of years, his Northern Soul Scene ran successful promotions. From the OKeh Soul Club in Keighley, Samson teamed up with DJ Chris King.

King looked older than his fifteen years, and managed to convince the management at the Nottingham Palais to give him a job as a DJ. Chris recalls how locals would ask him for soul records. "Everybody was coming and saying have you got these records, and I would say, yeah, I've had them for ages. They didn't believe me, but before long, on a regular Friday and Saturday night, I'd be playing things like Lou Johnson's "Unsatisfied", Patrice Holloway's "Love And Desire", things like that. It wasn't a Northern crowd, just regular punters who were in to have a drink and a punch up. We used to finish at two o'clock, and then go to Wigan. I knew so many of the records, and those I didn't, I made a beeline to get them. So, a totally naive thing to do, but with a friend, I went to the States. We found this little old guy, who used to live in Chicago, and he'd moved down to Miami. And he'd brought six sixty-foot trailers full of records. We were pulling stuff out of there, like five, ten copies of Mel Britt. Loads in boxes of twenty five. And I used them to trade for other records, and built my collection up from that.

Bobby Hutton

"I got talking to Richard and Russ, and everybody else at the Casino, and one night Russ says to me 'Have you got your records?' One of the other DJs hadn't turned up, so I did a spot and blew them away. Because I was a Mecca DJ, I could get the Mecca halls for all-nighters. I used to do Tiffany's at Coalville, which was a great all-nighter with about a thousand people in. Then I hitched up with Terry, and that was amazing. We were running Redditch, Birmingham Locarno, Nottingham's Tiffany's and Palais, Derby Assembly Rooms, Derby Kings Hall and Newcastle Tiffany's – both Stoke and the Geordie one. I remember one Bank Holiday Sunday, we had an all-dayer at Birmingham with fifteen hundred people, then an all-nighter at Derby with two thousand in. Terry drove to Chester-le-Street with fifteen hundred and another one in Nottingham with a thousand people. That's how huge it was. Now you're lucky to get five hundred at an all-nighter."

The Heart Of England ended on a high in 1976, with an all-dayer at the Blackpool Mecca, where Neil Rushton deejayed alongside Ian Levine, Colin Curtis, Richard Searling and Les Cockell, and an all-dayer at the Birmingham Locarno. For good measure, there was also what was advertised as a "Boxing Day Orgy" at the Ritz, Manchester.

Over twenty years after the event, Kev Roberts' *Togetherness Soul Review* printed a chart of the records that were played at the Ritz circa 1977. The play list was an eclectic mix of soul, current disco releases and obscure Seventies 45s. Top of the chart was Lou Pride's "I'm Comun Home In The Mornin", a rumbling steam train of a stomper from El Paso, Texas. This was Lou's first release, and since that auspicious start, Lou recorded for a host of small companies – Albatross, Gemco, Onyx, Black Gold – before Curtis Mayfield signed him to the Curtom label. The Tavares' brothers "Heaven Must Be Missing A Angel" was a new import release, the ninth successive R&B hit for the former Chubby & The Turnpikes. Bobby Hutton's "Lend A Hand", which had been a Mecca discovery, was from the album produced by Dee Ervin in 1973. Amongst the other twenty examples given, were Case Of Tymes' "Manifesto", Oscar Perry's "Main String", James Well's excellent "Baby I'm Still The Same Man", Bernie Williams' super rare "Ever Again", and former Steely Dan and Doobie Brothers' vocalist Mike McDonald's "God Knows".

Soul Sam, Poke and Johnny Manship had built up Cleethorpes' reputation by word of mouth, as the club was never advertised or promoted heavily through the usual soul publications. Sadly, for Mary Chapman's Lincolnshire Soul Club, pressure from the police forced the Cleethorpes all-nighter to close. The sessions at the Pier finished, following similar problems and only the Winter Gardens continued. Mary Chapman's belief that the publicity the scene was receiving was of the wrong kind had, unfortunately, come true. All-dayers became the order of the day, and the first was scheduled for 19th December 1976. These ran right through to 1981, with DJs Arthur Fenn, Rob Smith and the late Nev Wherry. Nev Wherry, DJ for the East Anglian Soul Club at St. Ives, was a popular character, who died in tragic circumstances on 28th February 1980. Over four hundred friends from the scene attended his funeral.

"Take it easy, please! Take it easy, DON'T PUSH! No pushing at the back!"

Wigan Bouncer on "This England" 1977

CHAPTER 19

It Ain't No Secret

THE ST. IVES ALL-NIGHTERS run by Ken Cox became a lifeline to the many Northern Soul fans living in East Anglia. Still not the most accessible part of the country, the East Anglian Soul Club flourished during 1977, until the St. Ivo Centre all-nighters were stopped because of police complaints to the management committee about drug offences. Regular DJs were Soul Sam, John Vincent, Ginger and Eddie, Hammy, Nev Wherry and Brian Rae, and big sounds heard during its heyday included the Barons "Since You're Gone", Prince Ella & Sydney Jones' "Baby Sugar I Love You", Betty Fikes' "Prove It To You", New People's "I'm Asking You", Burning Bush's "You Keep Putting The Burning On", Magnificent Men's "Keep On Climbing", Flaming Emeralds' "Have Some Everybody" and Bobby Diamond's "Stop". After the closure of St. Ives, the club carried on at the Peterborough Wirrina Stadium in Bishops Road, Peterborough.

The East coast developed into a thriving soul scene, with all-dayers at the Howard Mallett, in Cambridge, with DJs Richard Searling, Ian Clark and Tony Dellar, who had been deejaying at the Mallett since 1970. Terry Samson's Northern Soul Scene moved into the area and held their Loughborough first all-nighter on 10th September. There were all-nighters at King's Lynn, Great Yarmouth, and Norwich, where the weekly Back Street Soul Club is still going strong.

Andy Rix, DJ and researcher for Kent Records, lives in Boston, and first went to an all-nighter at the Wirrina Stadium when he was thirteen. "My eldest brother was at college and was friendly with a group of guys who frequented Cleethorpes Pier all-nighters. As an impressionable twelve-year-old, I used to listen to the 45s he borrowed and found that I liked them...I was intrigued by the stories of staying out all night dancing, listening to American soul records, and persuaded my parents to let me go to the local bash, which was where the bus to Cleethorpes left from. The DJ was called Eggy Molen and he used to play Northern and Motown. I'd known this guy for a few years as he had been a one-time boyfriend of my elder sister. His willingness to play things to me, coupled with meeting my brother's friends and buying records off them, led to a growing interest in the scene and, when I was thirteen, I went to my first 'niter at the Wirrina in Peterborough."

The division on the scene continued, and through the columns of *Black Echoes*, the spat between Ian Levine and Soul Sam continued. The Mecca DJ bitched: "It takes more skill to mix two records together than stop in-between each record and announce the title. I'd rather create a better dance floor atmosphere and keep the patrons on it than play to an empty dance floor like Soul Sam does to some records he plays." Ian Levine would eventually take his mixing skills to London.

Director Tony Palmer is no stranger to controversy. The history of popular music, *All You Need Is Love*, won him few friends when broadcast on television in 1976. *200 Motels*, co-directed with Frank Zappa, was condemned by *Time Out* as a "real dinosaur", and later productions, such as his nine-hour biopic, *Wagner*, were panned for being long-winded and riddled with illogical references. Much of the same criticism was aimed at his Wigan Casino documentary *This England*.

The thirty minute film, broadcast in December 1977, was rightly condemned for the Casino's supposed links to Wigan's grimy industrial past. Footage of derelict and faded buildings was interspersed with sepia library stills of Victorian mill workers, miners and gaunt street urchins. A connection Russ Winstanley became uncomfortable with, and although he had worked closely with the production team initially, he distanced himself from the proceedings and left. The soundtrack was limited to brief snatches of the MVPs, Rain, "Popcorn" Wylie, the Lovelites and Judy Street; and the inclusion of three awful folk songs – played in their entirety – was a pointless excercise – what the tale of the diligent ant and the grasshopper, "glad of sunshine", had to do with the soul scene was anybody's guess.

Although the club's members had voted against the filming, huge lights were suspended from the ceiling, and spoiled the Friday oldies all-nighter and the following Saturday for many of the regulars. Many complaints were voiced at Mike Walker, who had conducted the straw poll, and disappointment was compounded by the eventual screening.

The dancing was well-covered, but much of the action was filmed out of synch with the music, or dramatically slowed down. Bootleg videos of the programme, although of poor quality, contain unseen footage of the dancing and people crowded around the record bar. Tim Ashibende stands, arms crossed, watching soul fans flicking through the boxes of records. Without the distraction of the soundtrack, it's a far more evocative memory of the club. As is the opening sequence of the gum-chewing, all-nighter crowd, clutching holdalls, throwing the entrance money down, and pushing their way into the Casino.

Dave Withers, the film's spokesman for the soul crowd, gave an articulate summary of what the club meant to him. His final comments summed up for many, their strong bond with the club: "But the fact is, that, if Wigan shut down, if I heard during the week that there was to be no next week, I wouldn't know what to do. It'd be like instant nostalgia – that would be it. You'd think, God, I'm gonna be looking back for the rest of my life. I wouldn't really be able to cope – I'd have to sort my life out again. What am I gonna do now, where am I gonna go, I couldn't go to normal clubs…"

Without prior warning, the Highland Room at the Blackpool Mecca closed in October. The Mecca organisation were not making enough money from the whole complex during the winter months, and the decision was made to let out the Highland Room for private functions.

Black Echoes published an article entitled "Is It The End Of Northern Soul?", which attracted a response from Soul Sam. He reiterated that the Blackpool Mecca had had nothing to do with Northern Soul for the last two years and although its sudden closure was a disappointment for lovers of modern soul music, it was no loss to the Northern scene. Sam could see no reason why two distinct styles were being played together.

Following the fantastic turnout, for a farewell all-dayer at the Mecca, the management changed its minds and Saturday nights were allowed to continue.

Amongst the regular batch of records Russ Winstanley received from Simon Soussan in January 1978, was an acetate copy of an unissued Motown recording by Frank Wilson called "Do I Love You (Indeed I Do)". Originally scheduled for release on the company's Soul subsidiary in December 1965, the track had been withdrawn because of Wilson's reluctance to promote the song. He was more keen to develop a career as a songwriter and producer, which in the end proved to be a wise decision.

Motown had produced five hundred DJ copies of the disc, and the majority of these were destroyed when the record was removed from the release schedule. A file copy was kept with the master tape in the company's vaults, and this sample was borrowed by Motown employee and long time fan Tom DePerrio, who was working on a compilation of unissued recordings.

DePerrio worked at the company's offices on Hollywood's Sunset Boulevard and discovered hundreds of unreleased Motown recordings on acetates that were due to be thrown away. He sifted through the songs and compiled a list of over thirty outstanding tracks which he suggested would make a great compilation. The idea was rejected until he found himself employed as assistant to Iris Gordy, the Creative Division's vice-president. One morning, as she left the office for a manicure appointment, and being behind with her release schedules, Gordy asked DePerrio to put something together "if you know what's good for your ass". The previously unreleased material was collated and "From The Vaults" was quickly issued on the Motown subsidiary Natural Resources label in January 1979.

DePerrio lived with Lester Tipton, who had recorded the Northern favourite "This Won't Change" for Lou Beatty's LaBeat Records in Detroit. However, Tipton did not own a copy, so when Simon Soussan mentioned to DePerrio that he was in contact with Beatty, it seemed a great opportunity.

In a letter to DJ and collector Ian Clark, DePerrio explained how Soussan stole the Frank Wilson record from his apartment. "Simon Soussan at one time was a guest in my home one evening (as a matter of fact Lester was there at the time) and he went through all kinds of gyrations about how he could contact Lou Beatty…and get a hold of Lester's record for me. Okay, I have no reason to distrust. We're talking about a deal for his Uptown Festival record with Motown at the time, and I don't ever take anybody for anything 'til they show me. Anyway, I loaned him my Andantes single on VIP and my Frank Wilson single on Soul. But not to worry because why bother. He'll lose in the long run. Not I. But if anyone should ask you, yes…he stole it from me, booted it, and then sold my original."

Unaware of the circumstances relating to the record, Russ Winstanley covered the disc as "Do I Love You" by Eddie Foster. Foster had recorded "I Never Knew" for the West Coast IN label, which had been a popular cut at the Casino. The heavy metallicised acetate was adorned with a Motown label and Russ put a white sticker with the legend "EDDIE FOSTER" scrawled in felt tip. Almost immediately, the track became the biggest sound at the all-nighter. Rumours abounded that there were more copies in existence, but a few months later when it had become clear that it was as rare as first expected, Russ uncovered the disc.

The original surfaced in 1978, when Soussan sold his collection to Les McCutcheon, a dealer who traded under the name of Colin Bee. By this time, bootlegs of the record, credited to Eddie Foster, and pressed on the IN label, had sold nearly twenty five thousand copies. The disc was sold by McCutcheon for £250 to Jonathan Woodliffe, from Nottingham, who gradually moved away from the Northern Soul scene to become a modern soul DJ at events like the Southport Dance Weekender. Woodliffe knew that Kev Roberts had a large collection of twelve-inch promo singles from when he lived in the States. He approached Kev and

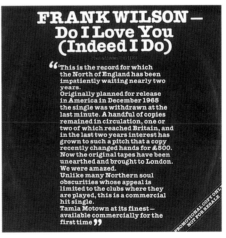

**FRANK WILSON —
Do I Love You
(Indeed I Do)**

"This is the record for which the North of England has been impatiently waiting nearly two years.
Originally planned for release in America in December 1965 the single was withdrawn at the last minute. A handful of copies remained in circulation, one or two of which reached Britain, and in the last two years interest has grown to such a pitch that a copy recently changed hands for £500. Now the original tapes have been unearthed and brought to London. We were amazed.
Unlike many Northern soul obscurities whose appeal is limited to the clubs where they are played, this is a commercial hit single.
Tamla Motown at its finest — available commercially for the first time"

offered to exchange the Frank Wilson single for about £350 worth of records. "For about seven years" remembers Roberts "people didn't take the record seriously. The problem was that it was a Motown record, and if I'd heard it once, I had heard it a thousand times in the States 'There's a warehouse with five hundred copies in'. But because the Northern scene was dwindling in the

Eighties, nobody actually rang me up and said 'Hey, can I come round and look at your Frank Wilson 45?' – there was no interest in it. Until 1989, when Tim Brown looked at it and asked if I was interested in selling it. I wasn't going to sell it, because I knew the offer would be about £500. When he came round the second time, he was setting up Goldmine Records, he said he wanted to buy Frank Wilson and offered £5000. I said OK, it's for sale!" The only other known copy turned up in 1990, when American Motown collector Ron Murphy sold his collection to Martin Koppell.

Murphy was a former Motown engineer, who Neil Rushton met in Detroit, when he was working with Inner City. "I was told about this guy" recalls Rushton "who was into Sixties soul, and I thought 'Yeah, probably never even heard of Ric-Tic', but I didn't realise that he had been a Motown engineer. The first thing he said was 'No, I haven't got the Magnetics, I haven't got Norma Jenkins.' And I wasn't bothered about Northern Soul, I thought he was being a bit cocky. But he was a lovely guy, and he played me all these unreleased Motown tracks – all on white labels. He'd just bought the D-Town catalogue master tapes that day, which he showed me. Things like Dee Edwards' "All The Way Home". And I asked the obvious question – 'Well, Ron, have you got Frank Wilson?', and he said 'Yeah' and pulled it out. I was making a lot of money then in Detroit with the techno stuff, so I offered him $2,000 for it, I don't know why, sort of nostalgia. But he wouldn't part with it. Then a couple of months later, I was in Chicago. I was with Kevin Saunderson, because he'd just had a hit, and I said 'Are you going to buy me a present, Kev?', so we drove from Chicago to Detroit and offered Murphy $5,000, but he still wouldn't sell it. And then, six months later, he sold his complete collection to Martin Koppell for $20,000."

This copy is now owned by Scottish collector, Kenny Burrell, who allegedly paid a staggering £15,000 for the Frank Wilson single. There are constant rumours of further copies existing; an American dealer is reputed to own the disc, and there is supposedly a photograph which shows somebody with an armful of copies.

Neil Rushton's Heart Of England Soul Club held a "Tear The Roof Off '78 All-Dayer" at the Ritz in Manchester, with what was advertised as "The North's Biggest Funk/Disco ALL-DAYER EVER!!!" Deejayed by Ian Levine and Colin Curtis from the Mecca, Graham Warr of Chaplin's, Birmingham,

Mike Shaft of Rufus, Manchester, Paul Schofield and Ian Dewhirst from Leeds Central.

"There was a whole thing going on in London where Chris Hill and Robbie Vincent were doing big all-dayers with different DJs." remembers Neil "And I thought that with the Ritz, we had moved on. It had gone from what was Northern Soul, to be a combination of older soul and brand new releases. I'd only just got into brand new disco, jazz funk and the rest. But it was really random and it was fantastic. The Northern stuff was becoming less and less relevant. The great thing was that we had the Cleethorpes crowd with Johnny Manship, Ian Dewhirst and Pat Brady from the Leeds area, Colin and Ian from Blackpool and Richard Searling was representing the Wigan side of it all. So there was a good combination. At the time, everyone was more and more obsessed with new music and we wanted to expel the Northern thing. So I thought let's try and take on the London guys."

On Friday 17th August, Wigan held a Mods '60s all-nighter. The Mod Revival had come to monopolise the popular music press that year, having developed from the Jam and similar bands on the punk scene. These groups included soul music covers in their sets, and inevitably the fans began to hunt the originals down. The mod revival towards the end of 1979, encouraged promoters on the Northern scene to run themed evenings. Chris King, advertised as "The King Of The Mods", Clive "Scooter Wiz Kid" Jones, "Mad Mod" Minshull, and "Mirror Maniac" Cockney Mick were the DJs at the event held at the Top Of The World, Stafford. At the Birmingham Locarno, Chris King and Brian Rae were offering prizes for the scooter with the most mirrors. Casino Classics' label issued a version of Booker T & The MGs' "Green Onions" but were losing out to an influx of import copies of the original. And in November, Tamla-Motown issued "20 Mod Classics".

Moses Dillard

CHAPTER 20

Young Mod's Forgotten Story

HOME GROWN R&B and soul acts were the mainstay of the club scene during the mid-Sixties. The Alan Bown Set, often featuring the vocal talents of Robert Palmer, were well received for their covers of songs by Little Anthony & The Imperials, Edwin Starr and the Temptations. Ferris Wheel, with Linda Lewis, and later Marsha Hunt, were a regular fixture – their "Number One Guy" was played at the Torch. And Herbie Goins & The Night Timers' "Number One In Your Heart" became a mod anthem all over the country. The fact that the majority of the bands' members were white, was incidental.

Records by white artists were regularly played alongside black American originals. Country veteran Charlie Rich's "Love Is After Me" was a much sought after disc, as were 45s by countless other white American acts. If the arrangement and rhythm fitted in with the real stuff, then that was OK by the club crowd – it wasn't only black artists and producers who copied the Motown sound, everybody did it.

Elvis Presley's B-side "Rubberneckin'" was played at the Twisted Wheel, and "Little Queenie" by Bill Black's Combo – the same musicians that played on many of Presley's early rock 'n' roll hits – was an enormously popular instrumental. While it was known that some of the records were by white singers – who knew or cared about the skin colour of Billy Harner, Barbara Mills, Dottie Cambridge, Rufus Lumley, April Stevens or Billy Joe Royal? Italian-American Frankie Valli's "You're Ready Now", was, for many, the first introduction to the Northern scene. Incidentally, when the Four Seasons had their first number one with "Sherry" in 1962, not only was it a massive R&B hit, but when an unscrupulous Italian promoter put a group together to masquerade as the genuine article, he used four black guys.

Tracks by American white acts were acceptable because they were unknown to the majority of the dancers. Spiral Starecase's "More Today Than

271

HOMER BANKS

Yesterday" was a million seller in the States, but the band were anonymous in Britain. Provided the white acts were not household names, the disc's credibility remained intact. When Simon Soussan found Paul Anka's "Can't Help Lovin' You", he covered it up as Johnny Caswell.

Tony Blackburn's third-rate interpretation of Doris Troy's "I'll Do Anything" had first been played by Keith Minshull as a practical joke. It went on to become the first release on the Casino Classics label, and the Wigan faithful greeted his personal appearance on the Casino stage with great applause. Soul Sam's spin of the theme from *Hawaii Five-O* was a gag that backfired, when hundreds bought the copies that Selecta Disc imported.

By the mid Seventies, with DJs becoming desperate in their search for the pounding stompers that Wigan loved, obscure B-sides and flops from the murky fringes of British pop provided an immediate alternative. Russ Winstanley had played Helen Shapiro's "Stop And You Will Become Aware", concealed as Dana Valery's "Stop Pretending", in early 1978, and by the summer, Richard Searling's playlist included ex-Seeker Judith Durham. It all became too much, when children's TV presenter Muriel Day's "Nine Times Out Of Ten" began to fill the floor.

The Blackpool Mecca's conversion to disco was absolute, and the struggle to find rare soul was abandoned. Nobody from the South of England was going to waste time and money travelling miles to hear records that could be heard in a local club. Or for that matter, journey to Wigan to hear Jackie Trent and Sandie Shaw. The film *Quadrophenia* had come out, and captured the imagination of teenagers, who quickly adopted the fashions and musical taste of the Mods. Many joined the soul crowd at Wigan, and disgruntled regulars were horrified when Russ played Prince Buster's "Al Capone".

Terry Davis, who had been one of the handful of London DJs to play Northern Soul records in the early Seventies, introduced a new format in April 1978. Advertised as a "60's Soul Party", the Wednesday evenings at The Prince of Wales in Hammersmith, West London, were unique in that, as well as playing oldies that were popular on the Northern circuit, Terry also introduced mid-tempo and the occasional slow record to the evening's play list. People travelled from all over the South of England; Worthing, Hemel Hemstead, Kent and Weybridge and filled a mid-week venue that was only open during regular licensing hours.

"I obviously enjoyed the Blackbyrds, Brass Construction and other music of the day, but was beginning to get withdrawal symptoms for Motown, Atlantic, Stax and the music we used to play. I suppose, in a way, we pioneered that whole Sixties revival thing, by insisting on playing records that were known in the Sixties. While we not averse to playing Northern records, we tended to choose the ones that were released in the UK, on Stateside, London, Pye International and so on. They were genuinely British releases that had been played in the clubs at the time. And I wanted to play deep soul records, as I found that even the dancers didn't mind the odd slow record. There's always scope for them, a few records every hour.

"I first met Randy Cozens there and of course, Ady Croasdell, who I knew from the record stall in Berwick Street market, and I believe used to go to the Wheatsheaf. When the Prince Of Wales came to a close, I was approached by Randy about running a similar thing elsewhere. I made a few trips up the West End, but we couldn't find anywhere suitable. So the next thing I knew, Randy had talked to Ady and found this place in Covent Garden. And I was asked, along with Tony Ellis and various others, about doing a deejay spot."

On 17th August 1979, Randy and Ady held a similar one-off night at Henri's Bar, downstairs at the Bedford Head in Covent Garden. Under the auspices of the "Southgate 60s Rhythm & Soul Club", a name taken from Dave Godin's early fanzine, the advertisement in *Black Echoes* proclaimed it would be the "Original Mod Revival – Rhythm & Soul is

274

back in the West End after well over a decade." With the doors closed by nine o'clock, faces from Brighton, Kettering, Southampton and Worthing were there en masse. Tony Rounce played the first record that night – Johnny Taylor's "Just The One I've Been Looking For".

Ady Croasdell, a soul fan since the days of Geno Washington, recalled his first introduction to the early days of the rare soul scene. "I'd been to my first all-nighter at this tiny little village just eight or nine miles outside Harborough called Kelmarsh. I'd always like soul music and at midnight about one hundred and fifty skinheads turned up. I was actually a long-haired skinhead, but these were serious skinheads, slick cool looking ones.

"It was a disused railway station about half a mile from the village and as well as the usual Stax, Atlantic and Tamla, I heard "The Entertainer", the Esquires and the Fascinations. This skinhead called George – the King of Kellmarsh – says to me 'Nice to have you along. Do you want any gear?' I had a pretty good idea what he was on about, but I'd never seen it before, or had it or knew anything about it. So I'm like 'Yeah, yeah, I love gear', so I bought ten shillings worth and got five green & clears. I pretended to swallow them and hid them in a matchbox. Anyway I stayed until five or six in the morning and had a really good time. I had these things in the matchbox in my pocket, and it was pretty dangerous then because if you got caught with them, you could get put inside. You could get three months for having some pep pills. I remember it was five or six miles back to my home, and luckily it was a quiet country road. But everytime I saw a car coming, I put the matchbox down, and carried on walking. When it had gone I turned round and picked the bastard up again. It took me five hours to get home.

"That was my first all-nighter, and shortly after someone must have told me about Jeff King on Leicester Market. I'd started asking about the records

THE SAPPHIRES
Swan Records
PM.: Bill Holmes
BO: Associated Booking Corporation

Carol Jackson, age 20; George Garner, age 23, and Joe Livingston, age 22, are the three talents that make up the popular singing group known as the Sapphires. They all come from Philadelphia, a city where pop competition runs high, but this group has not only held its own but is giving the rest of the country a run for its money. The group has been together for about two years and in that time has been polishing up its material in a night club and theater act. Jerry Ross, the producer. . . . . em, and the rest is record history. . . . . d dancing.

and so I got there and found all these records. I knew one or two, I'd probably got the naffer more cheap ones. He was playing me things like Human Beinz. He said it was really massive at the moment. I'd not heard it before, but with all that fuzz guitar I didn't like it. That was a tenner and Chubby Checker's "At The Discotheque" was a fiver. So I bought a couple of records and then I said: 'Oh, by the way, you haven't got any gear have you?'. He says 'Have a word with Batman'. This skinny looking mod bloke with a Twisted Wheel type blazer says 'Come here'. In the middle of Leicester Market, with hundreds of people milling about, walking up and down the stalls, and he opens his jacket and and he's got all these John Dickenson envelopes you put wages in. So he says 'Well, blues are so much…black bombers are so and so…green & clears are this much…'. ooh, so I says 'Bloody hell, I like them black bombers, I'll have some of them'. Jeff King was a lot older than me…I can't remember much about his personality except he was very amiable for a crook. The next time I went to the market he had pressings of the Poets' "She Blew A Good Thing" for sale at fifteen bob.

"At the next all-nighter I took three of them and this skinhead girl comes up to me and says 'Don't it make your head feel like it's got a hedgehog on it?' It was a good point, well made. She was the same girl who came up to me and said that it was nice to have a few wierdos here, 'cause I had long hair at the time. The Northamptonshire scene was going at the same time as The Wheel. I mean a lot of people say that it started there, but there were always people around Bedford, Luton, Corby and Kettering. We used to have all-nighters at this disused hen house in a village called Bletsoe, about ten miles north of Bedford. Somebody had hired a generator to get the decks going, bit like the rave scene. I remember dancing to Little Richard's "I Don't Wanna Discuss It'. I had Dr Martens on, doing some kind of fast moonhop. In the morning I had dust and chicken feed all over my trousers. This place wasn't even on the bloody road, you'd need an Ordnance Survey map just to find it."

Randy and Ady's club converted to the 6Ts Rhythm & Soul Club and a different venue – the Railway Hotel in West Hampstead. The pub had a long history as a soul haunt; during the Sixties it was known as Klooks Kleek and was a popular R&B venue, and in the early Seventies, it was The Bird's Nest, with Northern Soul nights run by Dave Rivers and Dave Burton.

The 6Ts Rhythm & Soul Club's first night was Friday 18th October. Situated in the upstairs Starlight Room, it became very popular and a regular complaint was of the difficulty in getting served at the bar. An eclectic mix of sounds included Maxine Brown, Spooner's Crowd's "Two In The Morning", the Impressions, Chuck Jackson, Solomon Burke, the Jewels and Nina Simone's "My Baby Just Cares For Me" which was an early favourite. It began attracting soul fans from all over the country: Russ Taylor from Flint, Richie Andrew and Bob Foster from Llandudno, John Farrell from Worcester and Ian "Ric Tic" Popple from Walsall. Torch regular and Peterborough all-nighter DJ Mick Smith, and Pete Widdison were seconded for turntable duty.

Amongst the records that set the 6Ts nights alight were John Farrell's discovery by Etta James "Mellow Fellow", Lenny O'Henry's "Across The Street", Junior Walker's B-side "Tune Up", a John Anderson find by The Cobra Kings "Big Limas", Googie Rene Combo's "Chic A Boo, Johnny Copeland "It's Me", Ray Johnson's "Sherry's Party", Paul Gayten's "Nervous

Boogie" – the parameters defined by the club's name being stretched to include Fifties sounds. When DJ Pete Widdison swung from the rafters at Christmas 1980, the manager, being less than impressed, decided enough was enough and stopped the club using the pub.

In 1980, Chris Savory, together with Nick Marshall and Dave Bell, started a Sixties soul night at the Bear Hotel in West Brampton near Newcastle in Staffordshire. This was a great success and became a

277

regular monthly event. The cellar bar was often packed with soul fans going on to the Friday oldies all-nighters at Wigan.

At the beginning of 1981, the 6Ts club held an all-nighter at Studio 21 in London's Oxford Street, the former site of the Last Chance. Then on Friday 20th February 1981, it moved to the 100 Club, the home of today's 6Ts all-nighters – and today one of the longest lasting clubs in London. Tony Rounce kicked off the evening with "If" by The Mayfield Singers. After a one-off at the Notre Dame Hall, off Leicester Square, 6Ts returned to the 100 Club and held its first all-nighter, with Roger Stewart spinning the first record.

Wigan Casino was a different kind of animal, when Iain Stewart revisited the club in August 1979, and reported the trip in his fanzine *Soul Symbol*. The last time Stewart had been to the club, it was a cool, friendly journey, but this time, "Ouch!…As we were moving out of the station, a crowd of lads came bursting back in – here we go I thought – well, nothing came of it but I was in for a shock when we hit the pavement. The Old Bill was everywhere, cars, dogs, patrolmen, the lot. I was still not sure what was going to happen, I soon found out. We were quickly herded together and then escorted to the Casino in case of an attack by the local murder squad. Strewth, what a start to the night."

The Friday oldies all-nighters had started in 1976, but the playlist was not ambitious or particularly daring. Iain wondered what the kids would have done if the DJs had played sounds like Brice Coefield's "Ain't That Right", the Master Four's "Love From The Far East", Frank Polk's "Love Is Dangerous" or Tony Middleton's "To The Ends Of The Earth"? At twenty four, Iain felt like a relic, surrounded by hundreds of seventeen and eighteen-year-olds, whose idea of oldies only goes

278

back two years. However, Stewart enjoyed himself dancing to the DJs that night, Keith Minshull, Brian Rae and Richard Searling.

The next night, Iain and his mates set off for the Saturday all-nighter which was considerably quieter. Russ was playing "Zorba" by Alan Reuss, a record that Ian and Siz Sayles, from Manchester, had discovered, and subsequently covered up as "High Energy" by the Broadway Band. Despite Ian unmasking the record, Winstanley had covered it again as "Destination Everywhere" by Derek & Ray.

Silvetti's "Spring Rain" filled the floor, and then Richard took over and played *the* unknown 45, then still only known as Joe Matthews. Stewart was impressed: "Everything that's been said about it is true. What a record! I love it, right down to the "1812 Overture" at the end (I kiddeth ye not)."

The record was Cecil Washington & The Group's "I Don't Want To Lose". At the height of its intrigue, Searling would be constantly plagued by soul fans' desperate attempts at guessing its true identity. In a scene notorious for huge sums of money being paid for vinyl, Richard turned down seven hundred and fifty pounds for his copy from a Southampton lad. Searling had bought the disc off Soul Bowl's John Anderson, who had discovered the record in Texas, on one of his regular visits to the States.

Later, Anderson while on a record buying trip to Detroit, met Johnny Mae Matthews, famed for discovering Mary Wells, Betty Lavette and the Distants, who later became the Temptations. She had recorded them for her Northern label before they signed to Motown. Johnny Mae, who was then in her eighties, was selling the rights to a track which had been popular in 1976; "Cut Your Motor Off", recorded by Black Nasty – a group made up of Matthews' children. John was looking through some records which she was selling, when he made an unusual discovery. "I was round her house, and she had a washing basket in the garage. I picked it up, and it was heavy. I took the washing off and underneath was a pile of Cecil Washington's. I don't know how they got there, or how she came to have them."

279

Ian Clark at Yate

The expected closure of the Yate all-nighters had been a little premature. The Second Anniversary, on 30th June 1979, was scheduled to be the final night. The ads promised Ian Clark, Jacko, Tony Ellis, Dave Thorley, Mac, Hippo and Dave Greet behind the turntables, and over one hundred pounds worth of prizes for the winners of the dancing competition final. A thousand people packed into the Stirling Suite, and were surprised to hear that the all-nighters were to continue. With the arrival of new management, it had been expected that the running of the all-nighters would be taken away from the Southern Soul Club. But Peter Aldous, the new manager, realised that the Northern Soul crowd were no trouble, and decided to take over the event.

Ian Clark, who started deejaying at the all-nighters in 1978, remembers one of the unsung events of the Northern Soul scene. "John Harvey's Inter-City Soul Club had run the first Yate all-nighter on 19th April 1975. Harvey asked Terry Davis along, and he shared the deejaying with Tony Ellis and myself. Then "Dinks" took over the running of the niter, as the Southern Soul Club. Every two weeks, I'd go down from London, where I was then living, riding shotgun in Tony's Ford Escort. His forte was the rare English stuff, while mine was mostly imports. I had some good tunes at the time, thanks to a USA trip with Ady Croasdell. This was before the 6Ts thing had started in London, but as soon as Yate got going, the West Hampstead crowd used to come down, especially on the anniversaries – the Sixties soul stuff was massively popular. By '78, we had Jacko, the late Paul Guntrip, Dave Thorley, Mac and Dave Greet. And it wasn't long before Jerry Hipkiss, alias Hippo, joined. "After the management changes, they ran it themselves under Mick McAvoy, who also ran a couple of good all-nighters in Swanage. The atmosphere, at times, was electric, the crowd really appreciated some excellent sounds. It was quite unique in many ways, what with the card schools, the backgammon and the cans of beer smuggled in! We all used to go to the other all-nighters, but Yate was special. There'd be people from the Midlands, Wales, Bristol, Gloucester, Newbury, Nottingham, Abingdon and London. But after the third management change it soon folded. The local police were never that keen,

and Northern Soul had started to lose its appeal. It all moved to London with the 6Ts and "Function At The Junction" nights. But while it was going we had some great nights, with DJs like Dave and Rod Shard and Soul Sam guesting."

"Now I won't say that the Northern Scene is dead but it sure is seriously ill. Remember the days, not too long ago, when certain people were talking about Northern Dance Music instead of Northern Soul Music? Those people are still around and still snipping away at the vitals of the scene. So what's going to happen is that the scene will continue to decrease steadily. Some people will give up altogether and others will go home to their collections and bide their time...but one thing I'm sure of, as eggs are eggs, is that the scene will rise again, with another club here and an all-nighter there, and before you know where you are we'll back to the usual state again."

Frank Elson Blues & Soul 1980

CHAPTER 21

Never Should Have Walked Away

BY THE TIME the Casino's seventh anniversary was celebrated on 25th September 1980, many Wigan names had departed. Billy Paul, Alan Rhodes, John Vincent, Martyn Ellis, Ian Dewhirst, Steve Russell and Pep, had all, for various reasons, left the club. And Soul Sam would soon go, after comments made in *Black Echoes* – about the sound systems at many Northern venues – were misinterpreted.

Any optimism at Wigan was draining away. Two months earlier, Casino manager Mike Walker had committed suicide, and his boundless energy and fire would be sorely missed when it was most needed. A black cloud still hung over the club, and unless the management heard differently, the Casino was scheduled to close in September. As notification had not been received, the club carried on under the assumption that the anniversary would be the last Wigan Casino all-nighter.

Even Russ Winstanley was in the dark about the Casino's future, when designing the seventh anniversary badge

As rumours circulated about the club's demise, Frank Elson reluctantly separated his "Checkin' It Out" column in *Blues & Soul* into two sections; one covering the modern soul world, and the other detailing events within the traditional Northern Soul venues. With an uncertain future, many of the scene's DJs seized every working opportunity – nobody was sure which direction Northern Soul would take.

Richard Searling, who had finally got his own radio show called *Soul Sauce*, on Sheffield's Radio Hallam, strove to maintain standards at Wigan.

During his spot at the seventh anniversary, Searling played a variety of quality Sixties soul and contemporary releases: Don Gardner's "Cheatin' Kind", J.B. Moore's "I Don't Ever Break That Rule", John & The Wierdest's "No Time", Court Davis' "Try And Think What You're Doing", the Professionals' "That's Why I Love You", Eddie Holman's "Hurt" and others by Bit's 'n' Pieces", Herman Hitson, the Nomads and David Porter.

24 Turin Drive Newcastle Staffs
ST5 2QL phone 0782 610833

The movers and shakers of the Seventies' Northern Soul scene, were moving on. After Colin Curtis left the Blackpool Mecca, Ian Levine was joined by Brian Wakelin, but by July 1979, he had also departed to work at Angels in Burnley. London's disco scene was calling. Neil Rushton was so sure of the death of the Northern Soul scene that he off-loaded twenty thousand pressings.

Dave Godin had taken another break from soul journalism to pursue his other love, the cinema, and he was at university studying for a degree in film history. Tony Cummings, after the critical acclaim of *The Sound Of Philadelphia*, had been approached by a publisher to write a book of his choice. A contract was signed for *The Strange World Of Northern Soul*, but Tony returned the advance, left the publisher in the lurch, and went to live in the USA, where he started researching a TV script for a black music series. Cummings left the soul scene after a year of living in Hollywood, and after seeing what black American music had become. As Tony remembers, he quickly became disenchanted.

"Here was a journo who'd gone from being a passionate R&B fan, writing for a mag run off on a duplicator, to a publicity department lackey who, when not stoned, was a bemused spectator of a corrupt record industry. I had entered black music journalism as a kind of populist scholar, trying to record for some imagined Academy of Black Music Studies all the information I could on every black American musician I came across. I left it disillusioned, with the giant-sized ego and the money-lust I was increasingly encountering and frightened by what my recanting of the black music religion might lead to. I dropped out, left behind my beloved record collection and returned to Britain, determined to leave journalism and R&B."

A spiritual experience in a black church became the turning point, and Tony found himself working with a Christian magazine, *Buzz*. As a freelance journalist in the Nineties, he began working as a producer and presenter with Cross Rhythms, a contemporary Christian music radio station.

The drawn out demise of the Wigan Casino began on 19th September 1981. As soul fans arrived for the expected wake, club members were surprised to be given a flyer announcing that there would be one more all-nighter. Understandably, this was greeted with considerable cynicism by many fans – though everybody still fought back tears as the lauded "Three Before Eight" were spun again and again, as the all-nighter came to a close. On 2nd October, another final all-nighter was held, and the lower attendance suggested that the majority of the club's brethren viewed the night with suspicion. Their mistrust was well-founded, as they discovered that there would be yet one more final all-nighter.

Edwin Starr thought that the ending was an anticlimax. "Fans had tattoos put on their body to commemorate the last night, only to find out it wasn't the last night!"

When the ultimate final night did come, in December, the club had remained empty since the previous all-nighter. As the morning came, accompanied by a barrage of soul clapping and relentless foot stomping, Wigan's Holy Trinity – Jimmy Radcliffe, Tobi Legend and Dean Parrish – were played and greeted with mass applause. They were repeated again, and Harry Green, the manager, climbed on stage to say a few words. Russ Winstanley thanked everybody for "eight incredible years. What more can I say?" And Frank Wilson's "Do I Love You" closed the proceedings at nine o'clock.

Prior to the Casino closing, Soul Sam had written in Steve Guanori's *Blackbeat*, that perhaps winding up would be a good thing. "It, along with the Northern scene in general, is largely living on its past reputation, its monthly oldies nights being the only real money spinner. At the same time, we should not forget the first five years when Wigan was probably the top niter in the country, though many who went to Cleethorpes and St. Ives would dispute that. What has led to the drop in attendances? The economic situation certainly, changing trends – yes, but could it also be the music policy there, with, Mr M's included, well over sixty per cent oldies, often the same ones. People are not going to travel weekly to hear records they can/do have on pressings. Newcomers are not going to be attracted to what is increasingly an outdated scene…I believe the DJ line-up at Wigan is diabolical. I'm not criticising the Mr M's set up either, as oldies up there are fine for those who want them, but of the ones downstairs, only Richard Searling seems to realise you cannot stand still, not only in trying to break new sounds, but adapting to newer styles and including album cuts. In the main room, there should be no place for anyone who just follows Richard, plays what he used to use or sticks to an oldies format."

When *Soul Survivors* was published in 1996, Russ Winstanley and Dave Nowell wrote: "Although a major body-blow to the soul scene, Wigan's demise heralded the start of a new era, and a new-look, and a more mature Northern Soul scene has emerged." But before things recovered, there were lean times ahead. Record dealer John Anderson remembers that by 1980, the collecting side had already dried up. "On my shelves, I had fifty copies of "Hit And Run", fifty copies of Silky Hargreaves, fifty copies of the Chandlers, and seventy five copies of Steve Mancha's "Did My Baby Come". I couldn't give them away. They went, over a few years, for just a few pounds each on the list. Of course, sales picked up in the late Eighties, but by that time I'd sold them all off."

The fanzines that were the life blood of the scene vanished. By 1980, Chris Savory's *Soul Cargo*, Dave McCadden's *Soul Time*, *It's The Beat* and *Nite Life*, Iain Stewart's *Soul Symbol*, and Chris Fletcher's *Soul Source* had all stopped publishing. Pat Brady's *Talk Of The North* also closed, but he went on to become a staff writer at *Black Echoes*. Brady, who has deejayed at over a thousand all-nighters, was one of the few not to leave the scene. He remembers when the scene shrank, and there were only a hardcore of about two thousand still on the scene.

The inpenetrable mystique of Northern Soul was slowly disappearing. Things had to change.

We asked DJs, collectors, promoters and soul fans to select their five all-time favourite tracks. These were featured in the weekly chart for ECHOES black music paper.

1. IAN CLARK

Collector, record dealer & DJ

1. Ronnie McNeir "Isn't She A Pretty Girl"   (DeTo)
2. Bobby Reed   "Time Is Right For Love"   (Bell)
3. Chuck Holliday "You Can't Trust Nobody Else" (Gloria)
4. George Pepp   "This Feeling Is Real"   (Coleman)
5. Lorraine Chandler "You Only Live Twice"   (RCA)

Over the coming months leading up to the publication of "The In Crowd", we will be featuring in ECHOES, a regular column listing the Top 5's of many of the DJs, collectors, dealers and soul fans we have interviewed for the book. And to kick off the series we start with Ian Clark's selection. A collector since the early Seventies, Ian later deejayed, to some acclaim, at the Yate All-nighters, and quickly became a main man on the scene. He was very helpful and encouraging when we first went to talk to him about the book.

"My favourite track, well for this week anyway, is the flip to "Sitting In My Class". It's just as atmospheric as the top side and a great Detroit production, a sound which to me is what's best about the Northern scene.

"The Bobby Reed track has been much overlooked, although it was played on the Modern scene about four years ago, and I gave it quite a few plays at the 100 Club. It's a great midtempo sound quite different to his other faster "Try Me" which came out on Brunswick.

"The Chuck Holliday 45 was played at Stafford, but it was only when Soul Sam picked up on it that it began to grow in popularity. Since then the price has rocketed from £15-20 to something around the £400 mark today. It's definitely one for the collectors.

"John Anderson at Soul Bowl got two original studio acetates of "This Feeling Is Real" from George Pepp in Detroit and I was lucky to get one, the other going to Mark 'Butch' Dobson".

"Lorraine Chandler's unreleased track was unearthed by Ady Croasdell, while trawling through RCA's vaults. This Pied Piper production finally saw the light of day on the Kent CD "Rare,Collectable And Soulful"."

2. RICHARD SEARLING

Jazz FM DJ & Togetherness promoter

1. Alice Clark   "You Hit Me Where It Hurts"
2. Frank Beverley   "If That's What You Wanted"
3. Linda Jones   "I Just Can't Live My Life"
4. Salvadors   "Stick By Me Baby"
5. Sandi Sheldon   "You're Gonna Make Me Love You

Those lucky enough to pick up Jazz FM in the North of England are well aware of Richard Searling's commitment to Black music. His early love of reggae was developed whilst listening to Radio Luxembourg where he first heard records by the likes of Pat Kelly and Ken Boothe, and by 1970 when he had met Judith, later to become his wife, he was introduced to deep soul music and subsequently the Northern Soul scene.

The Pendulum Club in Manchester was the turning point: "It was a fairly modern building behind the Manchester Evening News building on Hartman Street. I can remember guys walking around in there with Bobby Bland EPs...and I suddenly became aware of this magical scene...I can still remember my first visit, and ironically the record that stands out most was by a white group, Creation's "I've Got The Fever"...the DJs there – Barry Tasker and Dave White – were definitely a great influence." Richard was working at Global Records in Manchester, when he became the DJ at Va-Va's in Bolton. "It was a bit of a fluke really. I got asked to do it by this cool Jamaican guy from Bolton called Rick Barrett, who happened to be into soul music. He'd got wind that this place wanted a Friday all-nighter." Although Richard was only there for a few months, he managed to gather a strong following. "I remember Pep (Ian Pereira) more than anybody, and the lads from Doncaster – they were very loyal supporters."

After Kev Roberts had recommended Richard to Russ Winstanley, it was not long before Searling became one of the regular DJs at the Wigan Casino, the most enduring, and certainly most controversial, all-nighter of the whole scene.

3. NEIL RUSHTON

DJ, Promoter, All-4-U

1. Mayfield Singers	"Don't Start None"	(Mayfield)
2. Taboo	"Moving On In"	(Smoke City)
3. Charles Brimmer	"Show & Tell"	(Hayley's)
4. Brenda Holloway	"I'm So Happy"	(All-4-U)
5. Ann Byers	"I'm Happy Without You"	(Academy)

The forthcoming Highland Room re-union is a dream come true for Neil Rushton: "The line up at Blackpool is like a fantasy, which is why we have called the event 'Welcome to Dreamsville'. To me the whole Mecca vibe is summed up by the Carstairs' 'It Really Hurts Me Girl' and the idea of them reforming just to sing it at the Mecca is mindblowing."

Neil's current Top 5 is crowned by a Tony Rounce discovery, passed on to Neil via Ady Croasdell. "Sounds like it should have been played alomgside 'Double Cookin' at the Casino – the definitive stomper. The mix is a bit wierd but that doesn't detract." Another unissued track is a '70s production from Taboo, with none other than Chris Clark on vocals. "It sounds like a glorified demo, but it's still an awesome shuffler and fills the floor big time." Neil's third choice is the debut release on the new Coventry-based Hayley logo. Produced by Detroit soul veteran Clay McMurray this is a truly wondrous version of the Al Wilson classic. "I played this before Terry Callier went on at Soulvation and the crowd went apeshit."Neil and producer Ian Levine could not have dreamt how well the recording of Brenda Holloway's version of the Prince Phillip oldie came out. "Just before we laid down her vocals Brenda heard that she had just become a grandmother and so the song fitted her mood!"

"My last choice was first played in the Highland Room so this will no doubt get some action at the Mecca re-union gigs. Catchy intro leads into a fingersnappimg treat with Ann's vocals alternating between creamy and the occasional growl, as they slide over real sassy Philly backing vocals and harmonies. Plus there's a meaty sax buried in the mix which filnally gets released for a stonking solo towards the tension filled finale."

4. GINGER TAYLOR

Collector & DJ

1. Billy Butler	"The Right Track"	(OKeh)
2. Rubin	"You've Been Away"	(Kapp)
3. Hoagy Lands	"Next In Line"	(Stateside)
4. Contours	"Just A Little Misunderstanding"	(Gordy)
5. Al Williams	"I Am Nothing"	(Palmer/LaBeat)

Ginger Taylor first heard "The Right Track" at one of the last all-nighters of the Twisted Wheel in Manchester. "I've had the pleasure of working at gigs with Billy Butler, and I can't imagine it ever moving from my number one all-time favourite. A record with everything." Ignored at the time by EMI, soul fans had to wait until Dave Godin issued it on his Soul City label in 1969.

Rubin's hard-to-get American 45, is well known as the soundtrack to the Felix cat food commercial. "When it came over to this country it was bootlegged almost immediately, but it's 1 minute 56 seconds of sheer brilliance and just never lets up."

As a keen collector of English labels it didn't come as much of a surprise for Ginger to pick Hoagy Lands' rarity, a track which is still as popular today as ever, or, given his enthusiasm for the Motown sound, "Just A Little Misunderstanding": "I remember getting the Contours' on the import label, which at the time was my most expensive buy at 30 shillings. I was only sixteen and deejaying at the local youth club, and it's hard to believe that when it came out originally it was the 'B' side. I have moved on a bit since then and now own a copy on a red and white English demo – but that cost quite a lot more than 30 shillings!"

The inclusion of the Al Williams' Detroit rarity is the only difference to the top five Ginger featured in Mark Bicknell's excellent Soul Underground magazine.

Ginger's more recent crowd pleasers include Tommy Good's "I've Got To Get Away" and Jimmy Ruffin's "He Who Picks A Rose", both unissued Motown tracks, the Admirations' "You Left Me" (Peaches), the Montclairs' "Hey Girl Don't Fight It" (Arch) and the Magnetics' "I Have A Girl" (Ra-Sel).

5. ADEY CROASDELL

6T's Promoter, reluctant DJ & label manager

1. Kim Weston   "Helpless"   (Gordy)
2. Maxine Brown   "It's Torture"   (Wand/Kent)
3. Carla Thomas   "I'll Never Stop Loving You" (Stax/Kent)
4. Barbara Lynn   "This Is The Thanks I Get"   (Atlantic)
5. Impressions   "I Need You" (ABC)

On 17th August 1979, inspired by Terry Davis' '60's Soul Nights at the Prince of Wales in Hammersmith and similar events that had been run by Barry Quinnell in Brighton, Randy Cozens and Adey Croasdell started 'A Rhythm & Soul Night' at the Bedford Head in Covent Garden. Moving to the Railway Hotel, West Hampstead, it soon attracted a loyal following from the London soul crowd and Northern scene stalwarts like Richie Andrew, Bob Foster and John Farrell became regular visitors. After an all-nighter at the former 'Last Chance' Club the 6T's crowd moved to, what has been since 1981 their spiritual home, the 100 Club.

Adey's first master tape discovery was the Maxine Brown track which can be found on Kent's CD "Oh No Not My Baby: The Best Of". His efforts to unearth previously unreleased masters from record companies' vaults have led to many great discoveries, in fact one such find, Lorraine Chandler's "You Only Live Twice", was chosen by Ian Clark in our very first ECHOES Top 5.

Next year's proposed visit by Barbara Lynn is long awaited by her fans, and Adey is grateful to Randy for bringing the Texan soulstress' work to his attention. Released in 1968, "This Is The Thanks I Get" was her first recording for Atlantic, after her time at Tribe and Jamie.

Harboro Horace's final choice is from Chicago's finest the Impressions. Their classic "I Need You" was the closing record at Cleethorpes and the record still fills the 'final vinyl' spot at each and every 6T's all-nighter.

6. IAN LEVINE

Record producer & ex-Blackpool Mecca DJ

1. Charades   "Key To My Happiness"   (MGM)
2. Sandi Sheldon   "You're Gonna Make Me Love You" (OKeh)
3. Celeste Hardy   "You're Gone"   (Reynolds)
4. Yum Yums   "Gonna Be A Big Thing"   (ABC)
5. Jodi Mathis   "Don't You Care Anymore"   (Capitol)

Ian Levine, who was busy at the recent Blackpool Mecca Revival Weekender directing his film "The Strange World Of Northern Soul", gave us his Top 5 favourite tracks when we interviewed him for our book at his West London home earlier this year.

"My all-time favourites, without doubt, are the Charades and Sandi Sheldon. They both have this absolute 'hair on the back of the neck' tingling anticipation about them...the way they build up and never let you go. They're both very sophisticated musically and I would never part with them in a million years...nothing would ever prise those from my hands."

We expected Levine, the DJ most responsible for the sea change in Northern Soul to select more modern examples, such as the Carstairs' "It Really Hurts Me Girl", but as Ian explains: "At the time it made sense to go forward, but now you're asking me to look back, and these are my real all-time favourites".

Apart from the first two which are cast in stone, Ian found it difficult to whittle his many other favourites down to just five; and of the many other contenders which were considered for possible inclusion were the Invitations' "What's Wrong With Me Baby", Major Lance's "You Don't Want Me No More", PJ's "Tender Loving Care", Rose Battiste's "Hit And Run", Patrice Holloway's Capitol double-header "Ecstasy"/"Love & Desire" and Jackie Wilson's floater "I Don't Want To Lose You".

As can be seen from his choices and also-rans, Ian is not a big fan of the more earthy, R&B slanted tracks which make up a part of today's scene:"What I love are the wistful sounding tracks...mellow, jazzy chords with a dance beat...that epitomises Northern Soul to me".

7. KEV ROBERTS
Togetherness promoter & DJ

1. Willie Hutch	"The Duck"/"Love Runs Out"	(ABC Dunhill)
2. Mel Britt	"She'll Come Running Back"	(FIP)
3. Spyder Turner	"I Can't Make It Anymore"	(MGM)
4. Capitals	"Can't Deny That I Love You"	(Omen)
5. Barbara Lynn	"Take Your Love And Run"	(Atlantic)

From humble beginnings deejaying at clubs such as The Britannia near Trent Bridge in Nottingham, Kev quickly made his mark at Wigan Casino to become one of the venue's top DJs. Throughout the seventies he was a regular visitor to the USA, always on the look out for rare vinyl. Today, Kev's single minded approach amazes him: "I was totally focussed on records and had no other interest. I never went to the White House in Washington, I never went up the Statue of Liberty until about 1979. Simply because I was too busy, too intense."

Kev Roberts is also a part of the successful Goldmine set up with Tim Brown and Martin Kopple, and regularly promotes the popular Togetherness all-nighters and weekenders with fellow ex-Casino DJ Jazz FM's Richard Searling.

As Kev puts it, his venerable five is "a mixture of expensive collectors' items and more affordable classics", and his first choice certainly falls into the former category. Although one side – "Love Runs Out" – was released in the UK by ABC in the late seventies with Bobby Hutton's 1973 cut "Lend A Hand", the original US double header is still an elusive piece of vinyl.

Spyder Turner's 45 was a fairly common disc that turned up regularly during the early seventies in soul packs, however it soon became a worthy contender for the discerning soul fan's collection and grew in popularity. The track is featured on Spyder's "Stand By Me" album.

Kev's fave "Can't Deny That I Love You" was issued on the West Coast-based Omen label, known on the Northern circuit for dancers such as Brice Cofield's "Ain't That Right".

Barbara Lynn's perennial favourite ends Kev's selection, which he describes as "a varying degree of collectors items which all became proven dance floor winners."

8. MARK BICKNELL
DJ & "Soul Underground" editor

1. Jimmy Burns	"I Really Love You"	(Erica)
2. Eddie Parker	"I'm Gone"	(Awake)
3. JoAnn Courcy	"I Got The Power"	(Twirl)
4. Brooks Brothers	"Lookin' For A Woman"	(Tay)
5. Larry Clinton	"She's Wanted"	(Dynamo)

Mark Bicknell has DJ'd at many of the leading venues on the Northern scene – Top Of The World, Stafford; Keele; Winsford; Hinckley Leisure Centre; The 100 Club and numerous other weekenders and all-nighters. Despite the commitments of a family and the inevitable "day job", Mark also writes, edits and publishes the excellent fanzine Soul Underground.

Fortunate to have visited the States and met many of the original recording artists, Mark is an enthusiastic and knowledgeable collector – his Top 5 was accompanied by pages of background information.

Introduced to Jimmy Burns in Chicago in the late eighties, Mark managed to obtain a copy of "I Really Love You" from one of Jimmy's relatives; and on a later trip met Bobby James, the writer and original recorder of the song. Burns also recorded for the USA, Tip Top and Minit labels and John Anderson issued the track on Grapevine in the 70s.

Through good friend Rob Moss who lived in Canada, Mark acquired the Eddie Parker single which turned out to be producer Jack Ashford's file copy. A classic oldie.

"I Got The Power" was first heard by Mark at The Stars and Stripes All-nighter at Yate, spun by DJ Ian Clark. This Gregory Carroll production hails from New York City.

The Brooks Brothers' 45, which is on Dave Flynn's new "Sought After Soul" compilation is a gritty, hard-edged slab of Detroit Soul. Mark rates the disc highly: 'This is perfect Northern Soul of the highest order...for its pure energy and rich quality'.

Mark describes "She's Wanted" as 'a desert island disc'. Co-written by Eddie Holman, this was a Harthon production out of Philadelphia. Even though Mark has heard this track many times it still sends that 'magical shiver' down his spine. A recording that Mark acknowledges as truly 'The Heart Of Soul'.

9. DAVE BURTON
Collector

1. Triumphs	"I'm Coming To Your Rescue"	(OKeh)
2. Exciters	"Blowin' Up My Mind"	(RCA)
3. Vibrations	"Gonna Get Along Without You"	(OKeh)
4. Epitome Of Sound	"You Don't Love Me"	(Sandbag)
5. Rose Battiste	"Hit And Run"	(Revilot)

Dave Burton was one of the many behind-the-scene collectors who were responsible for introducing rare records to the DJs during the seventies. Working as manager of a branch of Harlequin Records in Berwick Street, Soho, Dave was a regular visitor to the Torch All-nighter and Blackpool Mecca. Together with Dave Rivers he also ran one of the few Northern soul venues in the South of England at the Birdsnest in Hampstead, where many of the rare sounds that were being spun at the Torch could also be heard.

It was at the legendary Stoke club where Dave first heard the Triumphs – which in the notes for the Kent OKeh compilation Ady Croasdell memorably describes as: 'possibly as fast as a record can go without bursting into flames'. Driven by a contagious bass line the 45 epitomises all that made the Torch the top club of its day. The Exciters' track appeared on their excellent "Caviar & Chitlins" album, and boasts lyrics in a class of their own. The song was rightly championed by Dave Godin in his Blues & Soul column – an essential read at the time.

On his first visit to the HIghland Room at the Blackpool Mecca, Dave recalls hearing the Vibrations' stomper; another release on the fabled OKeh label recorded by the quintet in New York in the mid sixties. Dave never tires of The Epitome Of Sounds' gem. "Simon Soussan thought it was a bit slow and sped up the bootleg, but I loved the girly chorus and the track's midtempo grace."

Those who were lucky enough to have seen Rose Battiste perform at the Blackpool Revival Weekend, will recall the encore of "Hit And Run" sung with the reformed Carstairs. As Dave had overslept (due to jetlag from his flight from Hong Kong where he now lives), Rose kindly sang the song again. And it was an ecstatic Dave who leapt up on stage to give his heroine a kiss.

10. NICK WASHER
Collector

1. Kim Weston	"Helpless"	(Gordy)
2. Velvelettes	"A Bird In The Hand"	(VIP)
3. Parliaments	"Don't Be Sore At Me"	(Revilot)
4. Marvelettes	"I Can't Turn Around"	(Tamla LP track)
5. Holidays	"Watch Out Girl"	(Golden World)

Nick Washer is another of the unsung heroes of the scene. A soul fan and collector since the early '60s, he brought many classics to the attention of fellow Londoner Dave Burton, who subsequently introduced them to DJs in the North of England.

Nick had written to *Record Mirror* to point out that the UK issue by the Debonaires' "I'm In Love Again" had been wrongly credited as a Holland-Dozier-Holland composition, when in fact it had been written by L. Ware and Mike Terry. The response from other readers was unbelievable, and amongst the replies was a letter from a guy in New Jersey called Kurt Schwartz.

"He had a spare copy of the Solid Hit American issue and wondered whether I'd like it? This led to a letter writing and record swapping deal that lasted for about seven years. He'd never heard of Northern Soul, but he had the most amazing collection of records and found duplicates with ease of tracks that nobody over here even knew existed. During those years hundreds of discs arrived from Kurt, together with interesting letters, reviews of what he had discovered and our own fortnightly Top 20, which towards 1978 I recall was more like a Top 200 with so many newly acquired gems bubbling under. It's impossible to remember all the titles he sent over, but these ring bells – Cissy Houston's "Bring Him Back", Edwin Starr "You're My Mellow", Doni Burdick's "Bari Track", Parliaments' "Heart Trouble", Patti & The Emblems' "I'm Gonna Love You A Long Long Time", Pat Lewis' "No One To Love", The Holidays' "I've Lost You", and Melvin Davis' "I Must Love You". I remember Dave playing Dean Courtney's "We Got A Good Thing" over the 'phone to Ian Levine. The whole shop could hear Ian at the other end screaming "I MUST HAVE IT, I MUST HAVE IT!". Two weeks later, another copy arrived and he did indeed have it."

11. BOB HARRIS

1. **Chuck Willis** "C.C.Rider" (Atlantic)
2. **Miracles** "You Really Got A Hold On Me" (Tamla)
3. **Artistics** "The Chase Is On" (Brunswick)
4. **Flamingos** "Boogaloo Party" (Philips)
5. **Sandi Sheldon** "You're Gonna Make Me Love You" (OKeh)

A familiar name and face to many of the regulars of the North of England's major clubs during the mid sixties, Bob Harris now lives and works in Hong Kong. Despite being unaware of the current resurgence of the scene, Bob shared his opinions and views regarding the formative years of Northern Soul.

"I feel that the resilience of the scene in the sixties was due not only to the impact of the music, but as much to the dance and drug scene. The record collectors kept in contact with each via the all-nighters, however the dance/amphetamine element were the instigators of the mid week meetings at pubs, small time clubs and the record and barbiturate sessions at each others' houses."

In Sheffield, Bob was a regular at Pete Stringfellow's King Mojo, the Esquire and Club 66 – where a diverse playlist would typically include favourite Harris tracks such as Don & Dewey's "Soul Motion" and Bob's first choice, the 1957 R&B hit by Chuck Willis. "I have to put this in the number one position as it is the only record I have in Hong Kong, and I bore everyone with it at parties. A very earthy track with a fantastic sax break."

"The most prolific experience I had in my days with music was witnessing Smokey Robinson perform "You Really Got A Hold On Me" in Sheffield. He was wearing a shark skin mohair suit and I can still see him dropping the microphone from his right hand to catch it six inches from the stage floor with his left hand on the third *hold me* of the chorus."

The Artistics' disc was given to Bob by friend and fellow club-goer Phil Merrill from Worcester. "An underestimated group – I think I have every single and album they ever recorded."

The final track is a classic that has appeared in many of the Top 5s we have received. "This has it all. Quality, great vocal and perfect to dance to. What a find."

12. DICK WATT

Collector

1. **Jock Mitchell** "Not A Chance In A Million" (Impact)
2. **Williams & Watson** "Too Late" (OKeh)
3. **Little Stanley** "Out Of Sight Loving" (Vance)
4. **Mr Lucky** "Born To Love You" (Stardom)
5. **Gail Nevels** "He Can't Do Without Me" (Dotty's)

It was 1974 and Carlisle collector Dick Watt was in King's Lynn visiting Soul Bowl, when owner John Anderson pointed out to him a small rack of about three to four hundred 45s. They were mostly mint condition white demos and included multiple copies of rarities such as Dena Barnes' Inferno gem *If You Ever Walk Out Of My Life* and the Honey Bees' "Never In A Million Years" on Garrison, and amongst these was Jock Mitchell's "Not A Chance In A Million". Dick has known John since he first began dealing in Glasgow. "There is no way I could have built up my collection without John's time and effort, and when he realised that I'd accept the odd water damaged label a copy of Eddie Parker appeared at no cost."

Larry Williams and Johnny 'Guitar' Watson's "Too Late" has to be one of the contenders for the title of most popular Northern sound – it has been a dancefloor favourite ever since it was first played at clubs like The Twisted Wheel. And although known to collectors via the 1967 UK-Columbia release "A Quitter Never Wins", the discovery of this Wheel favourite and other great OKeh tracks such as Larry Williams' "I Am The One" and "You Ask For One Good Reason" ignited an almost religious fervour for the label amongst collectors for what Ady Croasdell later identified as a 'Northern Soul Obsession'.

Unbelievably, Dick once swapped a Peugeot 206 GTI for a pile of records, amongst which was the Little Stanley 45. "I'm sure I lost out on the deal, but I always reckon that this was the one I got for the engine."

Gail Nevels' Detroit track "He Can't Do Without Me" is the same as Sue & Mel's version and was issued on James Riley's Dotty's label. Riley was a colourful character who also owned the Diamond Jim, Whip, Big D and Riley labels, but who sadly met an untimely death in 1971.

13. KEITH RYLATT
Soul collector & author

1. **Alvin Cash**   "Alvin's Boo-Ga-Loo"   (Mar-V-Lus)
2. **Alexander Patton**   "A Li'l Lovin' Sometimes"   (Capitol)
3. **O'Jays**   "Working On Your Case"   (UA)
4. **Ambassadors**   "Too Much Of A Good Thing" (Pee Vee)
5. **Vondells**   "Hey Girl You've Changed"   (Airtown)

Once the haunt of beatniks, the Left Wing coffee bar in Brazennose Street, Manchester, like many others in the city, transformed into a beat club after dark – and as The Twisted Wheel, pioneered the popularity of R&B in this country during the early sixties. After its move to Whitworth Street its all-nighters (and many great live acts) attracted soul fans from all over the North of England and the club is still highly revered despite having been closed for over twenty eight years. The history of the fabled club and thriving soul scene of the time is the subject of a book written and researched by Keith Rylatt and Phil Scott which is due to be published later this year.

Keith Rylatt who went to art college during the sixties chose Alvin Cash & The Registers' earthy "Alvin's Boo-Ga-Loo" as his all time favourite. The St Louis dance act once appeared at the Wheel, and although this was not put out by Stateside at the time of its US release it was later issued by President in 1968.

Patton's rare 45 was pressed up in huge quantities in the early seventies, but these are easy to spot as his name is spelt incorrectly on the label. In Keith's opinion: "The essence of rare quality soul", a view shared by all who remember this Wheel favourite – a disc which has since gone on to become an accepted Northern Soul classic. The O'Jays' "fusion of Uptown soul and group harmony" comes with the added bonus of another Northern classic on the flip side.

Keith considers the Ambassadors' cut to be "one of the best and rarest of Philly group sounds…and the Vondells' track was a side I could only dream of after collector Dick Watt introduced it to me – and its £500 price tag! Until one day in a crappy New York record store when I rescued it from this doo-wop collector's shelf, never to be seen again."

14. DAVE EVISON
DJ

1. **Impressions**   "I'm The One Who Loves You" (ABC/HMV)
2. **James Barnett**   "Keep On Talkin'"   (Fame)
3. **Ronnie Walker**   "You're The One"   (Philips)
4. **Melvin Moore**   "All Of A Sudden"   (Sky Hero)
5. **Montclairs**   "Hey You"   (Arch)

In Frank Elson's "Check Out The North" in *Blues & Soul* during the early '70s, Dave Evison's name would rarely feature without mention of Eddie Parker's all-nighter anthem "Love You Baby". When we last met Torch DJ Colin Curtis, he recalled making an endless tape of the Parker track especially for Dave, complete with Colin's barking dog in the background. Dave was deejaying alongside Wigan's Russ Winstanley and promoter Mike Prince at the Pembroke Halls in Walkden when Mike Ritson interviewed him for the book "The In Crowd".

Over the years Dave's taste in soul must have mellowed as ridin' high on his Top 5 is the Impressions' "I'm The One Who Loves You" from 1963. Memorably included on the UK "Big Sixteen" compilation, it was not a major US hit being issued before the Impressions' biggest smash "It's All Right". It is easy to forget how popular the trio's discs were on the early Northern circuit – despite the fact that none of the groups' treasures ever charted in this country, a bogus outfit billed as The Fabulous Impressions toured the UK successfully in the mid sixties.

Dave was educated at Millfield where he had the dubious honour of sharing French lessons with Tony Blackburn – a double entendre which the ex-Radio One DJ would have no doubt extracted considerable mileage out of. A stint in the army led to his first experience as a DJ at a Belfast NAAFI in 1970, and after finally putting the brakes on Chieftain tanks he returned to the mainland. Dave is best remembered as the oldies DJ at the Casino's Mr.M's.

Dave has since become a regular on Signal FM, where he has presented many features on Northern Soul – excerpts from his Wigan Casino special can be heard on the latest CD from Joe Boy which celebrates 25 years of this most famous club.

15. ROGER STEWART
Record Dealer & DJ

1. Seven Souls   "I Still Love You"   (OKeh)
2. Sam Williams   "Love Slipped Through My Fingers" (Tower)
3. Luther Ingram Orchestra "Exus Trek"   (HIB)
4. Sam Fletcher   "I'd Think It Over"   (Tollie)
5. Rose Batiste   "Hit And Run"   (Revilot)

Many of the rare items of memorabilia photographed for the book "The In Crowd" have kindly been loaned by Roger Stewart of Boogaloo Records. Besides running his competitively priced mail order service, Roger can often be heard deejaying at Ady Croasdell's 6Ts events – the next being the 100 Club's return to Trentham Gardens on 20th March. Rose Batiste, who Roger met at the Blackpool Mecca Revival will no doubt be performing his ultimate selection *"Hit And Run"* when she appears live at the all-nighter.

Roger's top choice is one of the rarer items on the cherished Chicago label, the Seven Souls' *"I Still Love You"* – a record which although not released in the UK was issued in France and Italy on the Epic label.

Another collectors' item is Williams' cut for the Capitol subsidiary Tower. Issued in the UK in the late seventies on John Anderson's Grapevine label (with another of producer Johnny Brantley's tracks Towanda Barnes' "You Don't Mean It"), this was a song that Anderson discovered had been recorded by ten different artists including the Ohio Players.

"Exus Trek", the atmospheric backing track to Luther Ingram's "If It's All The Same To You" was written by Detroit legend Richard 'Popcorn' Wylie. Ingram enjoyed the most successful period of his career at Johnny Baylor's KoKo label with the 1972 million-seller "(If Loving You Is Wrong) I Don't Want To Be Right", yet despite his acknowledged vocal prowess it was the haunting instrumental that became more popular in the Northern clubs.

Sam Fletcher's beat ballad came out on the Vee-Jay satellite Tollie in 1964, and was a favourite on the Belgium 'popcorn' scene during the early seventies – and if our memory serves us right was duly bootlegged.

16. JIMMY CLAVEN
Ex-Wheel Scene/Nighter-ite

1. Al Green   "Don't Leave Me"   (Stateside)
2. Chris Jackson   "I'll Never Forget You"   (Soul City)
3. Al Wilson   "Now I Know What Love Is"   (Liberty)
4. Stairsteps   "Stay Close To Me"   (Buddah)
5. Curtis Mayfield "Stay Close To Me"   (Curtom/Buddah)

It was Dave Godin's enthusiastic report – "The Up-North Soul Groove" – that first brought a thriving underground soul scene to the attention of Blues & Soul readers. Jimmy Claven was one of the names mentioned in Dave's original dispatches in the summer of 1970. Aged 13, Jimmy went to his first all-nighter at the Plebeians' Jazz Club in Upper George Yard, Halifax. Apart from the Twisted Wheel which was by then the leading soul club in the mid to late sixties, there were many excellent smaller venues dotted across the Midlands and North of England, and "Plebs" as the mods at the time shortened it to, attracted regulars from as far away as Sheffield and Burnley.

Jimmy needed little encouragement to sample the delights of other venues at the time and over the next few years regular haunts included the Cavern in Burnley, Birdtrap in Brierfield, the Twisted Wheel, and two other Manchester clubs which he feels were sadly underrated, the Blue Note and Top 20. Due to "JC", as he puts it "having to shoulder the responsibility" for maintaining the all-nighter crowds' energy levels he was sadly "unavailable" for the last night of the Wheel. He left England to live near Perpignan and on his return, CDs and compilations helped to re-acquaint him with the soul sounds missed in France. Ironically, it was Goldmine, based in Jimmy's home town of Todmorden, which did most to rekindle those great memories. And as with most of our compilers, Jimmy found it particularly hard to nail his perfect five and supplied a much longer list, which he thought would make a great compilation. Lastly, on a contentitious note, Jimmy listed four versions of the classic Motown song "Helpless", a track twice featured in previous Top 5s. In his order of preference they are by Bonnie Pointer, the Four Tops (from the "Second Album"), Kim Weston and...Manhattan Transfer.

17. DAVE RIMMER

Soulful Kinda Music Editor

1. Johnny Mae Matthews	"I Have No Choice"	(Big Hit)
2. Troy Dodds	"Try My Love"	(El Camino)
3. Joanne Courcy	"I Got The Power"	(El Camino)
4. Sam Fletcher	"I'd Think It Over"	(Tollie)
5. Cody Black	"I'm Slowly Molding"	(King)

The fastest Top 5 we have ever received is this selection from Soulful Kinda Music's editor Dave Rimmer. Halfway through the recent Trentham Gardens all-nighter we asked Dave if he could put one together, and one hour later, neatly written on the back of a Keele flyer, were his five choices together with 200 words of copy. A man who knows the meaning of the word deadline! Dave's magazine is highly recommended and a subscription for three issues at £10 can be obtained from 12 Winchester Rise, London Heights, Dudley DY1 2SE.

"Heresy, post-Wigan records. Whilst I spent a large portion of my youth at the all-nighters of the seventies, Wigan included, back in those days I wasn't DJing or collecting on a serious level. Who cared what label it was on? A break of almost ten years from the scene meant I missed Stafford Top Of The World completely. So when I did come back and start collecting again I had all those wonderful midtempo things to discover.

Yet my first choice is post-Stafford. I believe Gilly was the first to play this, but it really broke big on the scene from the Bretby Country Club soul nights run by Chris Anderton.

Troy Dodds is a Stafford record, and pure midtempo magic. Of all his records this stands head and shoulders above the rest. Joanne Courcy is Northern Soul in the traditional sense, urgent, uptempo and an instant floor filler. Sam Fletcher epitomises the Stafford period for me, midtempo, soulful and the business and still a hard one to turn up.

Cody Black – a long time want – Soul Sam was the first DJ I heard play it, but only because Uncle Ted Massey told me to request it. It took me three years to find a copy and eventually Butch sold me one.

So there we have it. Five records that show that the scene has moved on, and to be honest, for the better.

18. TIM BROWN

Goldmine Records

1. Darrell Banks	"Open The Door To Your Heart"	(Revilot)
2. Johnny Sayles	"I Can't Get Enough"	(St Lawrence)
3. Carstairs	"It Really Hurts Me Girl"	(Red Coach)
4. Barbara Lynn	"Take Your Love And Run"	(Jetstream)
5. Jock Mitchell	"Not A Chance In A Million"	(Impact)

"Throw in the flipside "Our Love Is In The Pocket" and you've got the greatest double-sider ever. I'm a little too young to have done the Wheel or the Torch, so "Open The Door" is picked on musical criteria alone. "Open The Door" combines singing ability, lyrical quality and production values to a level which elevates it to musical greatness beyond soul music *per se* even. Add the pathos of Banks' tragic demise a few years later, and you've got a bittersweet appreciation of true greatness and charisma in two minutes or so of music. Imagine my pride therefore when my own Goldmine label came to reissue not only this classic but virtually the entire output of Darrell Banks on one CD.

Johnny Sayles' "I Can't Get Enough" has an intro unlike any other in soul and whoosh! your feet don't touch the floor. How this one failed to sell when it was first released in Chicago I'll never know. True injustice. In 1974 at the Mecca, innovation was underway in the shape of sounds beyond the traditional Motown rhythm. I had no prejudice and accepted them all as part of a magical journey. James Fountain's "Seven Day Lover" pushes it close but eventually I plumped for the Carstairs' for no other reason than finding room for a harmony group sound amongst the solo guys.

"Take Your Love And Run" is pure adrenaline-style Northern. Originally on Jetstream and then Atlantic, it's also on her classic "Here Is Barbara Lynn" album – with the added bonus of a line or two more.

Back in Detroit for my fifth selection, a record that many moons ago taught me to follow my heart and be concerned with what sounded great rather than 'in vogue' records gone big. A classic oldie, Jock Mitchell's "Not A Chance In A Million" was a 'not-quite-made-it' Torch failure when I stumbled across it in 1975. The 45 instantly floored me particularly when it goes up a gear halfway through. It took another 10 years before most people woke up to how good it is.

19. DAVE SHAW

Collector & author of 'Casino'

1. The Group	"I Don't Like To Lose"	(Prophonics)
2. Michael & Raymond	"If Only You Knew"	(Giant)
3. Lovers	"Without A Doubt"	(Frantic)
4. Little Tommy	"Baby I Need You"	(Sound Of Soul)
5. Benny Mahan	"She Knows How"	(Pompeii)

Dave Shaw, from Nuneaton, is the author of a new book Casino to be published by Bee Cool later this year. Dave began what he considers to be "the most exciting, challenging and rewarding period" of his life after a visit to Wigan as a fourteen year old in 1975. Despite being sold forged tickets for his first visit – the club's second anniversary – with the help of two girls from Burnley Dave and his mate Steve eventually gained entry to the club by faking pass-out stamps on their wrists. This four year labour-of-love will bring back fond memories to those who were regulars at the club.

Dave's first 45, featuring the vocals of the Reverend Cecil Washington, will need little introduction. First played by Richard Searling under the alias of 'Joe Matthews' the disc remained under wraps for over two years before another copy was discovered by Kev Draper, a DJ at the Fleet all-nighter in Peterborough. With the Lovers' cut it epitomises for Dave everything the all-nighter stood for.

The Michael & Raymond track is probably a one-off and "finding a copy is the equivalent of finding another Turin Shroud at a car boot sale." He thinks that John Vincent was the last DJ to own a copy of the disc which surfaced briefly (or not) on Mel Collins and Joshie Jo Armstead's Chicago label.

Little Tommy's outing was a big sound for Soul Sam at Cleethorpes and is again attracting spins today.

Benny Mahan's midtempo killer from 1966 has never been a big club sound. Dave bought a copy for £10 in 1984 and grew to love the record with its "clever rhythm changes and vocal high spots". Former Wigan DJ Gary Rushbrooke was desperate to own a copy and persuaded Dave to part with the record at Stafford's Top Of The World. Another copy was unearthed but Dave was forced to sell it, when as he puts it "financial considerations became foremost in the deal".

20. ANDREW RIX

Collector, DJ & Ace/Kent Research Consultant

1. John & The Weirdest	"Can't Get Over These Memories"/	
	"No Time"	(Tie 101)
2. Cindy Scott	"I Wish You The World Of Happiness"	
		(Harthon/Virtue)
3. Ray Pollard	"This Time (I'm Gonna Be True"/	
	"No More Like Me"	(Shrine 103)
4. Larry Clinton	"She's Wanted"	(Dynamo 300)
5. Little Ann	"What Should I Do"	
		(Dave Hamilton Productions)

To pick a Top 5 is "Mission Impossible" as it changes from week to week, but here is my present choice.

The fabulous double-header from Johnny Hendley has everything needed for a class "Rare Soul" 45. The extremes of emotion portrayed here, grieving for departed love on one side and scorning her betrayal on the other, encapsulates something we've all experienced whilst coming to terms with a broken relationship. It probably all got too much for Johnny who, reportedly, currently requires long-term psychiatric care.

"World Of Happiness", which has the rhythm structure of Wigan biggie "Bird Walkin", blew me away when I first heard Butch play it. I finally tracked down an acetate of the finished version from the song's co-writer Eddie Holman. Hearing this version for the first time in James Solomon's basement in Philadelphia, with Eddie singing along, will always remain one of my most treasured memories.

Ray Pollard and I became good friends in the late 80's and this awesome double-header is a fitting tribute to one of the most under-rated singers of all-time.

Larry Clinton, one time flat mate of Jerry Williams, cut this "everything but the kitchen sink" tune for. Another Holman-Solomon composition that makes it simply because of its power. Finally the legendary Rose Valentine "When He's Not Around" cover-up, courtesy of Little Ann, that proves that many of the best songs were never issued at the time of their original recording. It's tracks like this that keep driving us to unearth those dusty old acetates and master tapes. Sheer femme perfection.

21. ALLAN S
Catacombs DJ

1. **Alexander Patton** "A L'il Lovin Sometimes" (Capitol)
2. **Dean Parrish** "Determination" (Stateside)
3. **Invitations** "What's Wrong With Me Baby" (Stateside)
4. **Lorenzo Manley** "Swoopdown On You" (Original Sound)
5. **Richard Temple** "That Beatin' Rhythm" (Mirwood)

Considering it only had a capacity of between three and four hundred and closed shortly after midnight, from 1967 until its closure in July 1974, The Catacombs in Wolverhampton was one of the most influential venues on the Northern Soul circuit. Situated in Temple Street, in what was formerly a lead smelting factory, the inside of the club retained many of the characteristics of the building with alcoves formed from the old furnaces. With no previous experience deejaying, Allan S managed to convince owner Steve Dobson to let him become the first DJ at the proposed new club. "Farmer" Carl Dene, who had made quite a name for himself at Chateau Impney in Droitwich joined shortly afterwards but was sacked by Dobson for promoting other venues where he deejayed. "Major" Bob Crocker, who worked at F.L.Moore's in Dunstable, one of the main sources for import 45s in the country, teamed up with Allan and together they became an irrepressible force. They went to inordinate lengths to unearth rare soul tracks to maintain the club's position at the forefront of the growing Northern scene. Richard Temple's "That Beatin' Rhythm" was a massive sound at the Catacombs and on the grapevine Allan learnt that Billy Butler, DJ at Liverpool's Mardi Gras club had an instrumental version. Refusing at first to let Allan have the disc, after a few drinks Butler eventually sold him the record, Jimmy Conwell's "Cigarette Ashes", for what was then the equivalent of two weeks' wages. Butler took Allan into the club where the record was on the floor of the DJ's booth in amongst a pile of other rare 45s.

Sadly, Bob Crocker was killed in a car crash whilst driving with Allan to visit bootlegger Jeff King in Leicester. Allan was hospitalised for three months but eventually returned to the Cats alongside "Blue" Max and Froggy.

22. RANDY COZENS
Soul Fan & Co-founder of 6T's Nights

1. **Maxine Brown** "Oh No Not My Baby" (Wand)
2. **Maxine Brown** "Your In Love" (Wand)
3. **Maxine Brown** "I Can't Get Along Without You" (Commonwealth United)
4. **Maxine Brown** "Don't Leave Me Baby" (Epic)
5. **Maxine Brown** "Raindrops" (unissued)

In 1979 under the auspices of "The Southgate 60s Rhythm & Soul Club", a tribute to Dave Godin's early soul association and fanzine, Randy Cozens and Ady Croasdell promoted an evening of R&B and mainstream sixties soul music. A re-birth of the Mod cult was in full swing and Randy's advertisement, in what was then titled Black Echoes, boasted that this event would be the "Original Mod Revival". It was from these small beginnings at Henri's Bar in London's Covent Garden that the 6T's long reign at the 100 Club would flourish.

A soul fan since the early sixties frequenting clubs such as The Discotheque and The Scene, it was at The Last Chance Saloon all-nighter in London's Oxford Street where Randy first heard "Oh No Not My Baby"; and he makes no apologies for his Top 5 being made up entirely of Maxine Brown tracks. Randy has never tired of this soul classic and confessed to having played it, one night, ten times on his local pub's juke box.

Apart from being the club where he was first introduced to the songs of his heroine, The Last Chance was also one of the few in the West End that had a 100% soul playlist. Typical records that could be heard included the Larks "The Jerk", Nella Dodds "Come See About Me", Gloria Jones "Finders Keepers" and dozens of other dancefloor favourites. It was one of Randy's ambitions to promote an all-nighter at the club which he finally succeeded with Ady Croasdell's help in 1981. And "Oh No Not My Baby" was, of course, the final record played that night.

Randy's wish to see her perform live on stage was eventually granted at Cleethorpes in 1997 when Ady finally persuaded one of soul music's true greats to return to the UK after an absence of over thirty years.

23. CHRIS BURTON
The Torch

1. Tony Clarke	"Landslide"	(Chess)
2. Dells	"Run For Cover"	(Cadet)
3. Billy Butler	"The Right Track"	(Soul City)
4. Major Lance	"Ain't No Soul"	(Columbia)
5. Jimmy Radcliffe	"Long After Tonight Is All Over"	(Stateside)

Chris Burton, a local promoter bought the Regent Cinema in Tunstall, Stoke-on-Trent in January 1965 for £27,000 and turned it into its final incarnation The Golden Torch. Originally a church built at the beginning of the 19th century, it then became a roller skating rink before conversion to a cinema. The first attraction to Burton's club was Billy J. Kramer & the Dakotas but it was not until 1967 that the first soul act played there – Inez and Charlie Foxx.

The original DJ was self-styled "Barmy Barry" who as well as playing the current pop music of the day also spun the likes of the Miracles, Martha & The Vandellas, Eddie Floyd and the Impressions. Although the club flirted with progressive rock, blues nights and reggae it eventually adopted a 100% soul music policy. The Golden was dropped from the title in around 1969 and local DJ Keith Minshull, Martyn Ellis from Manchester and Alan Day from Burton were brought in. When the Twisted Wheel closed in 1971, despite the efforts of other clubs to replace its place in the hearts of the growing soul scene's fans affections, the Torch quickly became the number one club. In March 1972 it opened for its first all-nighter.

Chris's favourites all bring back for him fond memories of the Torch, and topping the list is Tony Clarke's "Landslide" featuring the most distinctive drum introduction of any 45 played on the scene. Chris chose another Torch favourite, the Dells'"Run For Cover", as he is bringing the venerable vocal group to this country for the first time in July. Billy Butler's soul clappin' anthem "Right Track" and Major Lance's "Ain't No Soul" just had to be included. Major's "Live At The Torch", whilst not exactly a great soul album leaves you in no uncertainty of the unique atmosphere of the club. And Torch regulars will appreciate that Chris Burton's final selection could have been no other record.

24. RUSS WINSTANLEY
Wigan Casino

1. Steinways	"My Heart's Not In It Anymore"	(Oliver)
2. Phil Terrell	"Love Has Passed Me By"	(Carnival)
3. Florence Devore	"Kiss Me Now"	(Phi-Dan)
4. Sandra Richardson	"Don't Let Me Down"	(Inter/Soul)
5. Dottie Cambridge	"Cry Your Eyes Out"	(MGM)

Notwithstanding the regular promotions at nearby Lowton Civic Hall, it might be stretching the point to suggest that the Lancashire town is still at the forefront of today's soul scene, however Russ is still spinning the soul 45s that made his name. His book *Soul Survivors*, co-written with Dave Nowell, received a mixed reception from readers yet still sold thousands of copies, and the CD compilation of the same name for Telstar is arguably the biggest selling Northern compilation. Never one to shy away from the limelight, Russ can currently be seen on Richard and Judy's This Morning TV show in a regular feature with Rosemary Conley discussing ways of losing weight!

Russ recently he gave us his current most popular five tracks: "The Steinways' cut was always a Wigan favourite yet never quite made it to the 'classic' department. Lyrics by "Skiing In The Snow" writers, Linzer and Randell and arranged by Charles Calello. An outstanding disc coupled with a brilliant B-side.

"Phil Terrell's mid-tempo dancer has everything. Never pressed it is quite a rare disc, but is available on a Kent CD.

"Kiss Me Now" is a real sing-along girl track which was played at Wigan on its opening night.

As well as dusting off these classic oldies Russ is spinning other less well-known tracks. With its similar backing track to J.J.Barnes' "Real Humdinger" Johnny Barnes' "Real Nice" on Cap City is getting turntable action again, as is an unreleased version of the Velvelettes' "These Things Will Keep Me Loving You" recorded by Chris Clark.

Jazz bassist virtuoso Stanley Clarke's "Straight To The Top" is a 'haunting 70s sounding stormer in cross-over vein' and Chuck Jackson's 'usual mega vocals' can be heard on a Lambert and Potter song and production"You Gotta Hold On".

25. LEIGH SMART

DJ

1. Jerry Williams "If You Ask Me"   (Calla)
2. Harold Melvin "Get Out"   (Landa)
3. Dana Valery   "You Don't Know Where Your Interest Lies"
                                                     (Columbia)
4. Yvonne Baker "You Didn't Say A Word"   (Parkway)
5. Don Gardner   "The Cheatin' Kind"   (Sedgewick)

In 1973 whilst still at school, Leigh Smart was invited along with a group of older lads to a "soul do" at the Steam Machine in Stoke-on-Trent. He had no expectations of what it would be like, but that night made a lasting impression on Leigh and he has been well and truly hooked on all things Northern. The music he heard that night, mainly old Torch sounds, included Sam & Kitty, Dottie Cambridge, The Prophets and the record which is still his all-time favourite – Jerry Williams' "If You Ask Me". Soul fans in and around Tamworth, Hinkley, Nuneaton and Birmingham will probably have heard Leigh spin this classic.

He started frequenting all-dayers in the Midlands area and before long the all-nighters at Wigan. When the Casino opened Leigh was in his element: "It was like a breath of fresh air, a huge building with adequate room for dancers to strut their stuff, the balcony from which to watch the proceedings below and later Mr M's 100% oldies. Just a great place and records that blew your mind. The list of brilliant tracks is endless and you knew that to hear them it was vital to get to the Casino every week. It was a seemingly endless time of superb soul music and the live acts which were usually excellent." Leigh particularly remembers the Elgins, Jackie Wilson, Edwin Starr and the unforgettable night that Betty Wright performed.

His other choices include "Get Out", a massive track which he struggled to obtain before it was finally issued in 1975; Dana Valery's 45 brings back memories of the "sweaty, happy, brilliant atmosphere" at the Casino; the Yvonne Baker gem with its instantly recognisable James Bond-style introduction is "100% pure class that never seems to date" and Don Gardner's ultra-rare slice of vinyl is one that Leigh wishes Goldmine would issue!

26. DAVID CONWAY

Importer & Collector

1. Ray Agee   "I'm Losing Again"   Soultown)
2. Magnetics   "Lady In Green"   (Bonnie)
3. DC Magnatones "Does She Love Me"   (DC Magnatones)
4. Eric Mercury   "Lonely Girl"   (Sac)
5. Walter & Admirations "Man O Man"   (LaCindy)

Leaving no stone unturned, the intrepid half of the Bee Cool Twins, Mike Ritson was once again on the soul trail at Cleethorpes. The cognescenti (and usual suspects) were out in force to welcome back Little Ann and witness live for the first time in the UK Bobby "Lend A Hand" Hutton. Another rip-roaring success for Mr. Croasdell. Amongst the throng Mike met up with London-based collector and geography teacher Dave Conway. Since 1974 Dave's Trans Atlantic Sounds Inc has been hunting and tracking down those elusive Northern, 60s soul, R&B and Motown sounds, and in a suitable gap in the festivities he told Mike about his all-time five stunners.

Ray Agee's vintage Northern floorpacker is described by Dave as "primal perfection that grips you, chokes you then spins you around". Powerful stuff indeed.

The Magnetics' track is a legendary favourite and has been a highly-prized collectors item for quite some time. In his sleevenotes for the Goldmine CD "For Millionaires Only", Tim Brown recorded that it became the first Northern Soul record to sell for £2,000. Penned in Detroit in 1965 by Barney "Duke" Browner, "The Lady In Green" is "an infectious mid-pace dancer that never fails to strike a chord. Sheer brilliance."

As far as Dave knows the DC Magnatones' 45 is the only copy known to exist. It's an ace group sound in what Dave describes as "early Northern style". If you want to know what it sounds like you'll have to ask Dave to hear his copy!

Eric Mercury and the Soul Searchers' "Lonely Girl" is a storming uptempo dancer that "fires you through and through, relentless stuff".

Dave has left Walter & The Admirations' rarity until last. He considers "Man O Man (What Have I Done)" to be perhaps the best ever Northern record. A wall-of-sound and then some!

27. DAVE RIVERS
Torch Regular & ISC DJ

1. Robert Banks	"Mighty Good Way"	(Verve)
2. Clara Ward	"Right Direction"	(Verve)
3. Jerry Williams	"If You Ask Me"	(Calla)
4. Wonderettes	"I Feel Strange"	(Ruby)
5. Moses Smith	"Girl Across The Street"	(Dionn)

Since he returned to the scene for the Blackpool Mecca revival in November last year, Dave Rivers has accompanied us on many of our travels for the book. One particularly hectic night started at the Whitchurch Civic Centre, included a brief visit to Bretby Country Club in Burton and concluded with the Torch revival at Trentham Gardens. Our driver for the night was an ex-miner turned cabby whose geography was sadly lacking outside of Stoke. In light of the eventual two hundred mile round journey it was fortunate that Dave had the presence of mind to fuel himself for this arduous trip, the mini-bar being stripped of anything edible on Dave's arrival at the hotel. A mixed grill in Hanley at lunchtime was taken on board just in case.

In the early Seventies, Dave made regular journeys from London to the Golden Torch, more often than not in Mick Smith's Ford Anglia. The roof of which was dented by enthusiastic fists punching in the air to the taped soul pumping out of Mick's cassette recorder. He did his best to spread the word down South by running Northern Soul promotions at The Shack in Swiss Cottage and The Bird's Nest at West Hampstead with Dave Burton. Nobody else at the time was playing exclusively 100% rare sounds in the capital. The London crowd introduced many classic 45s to the North, one of Dave's most memorable being the Fuller Brothers' Soul Clock outing "Times A Wasting".

When Chris Burton instigated the International Soul Club to run events at various Top Ranks across the country, the two Daves deejayed at Watford, although at that time very few promoters had ventured far South and the attendances were poor. A year or so later, when the Northern scene was splashed all over the national media it might well have been a different story.

This Top 5 is the third that Dave has given us! We'd better print it before he changes his mind again.

28. ROGER BANKS
DJ, Collector & Light Entertainer

1. Yvonne Daniels	"Don't Want To Get Away From Your Love"	(Sterling)
2. Cody Black	"I'm Slowly Molding"	(King)
3. Willie Mae	"My Man Called Me"	(Peacock)
4. Spyder Turner	"I'm Alive With A Loving Feeling"	(MGM)
5. E.Wiliams	"Trade My Soul To The Devil"	(Jadee)

Roger Banks needed his sense of humour most when he travelling around the country supporting Grimsby FC in 1976. When they eventually escaped from Division Four in front of an ecstatic 26,000 crowd, Roger found welcome relief at the Winter Gardens in Cleethorpes. Fellow Mariners' fans had introduced him to the delights of soul music and since then has never looked back. Instead of trawling around the back waters of the Third Division's finest, his soul travels now took him to the likes of Loughborough where Soul Sam, John Vincent, John Manship and Kev Roberts did their best to entertain the soul folk; the KayGee-Bee in Sheffield, and the many soul clubs that spung up in the late 70s – like the East Anglian, Humberside, and the Wales & Cheshire. In Nottingham to borrow some examples from his collection of memorabilia, over tea and beetroot sandwiches he picked his Top 5.

Ms Daniels' gem, aided and abetted by the Peter Jim Orchestra was an ex-Cleethorpes' spin that has recently had a second lease of life. Another record played years ago by Soul Sam, and previously featured in Dave Rimmer's Top 5, is Cody Black's rarity "I'm Slowly Molding". Roger reckons it took a long time to break because it must be thick plastic!

Willie Mae is better known as Big Mama Thornton. A heavily-built, powerful singer who also played drums – it perhaps explains Roger's definition of this track as "soul with bollocks". The Spyder Turner track, a jewel from the Terra Shirma studios in Detroit, featured on his MGM album and was only issued in France on an EP. The final track was covered up as Eugene Jefferson and Roger thinks it is the only known copy.

29. TIM ASHIBENDE
Collector

1. Velvet Satins   "Nothing Can Compare To You"   (GA)
2. Keymen Strings "Try A Little Harder"   (Keymen)
3. Danny Monday "Baby Without You"   (Modern)
4. Lenny Curtis   "Nothing Can Help You Now"   (End)
5. Dobie Gray   "Out On The Floor"   (Charger)

"The In Crowd" would have to be at least twice as thick to include background details on every record featured on the Northern scene. But as it's the facts 'n' info that make it such a fascinating subject, we are doing our best to provide as many interesting snippets throughout the story. Tim Ashibende's *Tracks To Your Mind* is one of the many fanzines which have proved invaluable in getting to the nitty gritty of the rare soul scene. As the cover rightly states this is the fanzine for the "discerning rare soul collector".

The Velvet Satins' has been Tim's favourite track since he first heard it:"Everything about the record is textbook Northern; the introduction, the lyrics, the sax break…the excitement and atmosphere epitomises Wigan at its best. One minute fifty five seconds of magic. Soul without words doesn't sound possible but the Keymen Strings' backing to the Fi-dels is quite simply the best instrumental ever. It's so emotive, sensitive, in a word class!

"Danny Monday sums up for me Wigan in 1975. "Baby Without You" is the biz. It would be hard to find anything with a more compelling beat, it's relentless, pounding and those girls in the background make it an absolute classic. Lenny Curtis' great soul record is nothing less than a masterpiece. But what would you expect from Robert Bateman?

Dobie Gray might seem a strange one to include. Yes, it's over played, taken for granted perhaps but I'm not too purist to appreciate that it's still great. The words sum up how it feels when you're "Out On The Floor" dancing to a Northern record. If found now it would still be a classic which is the acid test. Just because we seem to have heard it forever doesn't make it a bad record. It's brilliant and always will be – old or not."

30. MICK SMITH
DJ & Dealer

1. Chuck Cockerhall "Have I the Right"   (Mala)
2. Vickie Labat   "Got To Keep Hangin' On"   (Shagg)
3. Mr. Soul   "Whatever Happened To Yesterday"
   (Genuine)
4. George Pepp   "The Feeling Is Real"   (Coleman)
5. Mr. Lucky   "Born To Love You"   (Stardom)

Danny Leno, DJ at the local Stevenage Mecca, who first introduced Mick Smith to the soul sounds that were taking the Northern clubs by storm: "Follow Your Heart", "(At The) Discotheque" and "Just A Little Misunderstanding". Before long, Mick was scouring local junk shops for deleted UK 45s, bargaining with F.L.Moore at his house in Leighton Buzzard, and travelling to Soul City in London. After a trip to Manchester's Pendulum Club, Mick never looked back. With Clive Everitt, they introduced many classic 45s to DJs on the circuit. You can argue amongst yourselves, but Mick and Clive found Tony Clarke's "Landslide", the Bobettes' "Havin' Fun" and "Happy Go Lucky Me", Velvet Satins, Lee David, Erma Franklin "Sweetest feeling", Kenny Gamble "Ain't It Baby" and countless others. One of their first sales was George Carrow's "Angel Baby", discovered in a shop in Hemel Hempstead and sold to Tony Jebb at the Mecca for £6. Kicking off the Smith five is Cockerhall's mid pacer. A massive sound for Mick at the 100 Club, and probably one of the hardest to find on the label.

Spun at Stafford, Vickie Labat's recording is a prime example of the overlooked gems from New Orleans. Incidentally, Mick's fourth choice, the in-demand track from George Pepp is another from the Big Easy.

Covered-up by Richard Searling as Maurice McAllister's "Your Love Is Slipping Away", the Mr. Soul track also surfaced in the States credited to Al Scott. A moody, mid-tempo classic that will be remembered by all who went to Wigan.

Mick's final pick is a raw and gritty soul sound from the West Coast, home to two of his current plays – John Simeone's "Who Do You Love", a 70s recording from the Hollywood-based TNT label and Milton Parker's "Women Like It Harder" on Closet.

Index

307

Photographs pages 222–223, 287, 288–289, 306 by Jonas Unger